John R. Sweney, Henry Lake Gilmour, William J. Kirkpatrick

Sunlit Songs

For Use in Meetings for Christian Worship or Work

John R. Sweney, Henry Lake Gilmour, William J. Kirkpatrick

Sunlit Songs
For Use in Meetings for Christian Worship or Work

ISBN/EAN: 9783337290160

Printed in Europe, USA, Canada, Australia, Japan

Cover: Foto ©Thomas Meinert / pixelio.de

More available books at **www.hansebooks.com**

SUNLIT SONGS:

FOR USE IN

MEETINGS FOR CHRISTIAN WORSHIP OR WORK.

EDITORS:

JNO. R. SWENEY, WM. J. KIRKPATRICK, AND H. L. GILMOUR.

"Upon them hath the light shined."
—Is. ix. 2.

PHILADELPHIA:

Published by JOHN J. HOOD, 1024 Arch St.

THE mists arise, the darkness flees,
    The east glows glints of gold ;
Glad song-birds trill the air with life,
    The drooping flowers unfold

II

There's sunlight on the mountain tops,
    There's brightness on the sea ;
There's gladness in the human soul,
    A living melody.

III

O Sunlit Songs of hope and heaven,
    Bright banners wide unfurled ;—
These, flaming in the light of God,
    Illuminate the world.

IV

O Church, the night of gloom is past,
    Go forth, in high employ,—
The sorrowing of earth enthuse,
    With Sunlit Songs of joy.

Ocean Grove, N. J., May, 1890.   E. H. Stokes.

· SUNLIT · SONGS ·

Sun of My Soul.

JOHN KEPLER.   Tune, HURSLEY. L. M.

1. Sun of my soul, thou Saviour dear, It is not night if thou be near:
2. When the soft dews of kind- ly sleep My wearied eye - lids gent - ly steep,

O may no earthborn cloud a- rise To hide thee from thy servant's eyes.
Be my last thought, how sweet to rest Forev- er on my Saviour's breast.

3 Abide with me from morn till eve,
For without thee I cannot live;
Abide with me when night is nigh,
For without thee I dare not die.

4 If some poor wandering child of thine
Hath spurned to-day the voice divine,
Now, Lord, the gracious work begin;
Let him no more lie down in sin.

5 Watch by the sick; enrich the poor
With blessings from thy boundless store;
Be every mourner's sleep to-night,
Like infant's slumbers, pure and light.

6 Come near and bless us when we wake,
Ere through the world our way we take;
Till in the ocean of thy love,
We lose ourselves in heaven above.

Praise God.

Tune, OLD HUNDRED. L. M.

Praise God, from whom all blessings flow ; Praise him, all creatures here below ;

Praise him above, ye heaven - ly host; Praise Father, Son, and ho - ly Ghost.

3

4

Zion Delivered.

Rev. F. G. McCauley. T. C. O'Kane.

Spirited.

1. Awake! arise! put on thy strength, In beauteous garments clothe thee now, From
2. Awake! arise, and shine in light, no darkness now enshrouds thy feet, With
3. Break forth and sing delightful strains, For God has heard thy contrite pray'r; The
4. Depart, depart and leave thy sin, Nor go by haste, nor leave by flight, For

death and darkness rise at length, With starry crown adorn thy brow, From
smiles, and gladness and delight, Thy Lord and Royal Master meet, In
Balm of Gilead soothes thy pains, For thee Jehovah's arm is bare. The
God his own shall welcome in, For thee the Lord of hosts shall fight; Break

dust and ash - es rise to joy, Let songs of praise thy lips employ.
ma - jes - ty and hon - or rise,—Behold, the morning gilds the skies.
watchman lifts his voice and sings,—While God his own to Zion brings.
forth and sing, O des - ert place, The King of Zi - on comes to bless.

CHORUS.

Behold! the Lord shall comfort Zion with end - less joy,
With endless joy, with endless joy,

And all his peo - ple shall in praise their time . . em - ploy.

F. G. BURROUGHS. Psalm 30. 5. H. L. GILMOUR.

1. O Lord, I will praise thee, For though thou wast angry, Thine anger is
2. O Lord, I will praise thee, Because thou hast saved me, And welcomed thy
3. O Lord, I will praise thee, For great is thy mercy, To par- don trans-
4. O Lord, I will praise thee, For though thou wast angry, Thine anger is

turned away ! By grace now is pardoned This heart that was hardened; From
prodigal home; Thy great love abiding Hath healed my back sliding; From
gressions like mine: Tho' summer had ended, Thine angels defend- ed, And
turned a - way! Thy comforts now cheer me, Thy presence is near me, Thou

CHORUS.

sin I am ransomed to - day. Ho- san - na! ho- san - na! The
thee I will nev - er more roam.
kept this late tro - phy of thine.
lov - est me free - ly to - day!

Lord is my banner, His an - ger is turned a - way! My chains have been

riv - en, My sins all for - given; O Lord, I will praise thee to - day.

Ask the Lord to Help You.

E. A. BARNES.

WM. J. KIRKPATRICK.

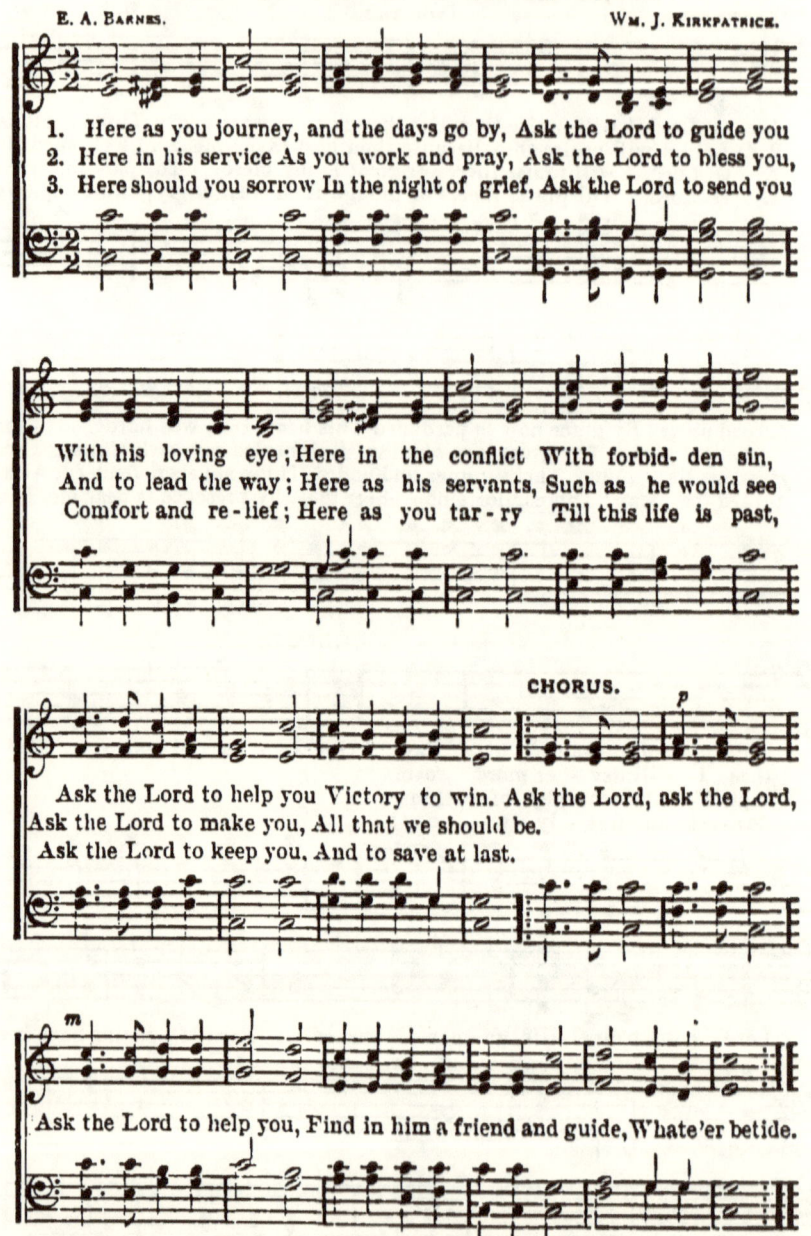

1. Here as you journey, and the days go by, Ask the Lord to guide you
2. Here in his service As you work and pray, Ask the Lord to bless you,
3. Here should you sorrow In the night of grief, Ask the Lord to send you

With his loving eye; Here in the conflict With forbid- den sin,
And to lead the way; Here as his servants, Such as he would see
Comfort and re-lief; Here as you tar - ry Till this life is past,

CHORUS.

Ask the Lord to help you Victory to win. Ask the Lord, ask the Lord,
Ask the Lord to make you, All that we should be.
Ask the Lord to keep you, And to save at last.

Ask the Lord to help you, Find in him a friend and guide, Whate'er betide.

E. E. HEWITT.

JNO. R. SWENEY.

1. Come to the throne of grace, Mercy is here; Seeking the Father's face,
2. Come to the throne of grace, Bring thy request; Christ is thy resting place,
3. Come to the throne of grace With thankful song, God's tender goodness trace
4. Come to the throne of grace, Known are thy needs; Look up to that high place

Humbly draw near. Come, by the "living way," O-pen for thee to-day,
Lean on his breast. Come, for his name is Love, Come, and his nature prove,
Life's path along. Come, for he waits to bless; His guardian care confess,
Where Jesus pleads. Oh, not for angel bands,—As our High Priest he stands,

CHORUS.

Come, hear thy Saviour say, "Be of good cheer." Come to the throne of grace,
He will thy sin remove, As east from west.
His promised gifts possess, Come, and grow strong.
Lifting his pierced hands, Still intercedes. Come, oh, come,

Mer-cy is here, Seek - ing the Father's face, Humbly draw near.

How should we Spend our Time?

"Redeeming the time, because the days are evil."

Maggie Metcalf.   Eph. v. 16.   Wm. J. Kirkpatrick.

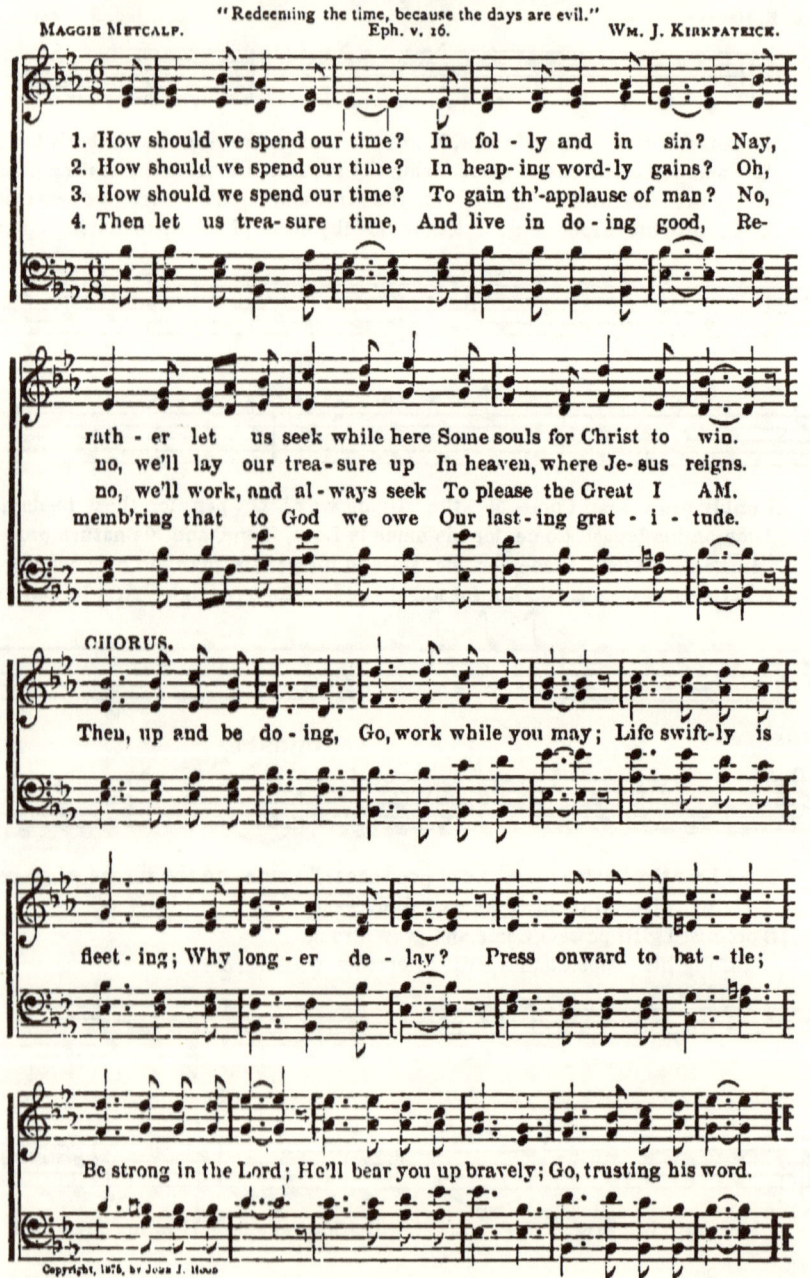

1. How should we spend our time? In fol - ly and in sin? Nay,
2. How should we spend our time? In heap-ing word-ly gains? Oh,
3. How should we spend our time? To gain th'-applause of man? No,
4. Then let us trea-sure time, And live in do-ing good, Re-

rath - er let us seek while here Some souls for Christ to win.
no, we'll lay our trea-sure up In heaven, where Je-sus reigns.
no, we'll work, and al-ways seek To please the Great I AM.
memb'ring that to God we owe Our last-ing grat - i - tude.

CHORUS.

Then, up and be do - ing, Go, work while you may; Life swift-ly is

fleet - ing; Why long - er de - lay? Press onward to bat - tle;

Be strong in the Lord; He'll bear you up bravely; Go, trusting his word.

Bear the Cross for Jesus.

"Take up the cross and follow me."—Mark x. 21.

Mrs. Annie S. Hawks.   R. Lowry. By per.

1. Bear the cross for Jesus, Bear it every day; Tho' the path be rugged,
2. Bear the cross for Jesus, Bear it thro' the strife, Or in pain and silence—
3. Bear the cross for Jesus; Would you know the pow'r Of his grace to save you

Bear it all the way; Bear the cross for Jesus, Whatsoe'er it be;
Whatsoe'er thy life? Bear the cross with patience Tho' you sigh for rest;
Save you hour by hour; Bear the cross for Jesus, Never mind its weight;

REFRAIN.

Bear it, and remember All his love for thee. Bear the cross, bear the cross,
   Just the one he gives you Is for you the best.
We shall leave our burden At the golden gate.

Bear it ev'ry day; Bear the cross for Jesus, Bear it all the way.

O My Saviour, Keep Me Ever.

FANNY J. CROSBY.   WM. J. KIRKPATRICK.

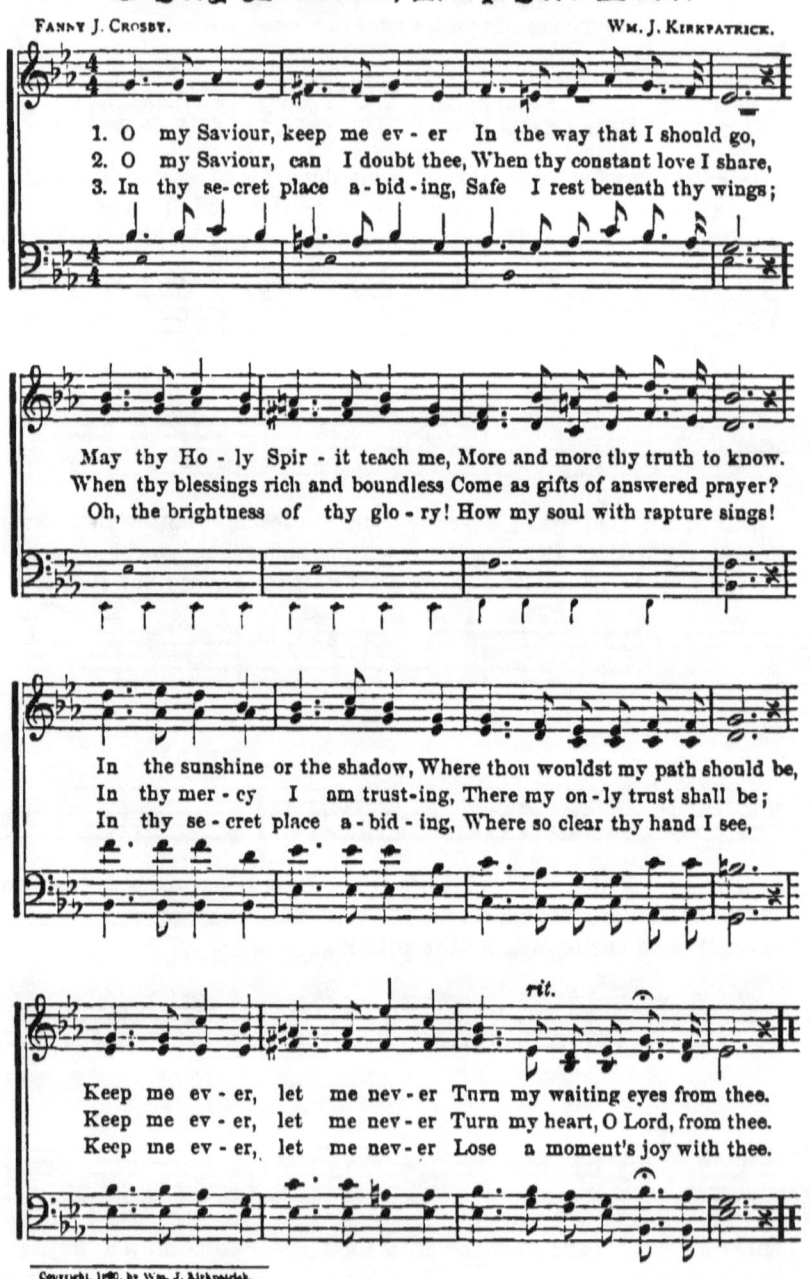

1. O   my Saviour, keep me ev - er   In the way that I should go,
2. O   my Saviour, can I doubt thee, When thy constant love I share,
3. In thy se - cret place a - bid - ing, Safe   I rest beneath thy wings;

May thy Ho - ly Spir - it teach me, More and more thy truth to know.
When thy blessings rich and boundless Come as gifts of answered prayer?
Oh, the brightness of   thy glo - ry! How my soul with rapture sings!

In the sunshine or the shadow, Where thou wouldst my path should be,
In thy mer - cy   I   am trust-ing, There my on - ly trust shall be;
In thy se - cret place a - bid - ing, Where so clear thy hand I see,

rit.

Keep me ev - er, let   me nev - er Turn my waiting eyes from thee.
Keep me ev - er, let   me nev - er Turn my heart, O Lord, from thee.
Keep me ev - er, let   me nev - er Lose   a moment's joy with thee.

I need this Very Saviour.

E. E. Hewitt.   Jno. R. Sweney.

1. I need the blood of Je - sus To take my sins a - way;
2. I need his power, transforming My in - most life and will;
3. I need his in - ter - ces - sions, Pre-vail - ing at the throne;
4. I need his new com - pas - sions, His love, to sweet - ly cheer;

I need his faith - ful coun - sel To guide me day by day.
I need, when storms are rag - ing, His whis - per, "peace, be still."
I need each word of prom - ise He gives me for my own.
I need the glad as - sur - ance, This Friend is al - ways near.

CHORUS.

I need this ver - y Sav - iour, Whom God provides for me;

His sav - ing grace so bound-less, His mer - cies great and free.

5 I need this very Saviour
   When joy breaks forth in song;
Or, when in desert places,
   The way seems hard and long.

6 I need him in death's valley,
   To bring the sunshine fair;
E'en up in heaven's glory,
   I need my Saviour there.

12 — Quit You Like Men.

F. G. BURROUGHS.   1 Cor. xvi. 13.   H. L. GILMOUR.

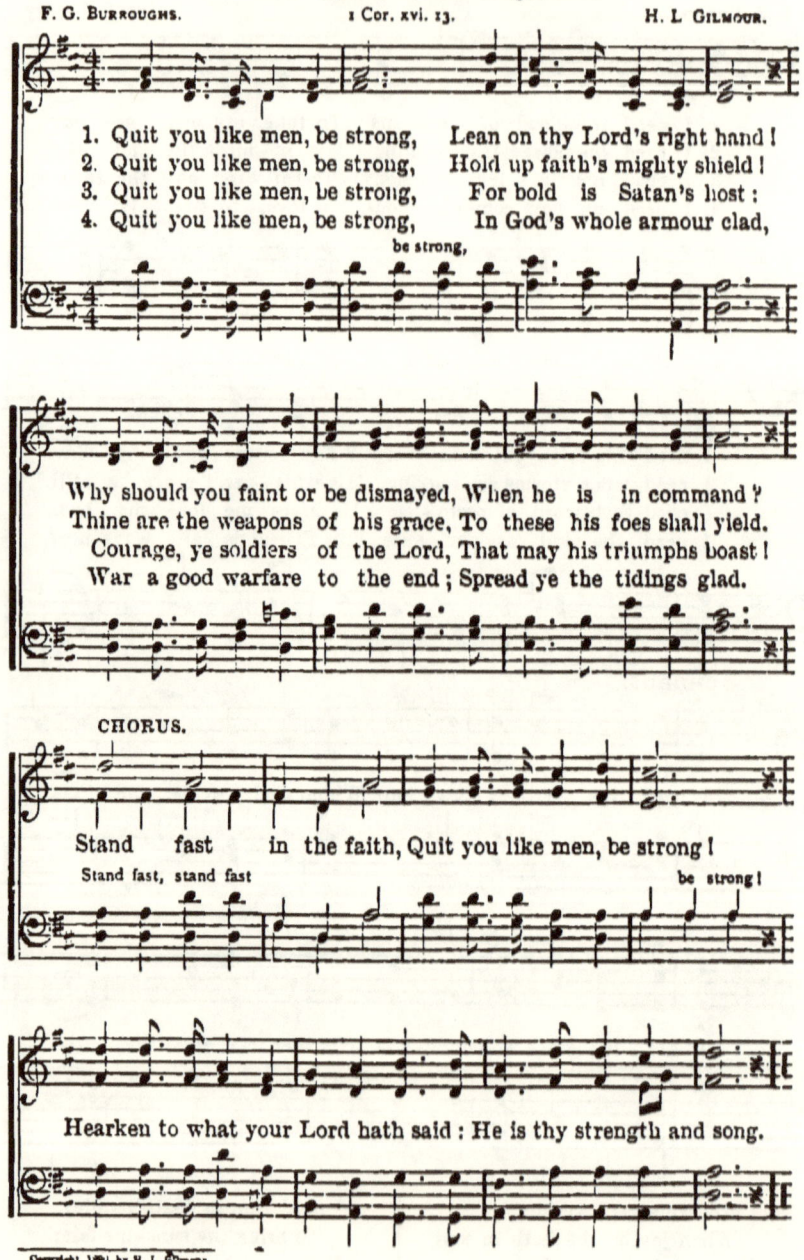

be strong,

1. Quit you like men, be strong,   Lean on thy Lord's right hand!
2. Quit you like men, be strong,   Hold up faith's mighty shield!
3. Quit you like men, be strong,   For bold is Satan's host:
4. Quit you like men, be strong,   In God's whole armour clad,

Why should you faint or be dismayed, When he   is   in command?
Thine are the weapons of his grace, To these his foes shall yield.
Courage, ye soldiers of the Lord, That may his triumphs boast!
War a good warfare to the end; Spread ye the tidings glad.

CHORUS.

Stand   fast   in the faith, Quit you like men, be strong!

Stand fast, stand fast   be strong!

Hearken to what your Lord hath said: He is thy strength and song.

"There is joy in the presence of the angels of God, over one sinner that repenteth." Luke xv. 10.

E. F. M.   E. F. MILLER.

1. There's re-joicing in the presence of the an - gels O - ver
2. Oh, how happy is the sinner who has tast - ed Of the
3. In the home where once was strife and pain and sorrow, There'll be
4. We will ral - ly round the standard of our Sav - iour, And to

sinners coming home, . All the heav'nly harpers, with a mighty
Saviour's wond'rous love, Love that bringeth peace and joy, which passeth
blessed peace and joy, . Prayer and praise to God around the family
oth- ers loud- ly call, . Come, ye sinners, and repent, believe in

coming home,

D. S.—dead's alive, the lost is found, and

Fine. CHORUS.

chorus, Now are praising round the throne. Then rejoice, . . all ye
knowledge, Ever giv- en from a - bove.
al - tar Will the pow'r of sin destroy.
Je - sus, He will freely pardon all.

then rejoice,

wand'rers Now are coming, coming home.

D. S.

ran- somed, Let your praises reach to heaven's highest dome, For the
all ye ransomed,   highest dome.

14 The Mind of Jesus.

E. E. Hewitt.   Jno. R. Sweney.

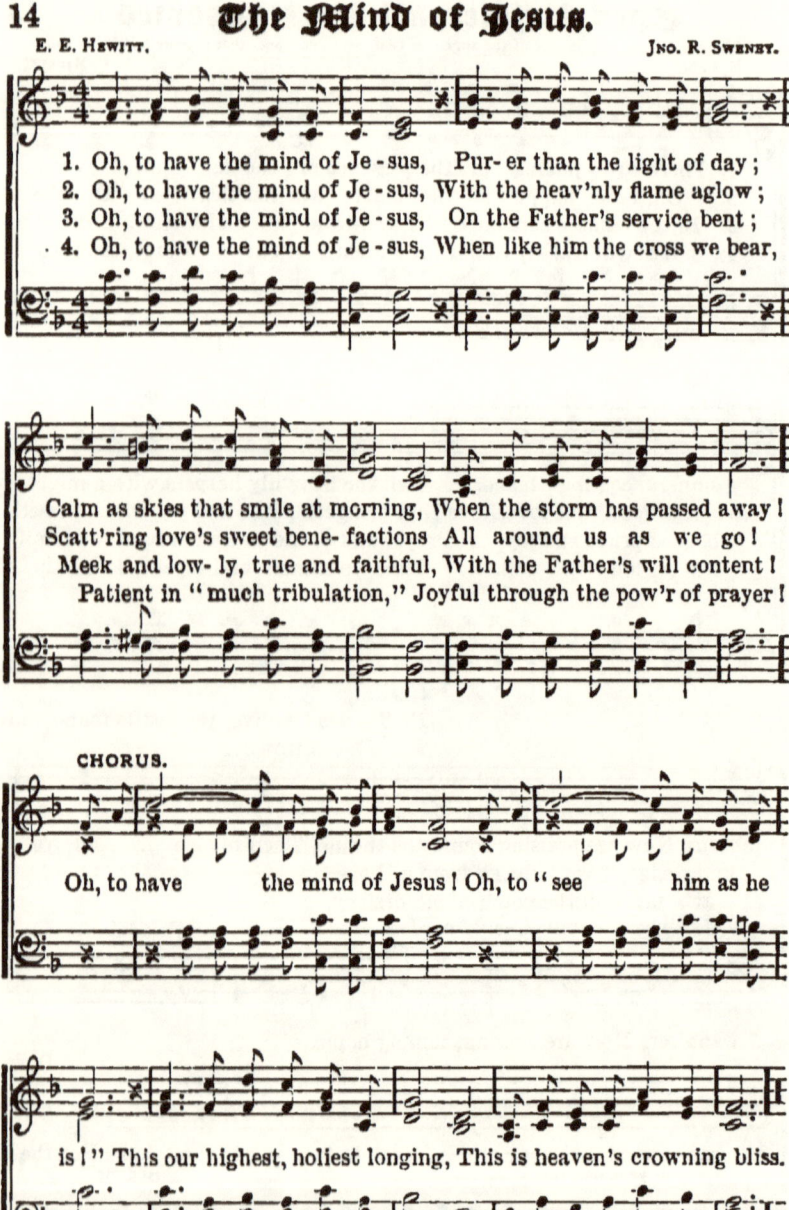

1. Oh, to have the mind of Je-sus,   Pur- er than the light of day ;
2. Oh, to have the mind of Je-sus, With the heav'nly flame aglow ;
3. Oh, to have the mind of Je-sus,   On the Father's service bent ;
4. Oh, to have the mind of Je-sus, When like him the cross we bear,

Calm as skies that smile at morning, When the storm has passed away !
Scatt'ring love's sweet bene- factions All around us as we go !
Meek and low- ly, true and faithful, With the Father's will content !
Patient in " much tribulation," Joyful through the pow'r of prayer !

CHORUS.

Oh, to have   the mind of Jesus ! Oh, to " see   him as he

is !" This our highest, holiest longing, This is heaven's crowning bliss.

SALLIE MARTIN.   WM. J. KIRKPATRICK.

1. Like an arm - y   we are marching, In the service of the Lord;
2. Like an arm - y   we are marching, With our banners, day by day,
3. Like an arm - y   we are marching, From the Sunday-school we come;
4. Like an arm - y   we are marching, Many tri - als tho' we meet,—

Marching onward to the vict- 'ry He has promised in his word.
Looking ev - er un - to Je - sus, Trusting him to guide our way.
Trained to fol- low our Commander, Till he brings us safe - ly home.
We shall count them scores of blessings, When we rest at Jesus' feet.

The Spirit and the Bride.

F. W. Faber. Rev. xxii. 17. H. L. Gilmour.

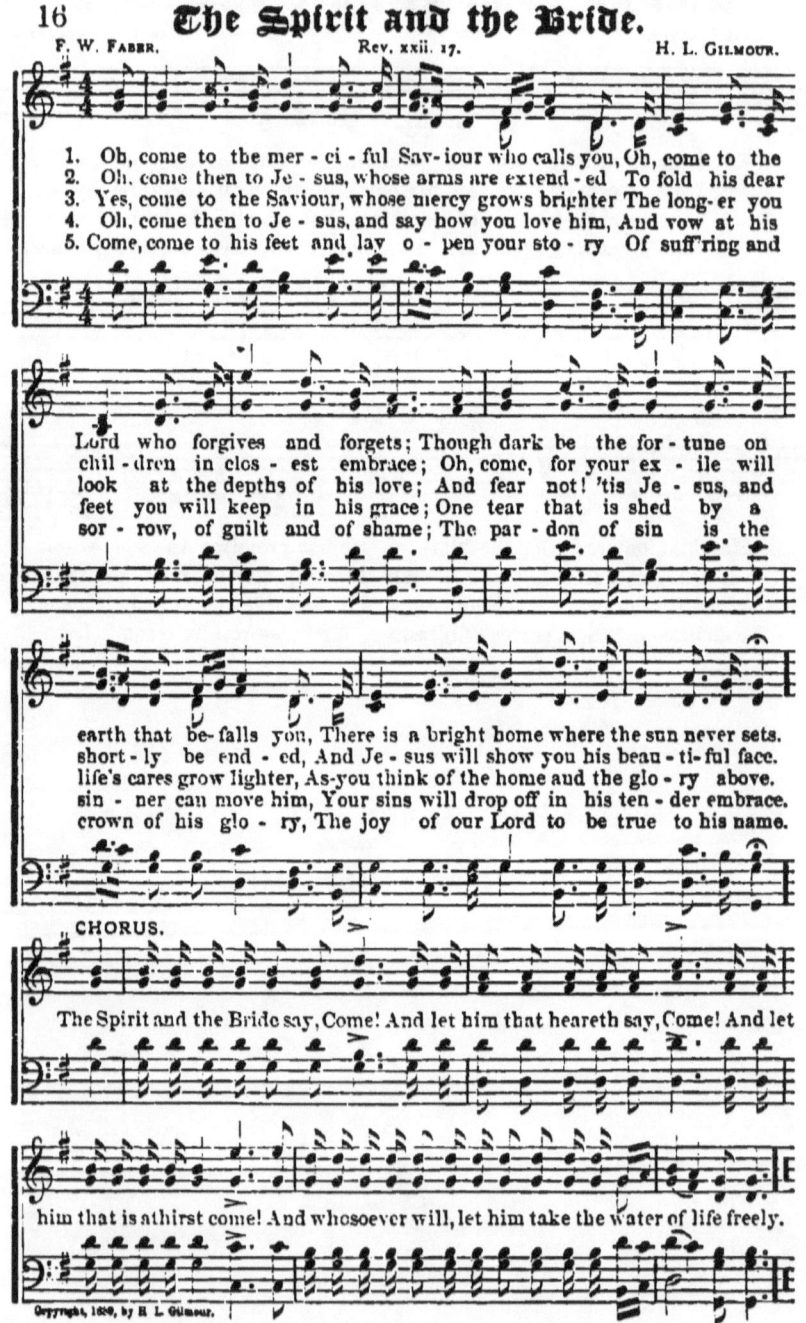

1. Oh, come to the mer - ci - ful Sav-iour who calls you, Oh, come to the
2. Oh, come then to Je - sus, whose arms are extend - ed To fold his dear
3. Yes, come to the Saviour, whose mercy grows brighter The long-er you
4. Oh, come then to Je - sus, and say how you love him, And vow at his
5. Come, come to his feet and lay o - pen your sto - ry Of suff'ring and

Lord who forgives and forgets; Though dark be the for - tune on
chil - dren in clos - est embrace; Oh, come, for your ex - ile will
look at the depths of his love; And fear not! 'tis Je - sus, and
feet you will keep in his grace; One tear that is shed by a
sor - row, of guilt and of shame; The par - don of sin is the

earth that be - falls you, There is a bright home where the sun never sets.
short - ly be end - ed, And Je - sus will show you his beau - ti - ful face.
life's cares grow lighter, As-you think of the home and the glo - ry above.
sin - ner can move him, Your sins will drop off in his ten - der embrace.
crown of his glo - ry, The joy of our Lord to be true to his name.

CHORUS.

The Spirit and the Bride say, Come! And let him that heareth say, Come! And let

him that is athirst come! And whosoever will, let him take the water of life freely.

Singing of Jesus.

E. A. Barnes.
WM. J. Kirkpatrick.

DUET.

1. Singing of Je - sus, singing his prais - es, Praising with joy
2. Singing of Je - sus, telling his mis - sion, Telling the life
3. Singing of Je - sus, telling his sto - ry, Bearing a - far
4. Singing of Je - sus, singing his prais - es, Bearing his name

our Lord and King; Singing his gos - pel, gift to all na - tions, Telling in
he free- ly gave; Bearing his mes - sage, full of salva - tion, Telling in
the hope of all; Showing his mer - cy, fount that is o - pen, Bearing in
'mid sin and strife; Singing of heav - en, home of the bless- ed, Telling in

CHORUS.

song what it will bring. Singing of Je - sus, singing of Jesus:
song, he died to save.
song his loving call.
song its perfect life.

Singing to-day, . . singing to-day, Singing his gos - - pel, his
Singing to day, singing to - day, Singing his gos - pel,

gos- pel of glo - ry. This is the mu - - sic of our way.
gos - pel of glo - ry, This is the mu - sic of our way.

Sunlit Songs—B

Jesus is Precious to Me

"Unto you therefore which believe he is precious." 1 Peter, ii. 7.

Priscilla J. Owens. W. J. Kirkpatrick.

1. Sweet is the name of my Lord, Hap-py his servants must be,
2. Precious his love that sus-tains, Precious in joy and de-light,
3. Precious in days of my youth, Precious in age and de-cline,
4. Precious the blood that he shed, Precious the tears that he wept,
5. Precious the cross that I bear, Sent as a to-ken of love,

Singing in joy-ful ac-cord, "Je-sus is precious to me."
Precious in conflict and pains, Precious in sor-row and night.
Precious the voice of his truth, Precious the hope that is mine.
Precious the ransom he paid, Precious the grave where he slept.
Precious the crown I shall wear, Radiant with glo-ry a-bove.

CHORUS.

Je-sus is precious to me, . . Je-sus is precious to me, . .
to me, to me.

Saved by his grace, so full, so free, Je-sus is precious to me. . . .
to me.

"And his name shall be called Wonderful."—Isa. ix. 6.

E. A. H.   ELISHA A. HOFFMAN. by per.

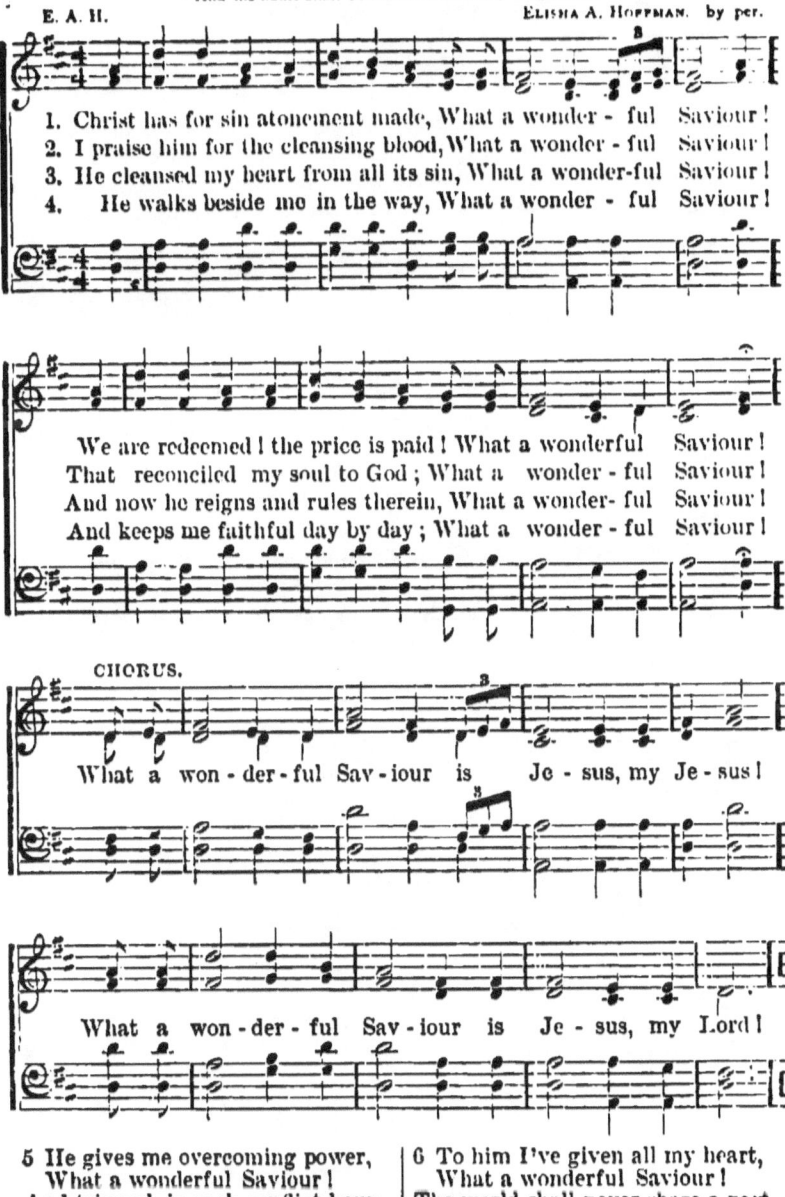

1. Christ has for sin atonement made, What a wonder - ful Saviour!
2. I praise him for the cleansing blood, What a wonder - ful Saviour!
3. He cleansed my heart from all its sin, What a wonder-ful Saviour!
4. He walks beside me in the way, What a wonder - ful Saviour!

We are redeemed! the price is paid! What a wonderful Saviour!
That reconciled my soul to God; What a wonder - ful Saviour!
And now he reigns and rules therein, What a wonder- ful Saviour!
And keeps me faithful day by day; What a wonder - ful Saviour!

CHORUS.

What a won - der - ful Sav - iour is Je - sus, my Je - sus!

What a won - der - ful Sav - iour is Je - sus, my Lord!

5 He gives me overcoming power,
  What a wonderful Saviour!
And triumph in each conflict hour,
  What a wonderful Saviour!

6 To him I've given all my heart,
  What a wonderful Saviour!
The world shall never share a part,
  What a wonderful Saviour!

It is the Lord my Saviour.

E. A. Harnes.   "In full assurance of faith." Heb. x. 22.   Wm. J. Kirkpatrick.

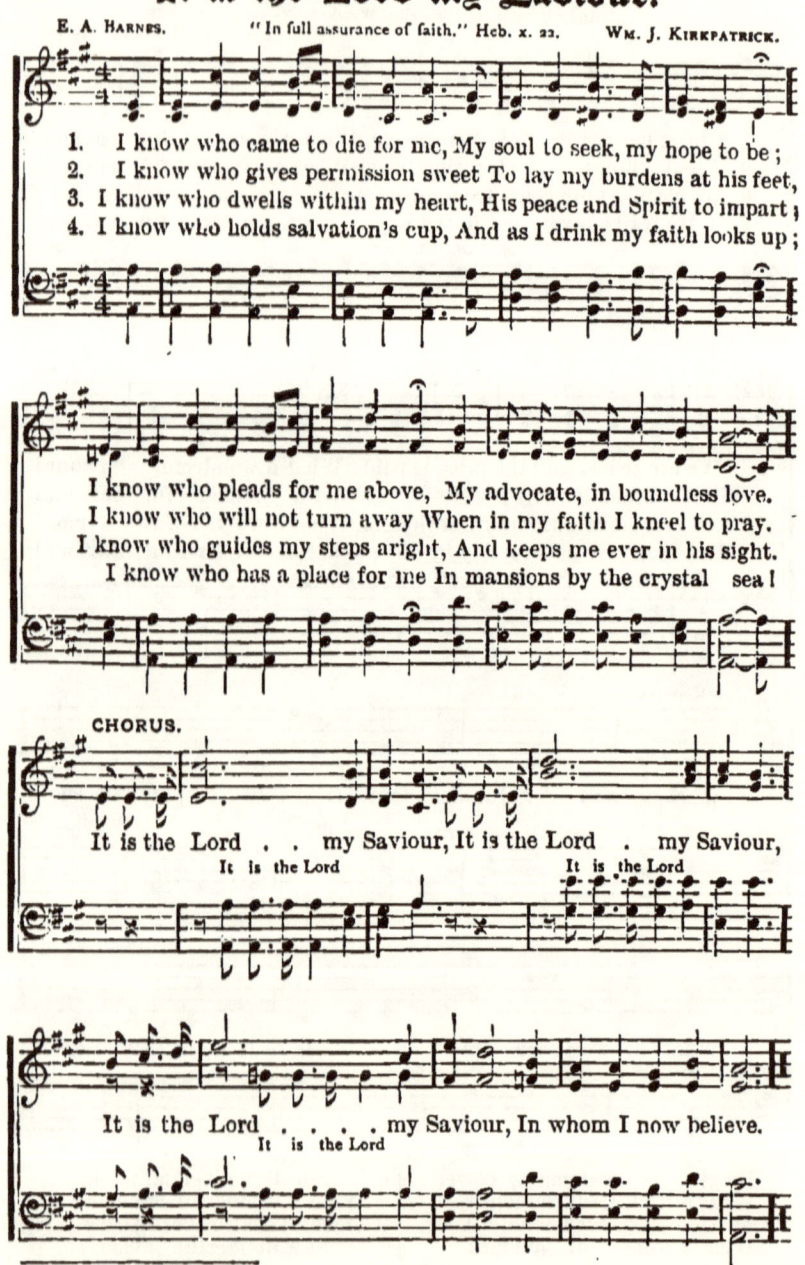

1. I know who came to die for me, My soul to seek, my hope to be;
2. I know who gives permission sweet To lay my burdens at his feet,
3. I know who dwells within my heart, His peace and Spirit to impart;
4. I know who holds salvation's cup, And as I drink my faith looks up;

I know who pleads for me above, My advocate, in boundless love.
I know who will not turn away When in my faith I kneel to pray.
I know who guides my steps aright, And keeps me ever in his sight.
I know who has a place for me In mansions by the crystal sea!

CHORUS.

It is the Lord . . my Saviour, It is the Lord . my Saviour,
It is the Lord   It is the Lord

It is the Lord . . . . . my Saviour, In whom I now believe.
It is the Lord

The Lord is Good to All.

E. A. BARNES.   Psalms cxlv. 9.   JNO. R. SWENEY.

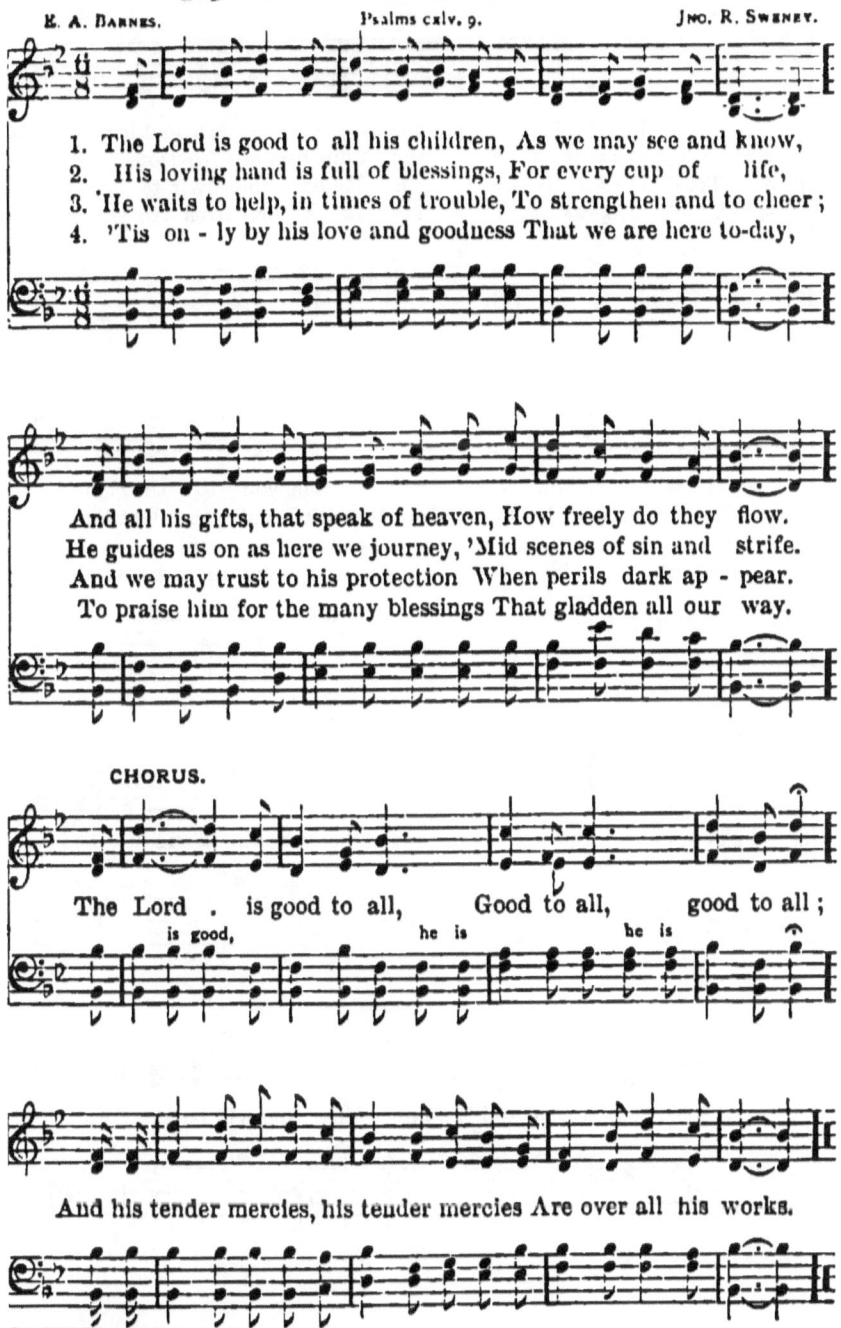

1. The Lord is good to all his children, As we may see and know,
2. His loving hand is full of blessings, For every cup of   life,
3. 'He waits to help, in times of trouble, To strengthen and to cheer;
4. 'Tis on - ly by his love and goodness That we are here to-day,

And all his gifts, that speak of heaven, How freely do they   flow.
He guides us on as here we journey, 'Mid scenes of sin and   strife.
And we may trust to his protection When perils dark ap - pear.
To praise him for the many blessings That gladden all our   way.

CHORUS.

The Lord . is good to all,   Good to all,   good to all;
is good,   he is   he is

And his tender mercies, his tender mercies Are over all his works.

Fix Your Thoughts on Jesus.

Minnie B. Lowry.   J. E. Hall.

1. Fix your thoughts on Je - sus, While life is fair and bright,
2. Fix your heart on Je - sus; Your best af - fec - tions give
3. Trust your all to Je - sus, He hath the pow'r to keep;
4. Thinking, speaking, do - ing, So by our lives to show

It will bring you com - fort, And guide you to the right.
To the cru - ci - fied One, Who died that you might live.
He will guide to heav - en, Tho' roads be rough and steep.
That we live for Je - sus, And la - bor here be - low.

CHORUS.

Fix your thoughts on Je - sus; Oh, wor - thy theme is he!

From earth's vain wish and low desire Your soul will be set free.

Open Doors.

E. E. Hewitt.   "I have set before thee an open door." Rev. iii. 8.   Jno. R. Sweney.

1. Open doors before us, See how wide they stand, Opened for his children,
2.   Open doors for service, Pass we not a-lone, Jesus going with us,
3. Doors for new achievement For our blessed King; He has set them open,
4.   Let him ever lead us In his chosen ways, Oh, what doors will open,

By our Father's hand; Let us gladly enter, Trusting in his might,
Makes our work his own; Paths of simple duty, Lit by him, shall prove
Touched the hidden spring; Shall we pause and falter, Dare to disobey,
"Jeweled gates of praise;" Death itself transfigured, Now an "open door"

CHORUS.

Trusting in his mercy Guiding us aright. Lord, we hear thee calling,
Avenues of blessing, Radiant with love.
When he calls us onward, In this gospel day?
To the shining mansions, "Pleasures evermore."

From the golden shore, "I have set before thee An o-pen door."

Working Together with Jesus.

E. A. Barnes.   1 Cor. iii. 9.   Wm. J. Kirkpatrick.

1. We work, as servants of Je - sus, We work 'mid gos - pel fields, While
2. We work to res - cue the er - ring, And bring them into the fold, While
3. We work where duty is call - ing, We work to reap and sow, While

Je - sus is leading us onward, Far out 'mid the precious yields; We
Je - sus is read - y to par - don, By rich- es of grace untold; We
Je - sus is giv - ing the increase, His goodness and love to show; We

work to tell of his gos - pel, Its tidings thus to spread, While Jesus, who
work to rescue the captives, Whose fetters are dark and strong, While Jesus is
work, and sweet is the service, And precious the sheaves we bring, While Jesus is

CHORUS.

go- eth be - fore us, Still of- fers the living bread. Working together with
near to de - liver, And teach them the victor's song.
blessing our la - bors, As gladly we work and sing.

Je - sus; Working in faith, working in love: Working togeth - er,

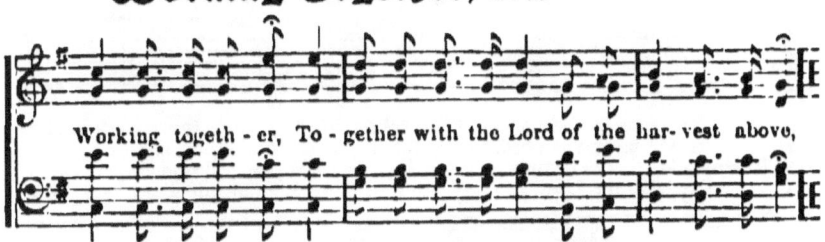

Working togeth - er, To - gether with the Lord of the har - vest above,

F. G. BURROUGHS.

Lo, I am With You.

ADAM GEIBEL.

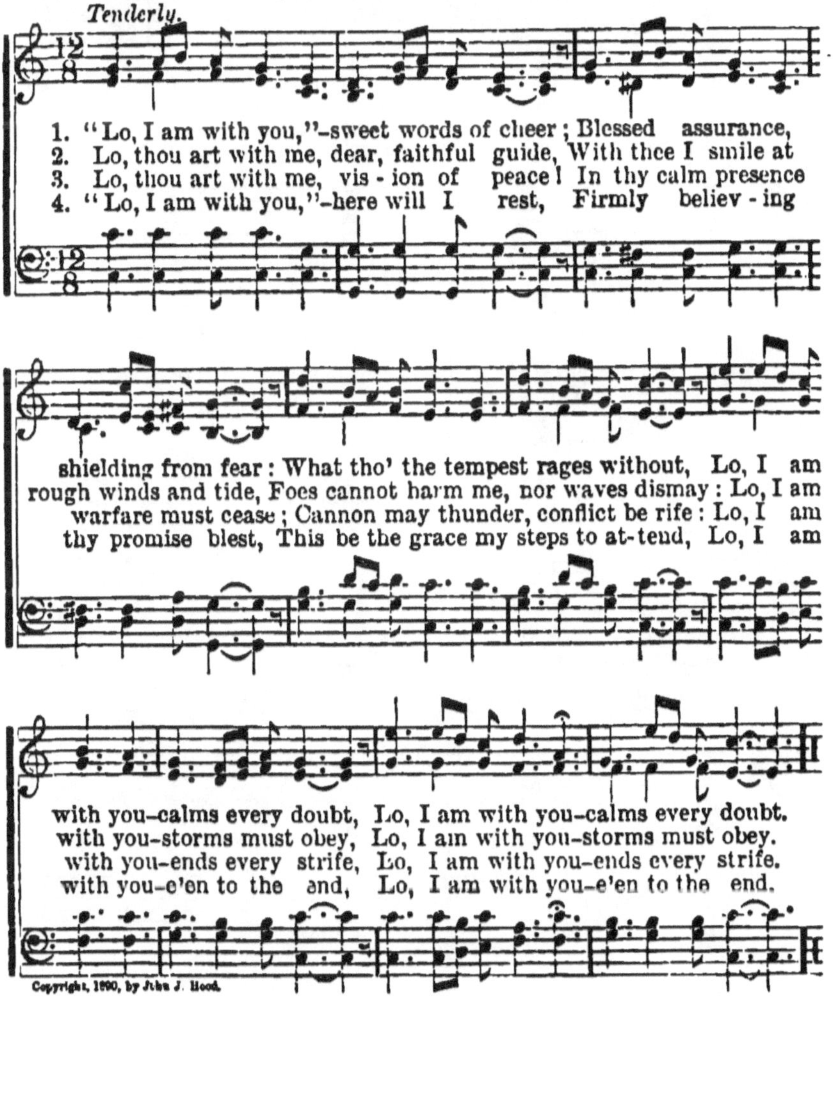

Tenderly.

1. "Lo, I am with you,"—sweet words of cheer; Blessed assurance,
2. Lo, thou art with me, dear, faithful guide, With thee I smile at
3. Lo, thou art with me, vis - ion of peace! In thy calm presence
4. "Lo, I am with you,"—here will I rest, Firmly believ - ing

shielding from fear: What tho' the tempest rages without, Lo, I am
rough winds and tide, Foes cannot harm me, nor waves dismay: Lo, I am
warfare must cease; Cannon may thunder, conflict be rife: Lo, I am
thy promise blest, This be the grace my steps to at-tend, Lo, I am

with you—calms every doubt, Lo, I am with you—calms every doubt.
with you—storms must obey, Lo, I am with you—storms must obey.
with you—ends every strife, Lo, I am with you—ends every strife.
with you—e'en to the end, Lo, I am with you—e'en to the end.

Be Strong in the Lord.

E. E. Hewitt.   Wm. J. Kirkpatrick.

1.   Be strong in the Lord, In his royal might; Thy rock, thy salvation, Thy
2.   Be strong in the Lord, Living for the right, For all that is worthy In
3. Be strong in the Lord, Can we doubt his pow'r? His strength is made perfect In
4.   Be strong in the Lord, In the peace that flows Like broadening rivers Thro'

song, and thy light; With the shield of faith, In his armor clad, Go forth to life's
God's holy sight; In the midst of ills Be thou not dismayed, For whither thou
life's darkest hour; Trusting not thyself, But his grace divine, The crown of thou
fields of repose, In the joy that sings Thro' the darkest days, A clear, ringing

CHORUS.

conflicts Triumphant and glad. Be strong in the Lord, Be strong in the Lord,
goest His arm gives thee aid.
victor Shall one day be thine.
prelude To heavenly praise.

Strengthened by his Spirit, Strengthened by his word; Pressing on to vict'ry

All the way along; Be strong in the Lord, oh, be strong, be strong!

You and I Will be There.

FANNY J. CROSBY.   JNO. R. SWENEY.

1. By his an - gel host at - ten - ded, When the Son of Man shall come,
2. On the day of fi - nal judgement, When the dead his voice shall hear,
3. Soul and body re - u - ni - ted, What rejoic - ing there will be,
4. Then be ready, oh, be read - y For the com - ing of the King,

In the glo - ry of his Fath - er, And shall take his peo - ple home,
And the sounding of the trum - pet Calls the nations far and near,
What a hal - le - lu - jah cho - rus, When our Saviour we shall see.
And the vast and countless numbers That in triumph he will bring.

CHORUS.

You and I will be there, In our
You and I will be there, will be there.

robes. white and fair, Caught up with a shout,
In our robes white and fair

We shall meet him in the air, We shall meet him in the air.

Let Us Endeavor.

E. E. HEWITT. (Christian Endeavor Song.) WM. J. KIRKPATRICK.

1. Let us endeav - or to speak for the Master; Surely he's worthy our
2. Let us endeav - or to work for the Master; Serving in gladness wher-
3. Let us endeav - or to live for the Master; Live for his glo - ry who

heart-i - est praise; Worthy our loyal and loving con-fes -sion; Worthy the
ev - er we go, Keeping our lamps shining out in the darkness, Till others
died for our sin; Yielding our all in a true con- se- cra- tion, Trusting, o-

CHORUS.

hymns of thanksgiving we raise. Help - ing us ev - er
fol - low the heaven- lit glow.
bey - ing, his blessing we win. Helping us ev - er, In each endeavor,

In each endeav - or, Je - sus stands by us to
Helping us ev - er, In each endeavor, Jesus stands by us to give us success,

give us suc - cess; His arm upholding, His love en-
Jesus stands by us to give us success;

Let Us Endeavor.—CONCLUDED.

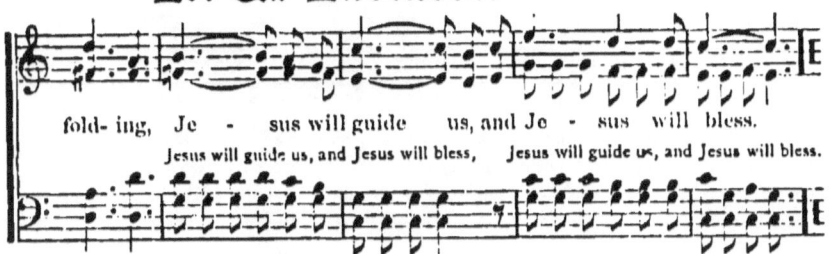

fold- ing, Je - sus will guide us, and Je - sus will bless.

Jesus will guide us, and Jesus will bless, Jesus will guide us, and Jesus will bless.

Live by the Promises.

E. E. HEWITT.   JNO. R. SWENEY.

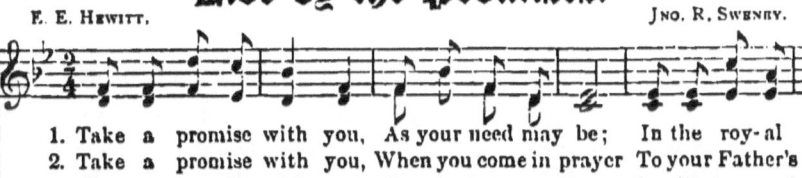

1. Take a promise with you, As your need may be; In the roy-al
2. Take a promise with you, When you come in prayer To your Father's
3. Take a promise with you, In the bus - y throng; It will cheer and
4. Take a promise with you, In your work for God; In the strength he

CHORUS.

storehouse, Rich supplies and free. Live by the prom-is-es, Precious
pres -ence Plead his own word there.
com - fort, Help your soul a - long.
gives you Spread the truth abroad.

words of love! Gol- den links in mercy's chain, Drawing us a - bove.

I'm Happy, so Happy!

LIZZIE EDWARDS.

JNO. R. SWENEY.

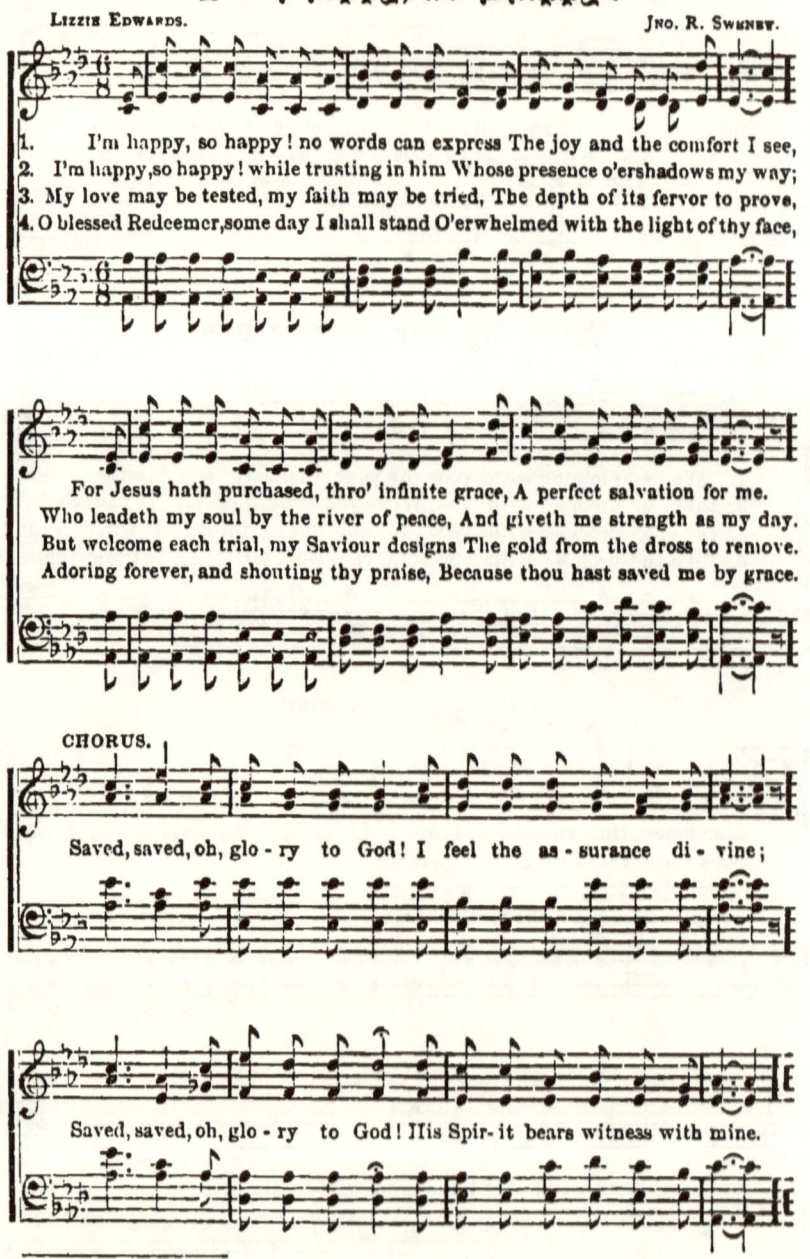

1. I'm happy, so happy! no words can express The joy and the comfort I see,
2. I'm happy, so happy! while trusting in him Whose presence o'ershadows my way;
3. My love may be tested, my faith may be tried, The depth of its fervor to prove,
4. O blessed Redeemer, some day I shall stand O'erwhelmed with the light of thy face,

For Jesus hath purchased, thro' infinite grace, A perfect salvation for me.
Who leadeth my soul by the river of peace, And giveth me strength as my day.
But welcome each trial, my Saviour designs The gold from the dross to remove.
Adoring forever, and shouting thy praise, Because thou hast saved me by grace.

CHORUS.

Saved, saved, oh, glo-ry to God! I feel the as-surance di-vine;

Saved, saved, oh, glo-ry to God! His Spir-it bears witness with mine.

E. E. Hewitt. Wm. J. Kirkpatrick.

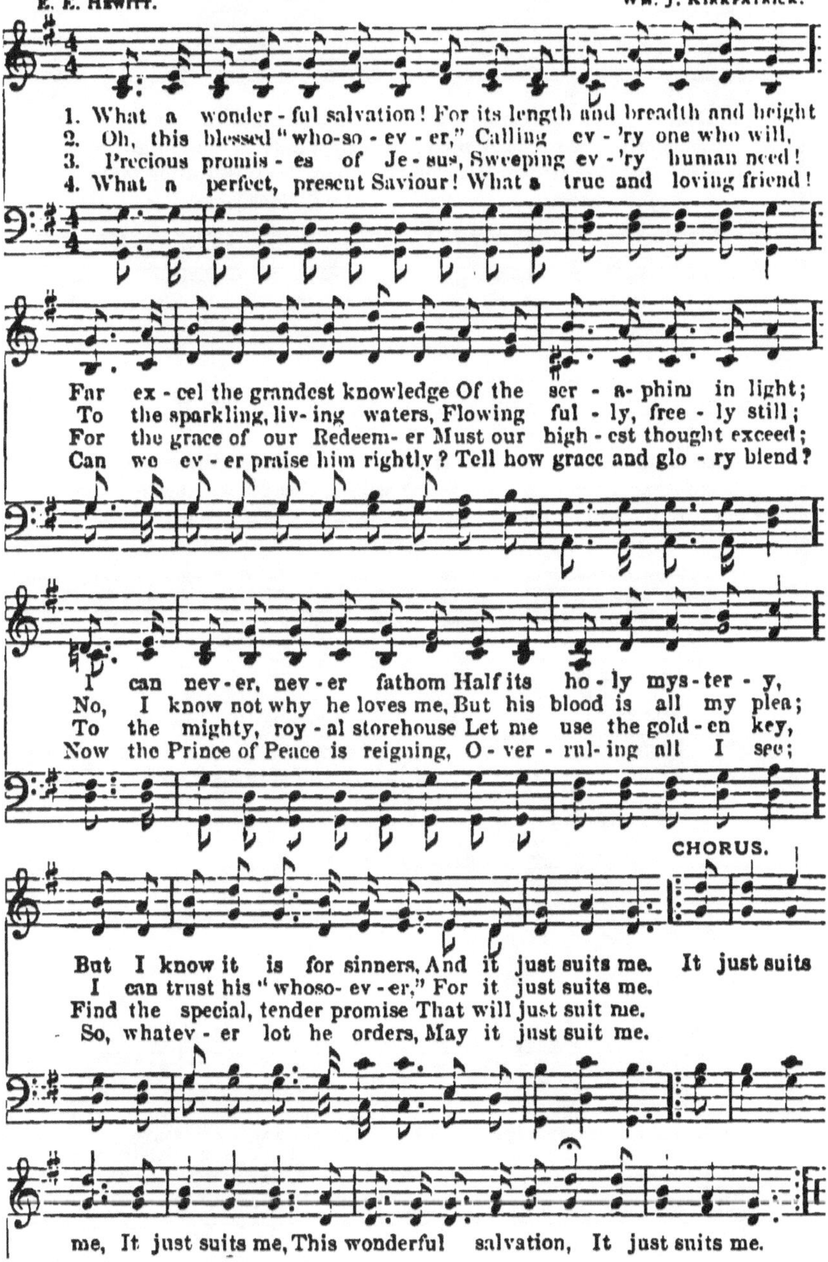

1. What a wonder-ful salvation! For its length and breadth and height
2. Oh, this blessed "who-so-ev-er," Calling ev-'ry one who will,
3. Precious promis-es of Je-sus, Sweeping ev-'ry human need!
4. What a perfect, present Saviour! What a true and loving friend!

Far ex-cel the grandest knowledge Of the ser-a-phim in light;
To the sparkling, liv-ing waters, Flowing ful-ly, free-ly still;
For the grace of our Redeem-er Must our high-est thought exceed;
Can we ev-er praise him rightly? Tell how grace and glo-ry blend?

I can nev-er, nev-er fathom Half its ho-ly mys-ter-y,
No, I know not why he loves me, But his blood is all my plea;
To the mighty, roy-al storehouse Let me use the gold-en key,
Now the Prince of Peace is reigning, O-ver-rul-ing all I see;

CHORUS.

But I know it is for sinners, And it just suits me. It just suits
I can trust his "whoso-ev-er," For it just suits me.
Find the special, tender promise That will just suit me.
So, whatev-er lot he orders, May it just suit me.

me, It just suits me, This wonderful salvation, It just suits me.

Jesus is Waiting to Save.

E. A. Barnes.   Jno. R. Sweney.

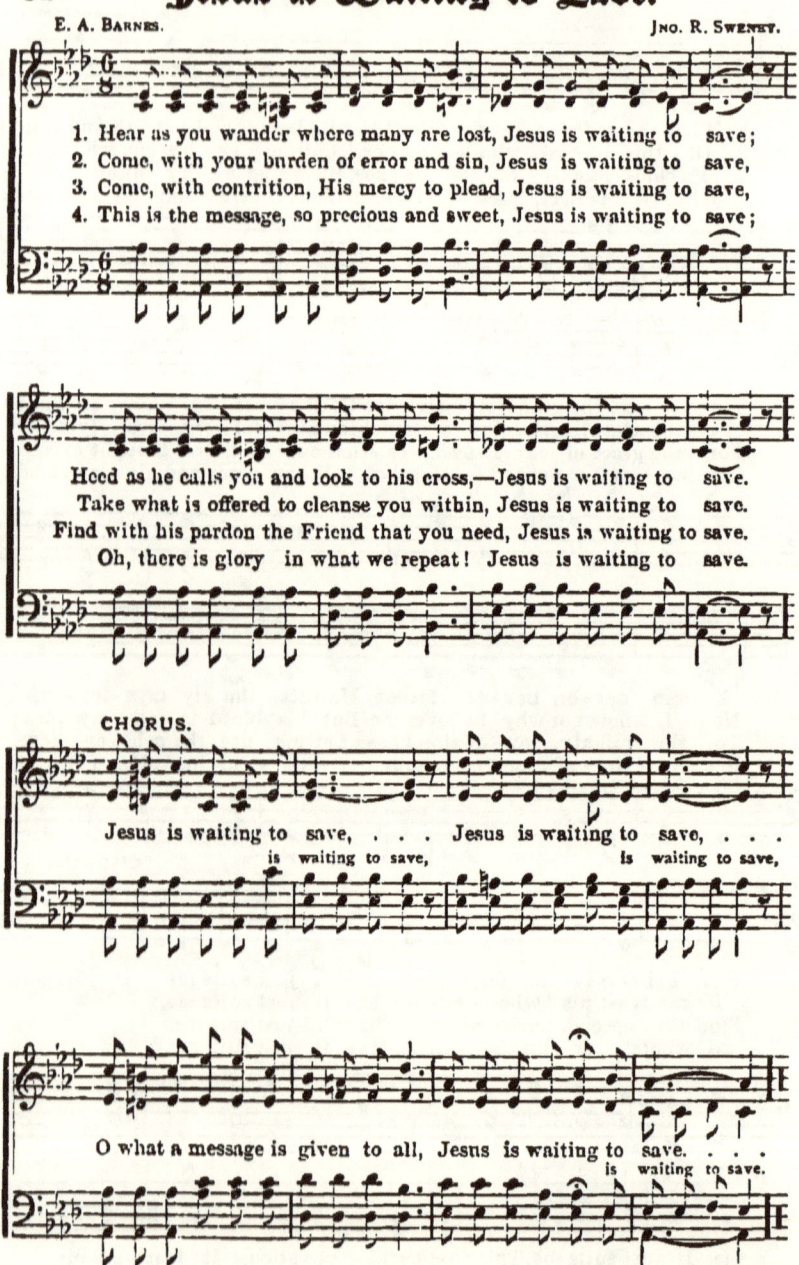

1. Hear as you wander where many are lost, Jesus is waiting to   save;
2. Come, with your burden of error and sin, Jesus is waiting to   save,
3. Come, with contrition, His mercy to plead, Jesus is waiting to save,
4. This is the message, so precious and sweet, Jesus is waiting to   save;

Heed as he calls you and look to his cross,—Jesus is waiting to   save.
Take what is offered to cleanse you within, Jesus is waiting to   save.
Find with his pardon the Friend that you need, Jesus is waiting to save.
Oh, there is glory   in what we repeat! Jesus   is waiting to   save.

CHORUS.

Jesus is waiting to   save, ...   Jesus is waiting to   save, ...
is   waiting to save,   is   waiting to save,

O what a message is given to all, Jesus is waiting to   save. . . . .
                                                        is   waiting to save.

Abbie Mills.　　　　　　　　　　　　　　Wm. J. Kirkpatrick.

1. Heirs to the kingdom of Jesus the Lord, Go tell the world of his love;
2. Think how he labored that we might have rest, Go tell the world of his love;
3. Plead to the lost ones to come while they may, Go tell the world of his love;

Publish the blessings that flow from his word, Go tell the world of his love;
Think how he suffered that we might be bless'd, Go tell the world of his love:
Jesus is waiting, he'll save them to-day, Go tell the world of his love:

Love that has purchas'd redemption from sin, Love that makes happy the spirit within
Sav'd by his mercy, upheld by his care, Tell of the goodness we constantly share;
Love that is nearest when earth joys are past, Lighting our pathway by clouds overcast;

Love that will help us our conquest to win, Go tell the world of his love.
Fill'd with his fulness, no longer forbear, Go tell the world of his love.
Love that will bring us to glo-ry at last, Go tell the world of his love.

D.S.—Heirs to the kingdom of Jesus the Lord. Go tell the world of his love.

CHORUS.　　　　　　　　　　　　　　　　　　　　　*D. S.*

Go tell the world, Go tell the world, Go tell the world of his love of his love;

Sunlit Songs-C

God is Here.

Sallie M. Smith.　　　　　　　　　　　　　　　　Jno. R. Sweney.

1. 'Tis the hour   of so - cial meeting, Blessed hour   we love so   dear!
2. Tho' from him   we oft have wandered, If a - gain   we seek his   face,
3. He who knows our ev - 'ry weakness Bids us now   to him draw near,
4. Blessed hour   of pure de - vo - tion! On its wings our spir - its   rise,

Ho - ly thoughts, like music stealing Soft- ly   whis - per, God is   here.
To his   fa-   vor he'll restore us, Thro' his   free,   abundant grace.
Lights the lamp   of faith within   us, Brings a   balm our souls to cheer.
And re- ceive   a precious foretaste Of a   home beyond the skies.

CHORUS.

God is   here,   we feel his presence, God is   here,   and that to   bless;

Oh, the bliss   of such a moment Mortal tongue can ne'er ex- press.

That Mansion of Mine.

EDGAR PAGE. CHO. by H. L. G.   H. L. GILMOUR.

1. I think oft - en-times of that man-sion of mine, A-wait-ing me
2. O mansion in glo - ry, my Father hath reared; O rest for the
3. O mansion of mine,'neath the palm-bearing trees,'Mid flow'rs ev-er
4. O mansion of mine, for I hope to be there, The saints of the

there, o'er the bounda - ry line, The light of its glo - ry seems
wea - ry, by Je- sus prepared: I'm near-ing thy por- tals, thy
bloom - ing, the white-robed to please; O riv - er of life, with thy
Lord in thy glo - ry shall share: We'll tell it all o - ver, how

saying, "Come home," The Spir - it within sings my soul sweetly on.
wide o - pen door, Be near, my dear Saviour, to lead safe- ly o'er.
sil - ver- y flow, The taste of thy wa - ters I'm long-ing to know.
Je - sus we found, While harps shall be tuned, and our songs shall resound.

CHORUS.

In my Father's house are many mansions, Where all the blood-washed roam
ma- ny, ma- ny,   Far be-

yond the pearly gates, Where a loving Saviour waits, To welcome the ransomed
home.

Lend a Helping Hand.

James L. Black.

Jno. R. Sweney.

1. Take the balm of consolation To the lonely hearts that grieve; Far more
2. Go and leave a word of kindness At a weary neighbor's door, It may
3. As the streams that from the mountain Ripple down its mossy side, Giving

blessed, said the Master, 'Tis to give than to re-ceive; Like the
touch a chord of feel-ing He has nev - er known be-fore; Though our
forth their crystal wa-ters, Seem expand-ing while they glide; Thus our

sun that nev - er wearies, Like the dew and rain that fall, With a
hands no wealth can offer, Though we have but words to give, Yet the
ev - 'ry ser-vice, rendered In the name of Christ our Lord, Shall on

CHORUS.

cheerful, lov-ing spir-it, Lend a help-ing hand to all. Hear the
good we' do for Jesus Through e - ter - nal years shall live.
earth receive a blessing, And in heaven a bright reward.

call, oh, hear the call, Lend a help-ing hand, a

Hear the call, oh, hear the call,

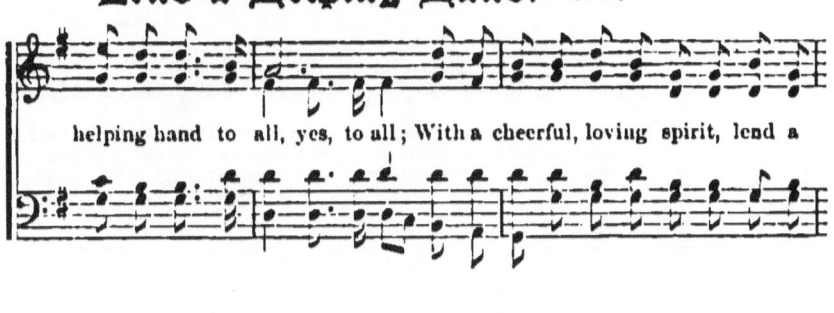

helping hand to all, yes, to all; With a cheerful, loving spirit, lend a

helping hand to all, Lend a helping hand, a helping hand to all.

Precious Saviour Mine!

MARTHA J. LANKTON.   WM. J. KIRKPATRICK.

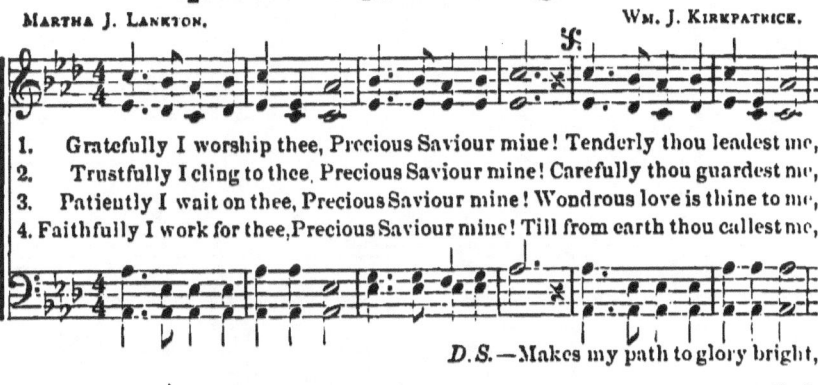

1. Gratefully I worship thee, Precious Saviour mine! Tenderly thou leadest me,
2. Trustfully I cling to thee, Precious Saviour mine! Carefully thou guardest me,
3. Patiently I wait on thee, Precious Saviour mine! Wondrous love is thine to me,
4. Faithfully I work for thee, Precious Saviour mine! Till from earth thou callest me,

D. S.—Makes my path to glory bright,

Fine. CHORUS.   D S.

Precious Saviour mine! All the day, and all the night, Peace, with calm and steady
light,

Precious Saviour mine!

Now I Am the Lord's.

L. H. Edmunds.

W. J. Kirkpatrick.

1. Tempt me not with worldly pleasures, I no more their pow'r can own,
2. Now a stronger power attracts me, Draws me ev - er to his side,
3. 'Tis the power of love constraining, Mighty power of sovereign grace;
4. May I know a growing nearness To the Saviour whom I love;

Jesus has sought me, Jesus has bought me, Made me his a - lone.
Draws me so sweetly, binds me completely, Here would I a - bide.
Sunlight is beaming, heaven is streaming, From my Saviour's face.
Trusting him ev - er, leaving him nev- er Till I mount a - bove.

CHORUS.

Now I am the Lord's; he made me his for- ev- er, When up - on the

cross the ransom-price he paid; Yes, I am the Lord's, and

poco rit.

Je- sus is my Saviour, Praise to his name! the full atonement's made.

I Will Go.

F. G. BURROUGHS. H. L. GILMOUR.

1. I will go in the strength of the Lord, To the work he has
2. I will go at his gen-tle command, Tho' I know not the
3. I will go in the strength of the Lord, And no e-vil shall
4. I will go, in his pan-op-ly clad, And undaunted by

giv'n me to do, In the strength that is mighty to save, To the
way of his choice; But the Lord knoweth me by my name, So I'll
cause me to fear; Thro' green pastures, or thro' death's dark vale, I will
migh-ti-est foe: For no weapon can pierce faith's strong shield,—In the

CHORUS.

field where the lab'rers are few.
fol-low my kind Shepherd's voice. I will go, where he
go, with my Com-for-ter near.
strength of the Lord I will go.

I will go,

leads, In my weakness his pow'r I shall know: I shall know:
where he leads,

All things, by his grace, I can do,— In the strength of the Lord I will go.
by his grace, I can do,—

Copyright 1890, by H. L. Gilmour.

40 Blessed Light of God.

E. A. BARNES. "His marvellous light." 1 Peter. ii. 9. JNO. R. SWENEY.

1. Day by day we journey here, In the light of God: Shadows lift and
2. We have gospel words to speak, In the light of God; We have err- ing
3. All our joys so sweetly blend, In the light of God; And our joys will

dis - appear, In the light of God. Here his precepts we obey, Here 'tis
ones to seek, In the light of God. Life its cares and duties bring, Yet 'tis
nev - er end, In the light of God. We have words of love and cheer, And we

sweet to sing and pray, And our hope fades not away, In the light of God.
sweet to work and sing, As its days are on the wing, In the light of God.
never need to fear While in faith we journey here, In the light of God.

CHORUS.

In . . . the light, Blessed light of God, . In the light, in the light,
In the light, . . in the light, Blessed light, - light of God,

Blessed light of God! We all rejoice as we journey home, In the light,

in the light, We all rejoice as we journey home, In the blessed light of God.

Father all Holy.

E. E. HEWITT.　　　　THE LORD'S PRAYER.　　　　WM. J. KIRKPATRICK.

1. Father all ho - ly, bend we so lowly, Glowing with love's tender flame,
2. Angels adore thee, waiting before thee, Swift thy commands to fulfil:
3. From sin deliv - er, keep us forev - er, Kingdom and glory are thine,

Father in heaven, praises be giv - en, Hallowed forev - er thy Name.
Grant us, we pray thee, grace to obey thee, Choosing and serving thy will.
Thine, too, the power, hear us this hour, Father, our Father divine!

Telling the story, spreading thy glory, Send forth thy people, we pray,
Father, now lead us, day by day feed us, Ever provide and defend;
Jesus is pleading, still interceding For his redeemed ones again,

Till every nation know thy salvation, Under thy kingdom's full sway.
Trespass confessing, seeking thy blessing, Pardon and peace without end.
For his sake hear us, in his name cheer us, He is the faithful "Amen."

I Have Come to the Fountain.

In that day there shall be a fountain opened for sin and for uncleanness.

Rev. Wm. M. Carr.

W. J. Kirkpatrick.

1. I was once far a-way from my Saviour, Far a-way from his
2. His Spir-it sought out my poor refuge, Sent con-vic-tion and
3. Just now I plunge in-to the fountain, Just now I hear,
4. I will bless him for-ev-er and ev-er Who saved a poor

kind, loving care; I had injured him times without number, I was
knowledge of sin, I sought for my Lord till I found him, And
"go, sin no more," My heart is washed clean, I will praise him! My
reb-el like me, In life will proclaim him to others, And

CHORUS.

down in the depths of despair.
knew that my soul was redeemed.
soul as an ea-gle doth soar.
praise him e - ter - nal-ly.

I have come to the Fountain of

cleansing, To the Fountain of cleansing from sin; Washed and made

free from all sin would I be, Just now I am en-tering in.

Jesus is Waiting.

Charlotte Murray.

H. L. Gilmour.

With feeling.

1. Je - sus is waiting to welcome the weary, Worn with the world's fruitless
2. Je - sus is waiting—He standeth and knocketh, Calling in love up - on
3. Will you not come? You need no preparation : Stay not to think, but come
4. "Oh! I am yearning to see you unburdened, Death did I suff - er that

striv - ing for peace, Tired with a night-watch that knoweth no morning,
each one oppressed—"Come unto me, sin - ner, wea - ry and la - den,
just as you are; Bring nothing with you, for love giv - eth freely,
you might be free; Will you not come? and by life - con - se - cration

REFRAIN.

Sick with a heart-ache that earth cannot ease. "Come un - to me,
I will refresh you and give you my rest."
Peace—per - fect peace—that no sorrow can mar.
Try to win oth - ers, and bring them to me?"

all ye that la - bor, And are heavy laden, and I will give you rest," Take

my yoke upon you and learn of me, 'Tis ea - sy, my burden is light.

O Kedron.

James. L Black.

JNO. R. SWENEY.

DUET.—Soprano and Tenor.

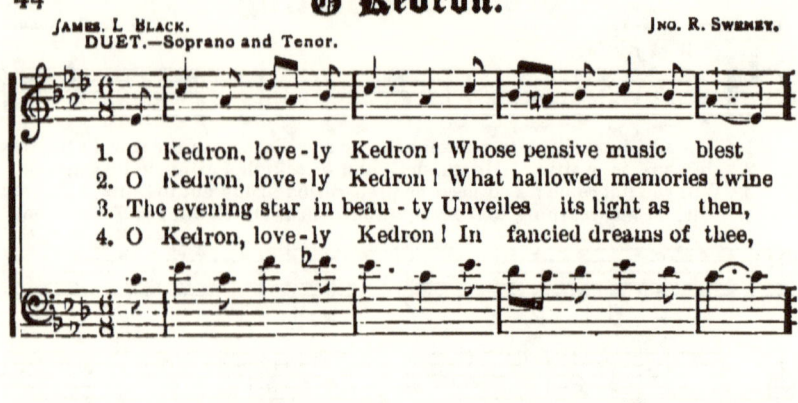

1. O Kedron, love-ly Kedron! Whose pensive music   blest
2. O Kedron, love-ly Kedron! What hallowed memories twine
3. The evening star in beau-ty Unveiles   its light as   then,
4. O Kedron, love-ly Kedron! In   fancied dreams of thee,

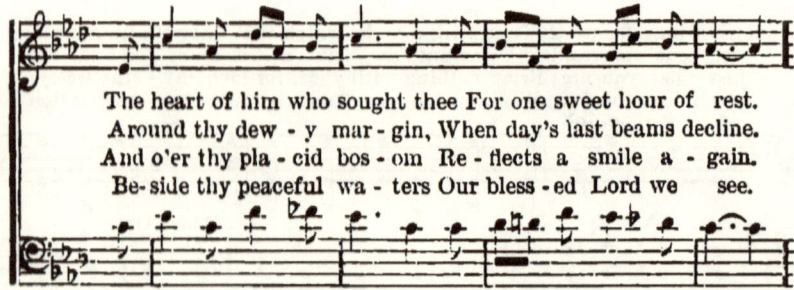

The heart of him who sought thee For one sweet hour of rest.
Around thy dew - y mar-gin, When day's last beams decline.
And o'er thy pla - cid bos-om Re - flects a smile a - gain.
Be- side thy peaceful wa - ters Our bless - ed Lord we   see.

CHORUS.

As he, our Sav - iour, lingered A - mid thy frag - rant   air,

We steal a- way, at close of day, For ono sweet hour of prayer.

Sing the Dear Name Softly.

E. E. Hewitt.　　　　　　　　　　　　　　　　　　Wm. J. Kirkpatrick.

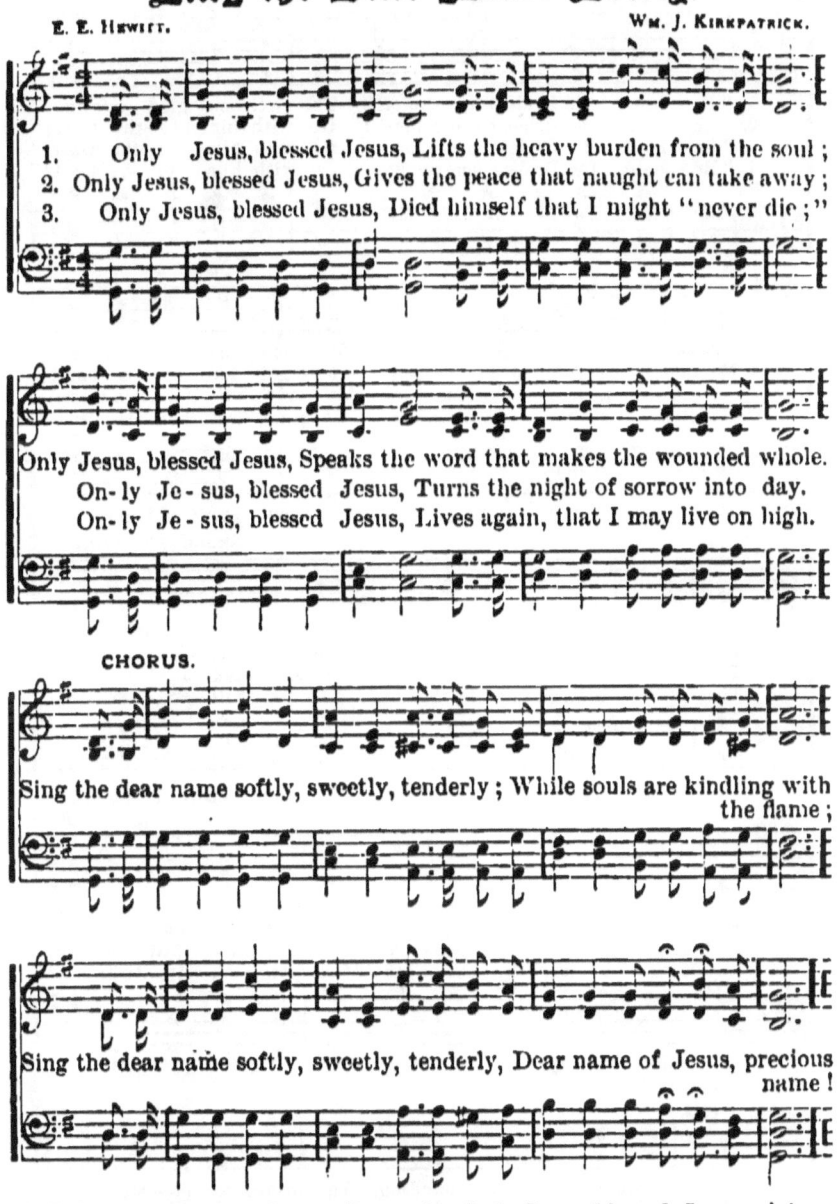

1. Only　Jesus, blessed Jesus, Lifts the heavy burden from the soul ;
2. Only Jesus, blessed Jesus, Gives the peace that naught can take away ;
3. Only Jesus, blessed Jesus, Died himself that I might "never die ;"

Only Jesus, blessed Jesus, Speaks the word that makes the wounded whole.
On-ly Je-sus, blessed Jesus, Turns the night of sorrow into day.
On-ly Je-sus, blessed Jesus, Lives again, that I may live on high.

CHORUS.

Sing the dear name softly, sweetly, tenderly ; While souls are kindling with the flame ;

Sing the dear name softly, sweetly, tenderly, Dear name of Jesus, precious name !

4 Only Jesus, blessed Jesus ; [heart;
Let him write that name upon my
Only Jesus, blessed Jesus ;
From his service never to depart.

5 Only Jesus, blessed Jesus ; [ring ;
With his praise, the heavenly arches
Only Jesus, blessed Jesus ;
In his beauty I shall see the King.

Are You Prepared? Am I?

Helen E. Brown.　　"And at midnight there was a cry made." Matt. 25: 6.　　H. L. Gilmour.

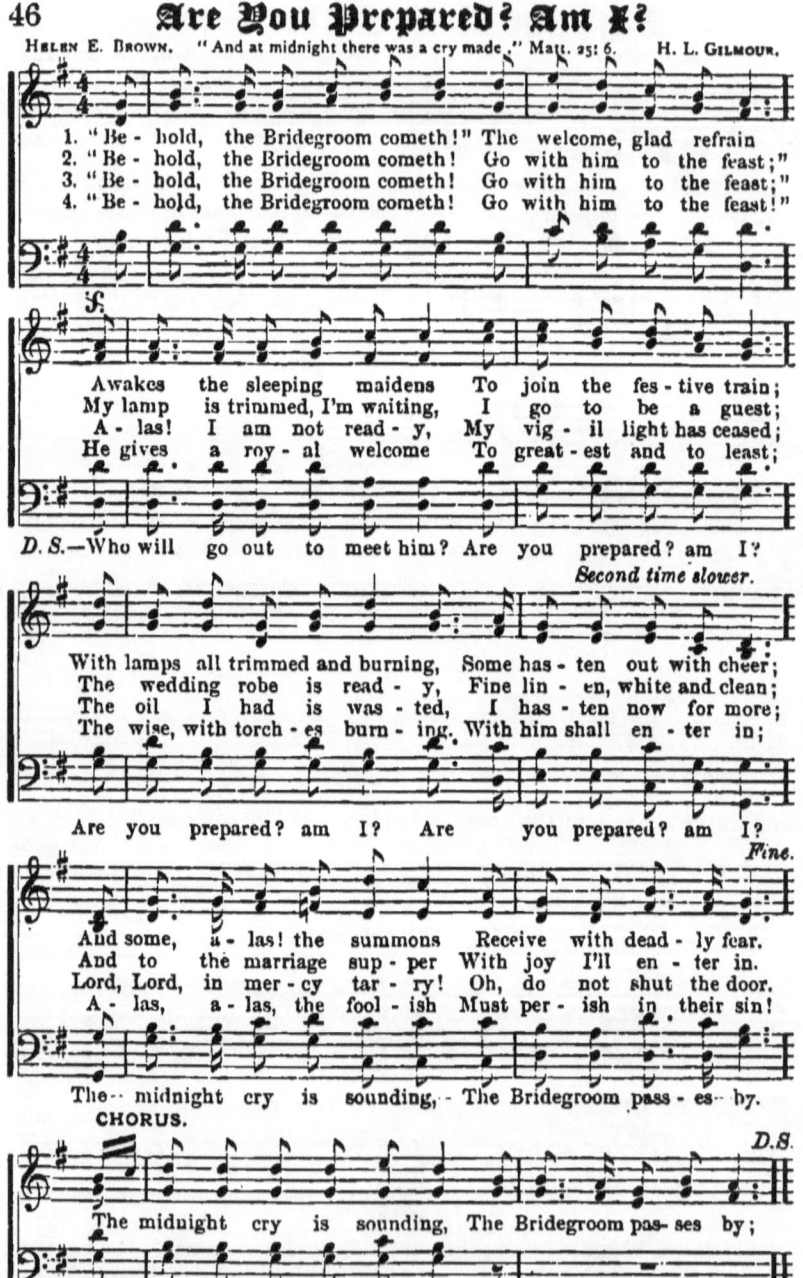

1. "Be - hold, the Bridegroom cometh!" The welcome, glad refrain
2. "Be - hold, the Bridegroom cometh! Go with him to the feast;"
3. "Be - hold, the Bridegroom cometh! Go with him to the feast;"
4. "Be - hold, the Bridegroom cometh! Go with him to the feast!"

Awakes the sleeping maidens To join the fes - tive train;
My lamp is trimmed, I'm waiting, I go to be a guest;
A - las! I am not read - y, My vig - il light has ceased;
He gives a roy - al welcome To great - est and to least;

D. S.—Who will go out to meet him? Are you prepared? am I?

Second time slower.

With lamps all trimmed and burning, Some has - ten out with cheer;
The wedding robe is read - y, Fine lin - en, white and clean;
The oil I had is was - ted, I has - ten now for more;
The wise, with torch - es burn - ing, With him shall en - ter in;

Are you prepared? am I? Are you prepared? am I?

Fine.

And some, a - las! the summons Receive with dead - ly fear.
And to the marriage sup - per With joy I'll en - ter in.
Lord, Lord, in mer - cy tar - ry! Oh, do not shut the door.
A - las, a - las, the fool - ish Must per - ish in their sin!

The-- midnight cry is sounding, - The Bridegroom pass - es-- by.

CHORUS.

D.S.

The midnight cry is sounding, The Bridegroom pas- ses by;

Go to Thy Saviour.

Sallie E. Smith.

Jno. R. Sweney.

47

1. Go to thy Saviour, O sad and op - prest, Pillow thy head on his
2. Hast thou temptations? he knoweth them all,— Seeth thy tears, like tho
3. Art thou discouraged thy la- bor to see Yielding no fruit of re-
4. Leave to the Saviour the work thou hast wrought, Think not thy seed has been

kind, loving breast; Never a tri - al but Jesus can feel, Never a
raindrops that fall; Hast thou been watching while others have slept? Over thy
joicing for thee? Weary of sowing thy seed on the plain, Waiting the
scattered for naught; Jesus has guarded each blade as it grew, He has re-

CHORUS.

sorrow his love will not heal. He was af- flict - - ed and troubled as
spir - it a watch he has kept.
harvest and reaping in vain.
freshed it with sunlight and dew.

thou, Go to thy Sav - - iour, he calleth thee now; Go with thy

burden, whatever it be, Jesus will tenderly share it with thee.

48 I am Weary of Sin.

MARTHA J. LANKTON.   WM. J. KIRKPATRICK.

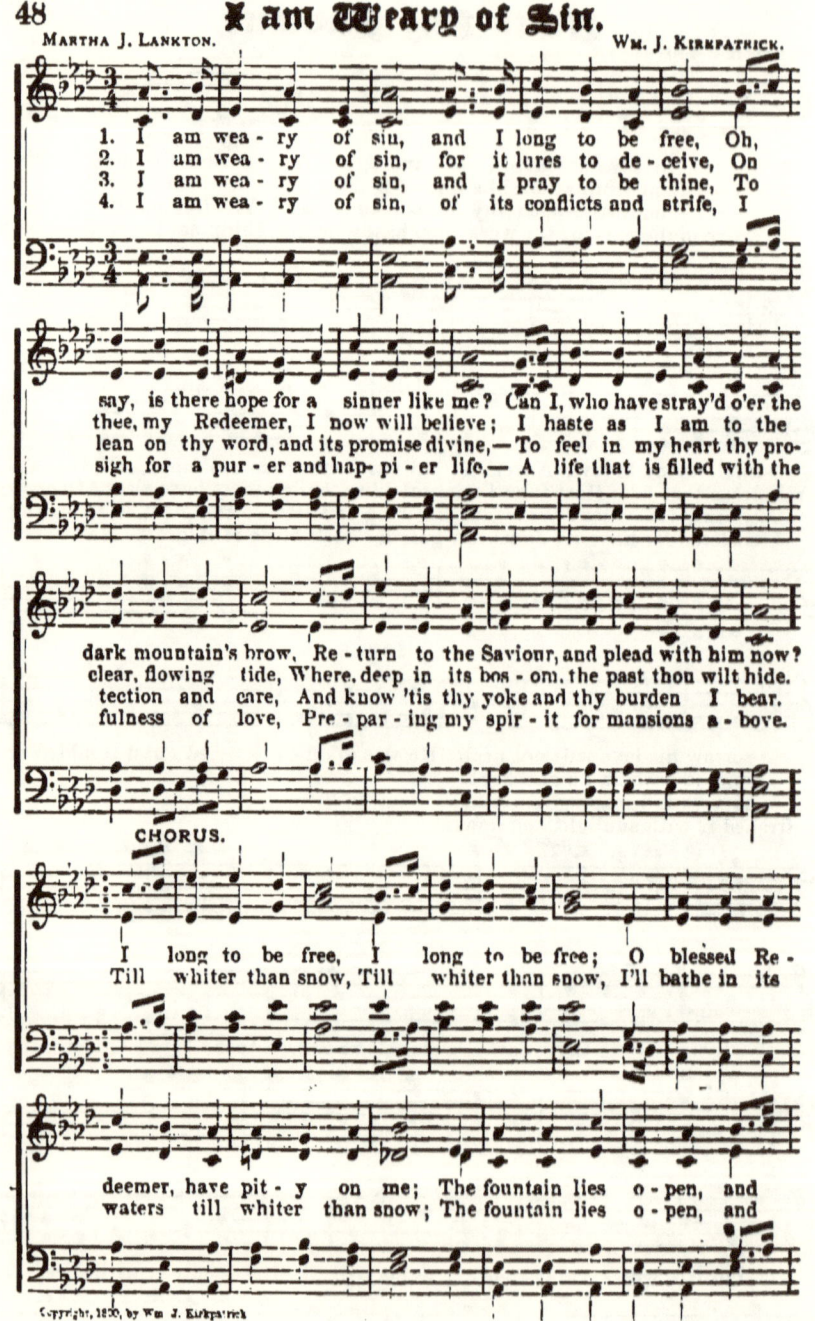

1. I am wea - ry of sin, and I long to be free, Oh,
2. I am wea - ry of sin, for it lures to de - ceive, On
3. I am wea - ry of sin, and I pray to be thine, To
4. I am wea - ry of sin, of its conflicts and strife, I

say, is there hope for a sinner like me? Can I, who have stray'd o'er the
thee, my Redeemer, I now will believe; I haste as I am to the
lean on thy word, and its promise divine,— To feel in my heart thy pro-
sigh for a pur - er and hap- pi - er life,— A life that is filled with the

dark mountain's brow, Re - turn to the Saviour, and plead with him now?
clear, flowing tide, Where, deep in its bos - om, the past thou wilt hide.
tection and care, And know 'tis thy yoke and thy burden I bear.
fulness of love, Pre - par - ing my spir - it for mansions a - bove.

CHORUS.

I long to be free, I long to be free; O blessed Re -
Till whiter than snow, Till whiter than snow, I'll bathe in its

deemer, have pit - y on me; The fountain lies o - pen, and
waters till whiter than snow; The fountain lies o - pen, and

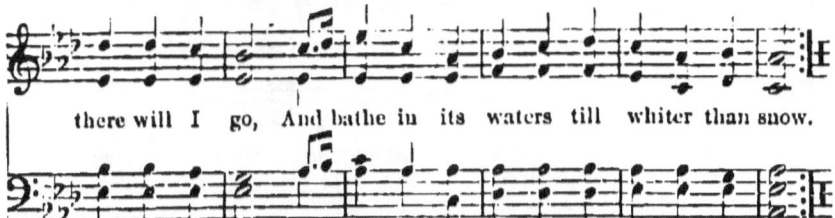

there will I go, And bathe in its waters till whiter than snow.

Hold On, My Soul.

Wm. H. Jones.   Jno. R. Sweney.

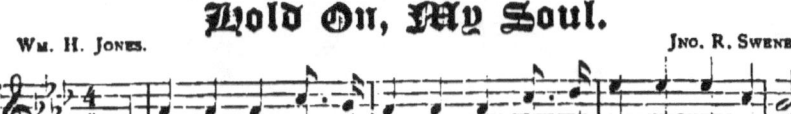

1.   Hold on, my soul, to the end hold out, With a faith no storm can shock;
2.   Hold on, my soul, tho' the lightenings flash, And thy sails all torn may be,
3.   Hold on, my soul, tho' the waves run high, For the night and storm shall cease,
4.   Hold on, my soul, for the end draws near, And thy voyage is well nigh o'er,

Fine.

Stand firm, stand fast, for the Lord has said He will hide thee in the rifted rock.
For thy hope still points to the polar star, Brightly shining thro' the clouds for thee.
There is light beyond, 'tis the morning breaks, Thou art coming to the port of peace.
And the welcome-home thou hast longed to hear Soon will greet thee on the golden
shore.

D.S.—on, my soul, for the Lord has said He will hide thee in the rifted rock.

CHORUS.   D S.

Hold on, (hold on,) hold on.(hold on,) With a faith no storm can shock, Hold

Sunlit Songs—D

Bear ye One Another's Burdens.

E. A. BARNES.   Galatians, vi. 2.   WM. J. KIRKPATRICK.

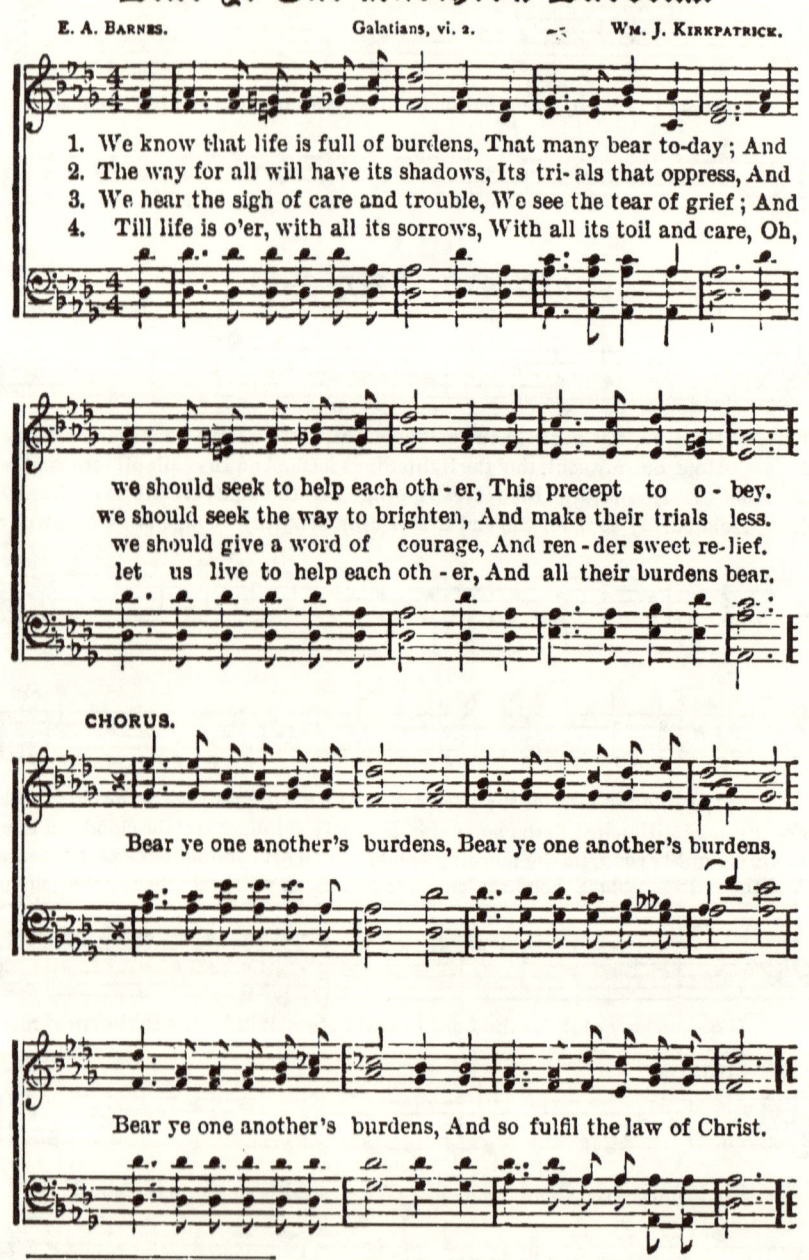

1. We know that life is full of burdens, That many bear to-day ; And
2. The way for all will have its shadows, Its tri-als that oppress, And
3. We hear the sigh of care and trouble, We see the tear of grief ; And
4. Till life is o'er, with all its sorrows, With all its toil and care, Oh,

we should seek to help each oth-er, This precept to o-bey.
we should seek the way to brighten, And make their trials less.
we should give a word of courage, And ren-der sweet re-lief.
let us live to help each oth-er, And all their burdens bear.

CHORUS.

Bear ye one another's burdens, Bear ye one another's burdens,

Bear ye one another's burdens, And so fulfil the law of Christ.

Redemption's Story.

51

Wm. T. Ortlip. Jno R. Sweney.

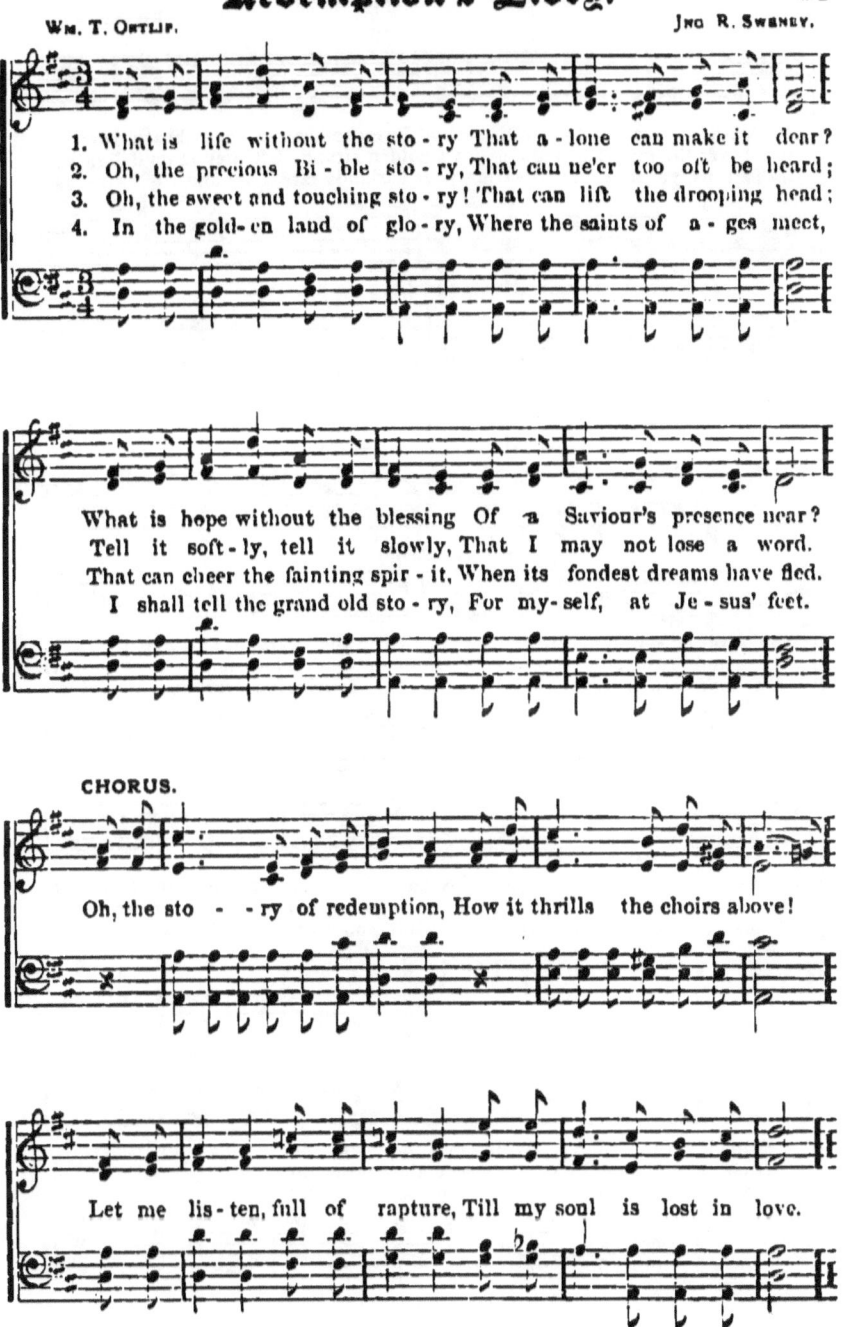

1. What is life without the sto-ry That a-lone can make it dear?
2. Oh, the precious Bi-ble sto-ry, That can ne'er too oft be heard;
3. Oh, the sweet and touching sto-ry! That can lift the drooping head;
4. In the gold-en land of glo-ry, Where the saints of a-ges meet,

What is hope without the blessing Of a Saviour's presence near?
Tell it soft-ly, tell it slowly, That I may not lose a word.
That can cheer the fainting spir-it, When its fondest dreams have fled.
I shall tell the grand old sto-ry, For my-self, at Je-sus' feet.

CHORUS.

Oh, the sto - - ry of redemption, How it thrills the choirs above!

Let me lis-ten, full of rapture, Till my soul is lost in love.

Music and Love.

S. Martin.   Wm. J. Kirkpatrick.

1. Ten-der-ly, soft and clear Music and Love we hear, In our Sabbath dwelling,
2. O- ver the morning land, over its golden strand, Oft they roam delighted,
3. Tell us, ye sisters fair, wearing your garlands rare, Rose and lily twin-ing,

D.S.—soft and clear Music and Love we hear, etc.

songs of rapture swelling, Gently their wings they bend, sweetly their voices blend,
hand in hand u-nit-ed, Over the land of flowers, over its vernal bow-ers,
all their charms combining, Tell us of Him whose eye watcheth beyond the sky,

Fine.

Songs of ho - ly rap-ture swelling; List to their carol. joyful now they say,
Love and Music roam u - ni - ted, Now, on their pinions, fair and snowy white,
O'er our path, in beauty shining; Still they are singing, hear their tuneful lay,

Come to the Sa - viour; glad-ly haste a-way, Come to the ban-quet
Laved in a fountain, sparkling, pure and bright, Quick as an ar - row,
Come to the Saviour, trust him while you may, Come to the ban-quet

Rit. ad lib.   D. S.

wait-ing you to- day, Wait-ing for one and all. Ten-der-ly,
from the vales of light, Com-fort they bring to all.
wait-ing you to- day, Wait-ing for one and all

Stepping in the Light.

53

L. H. Edmunds.   W. J. Kirkpatrick.

1. Trying to walk in the steps of the Saviour, Trying to follow our
2. Pressing more closely to him who is leading, When we are tempted to
3. Walking in footsteps of gen - tle forbearance, Footsteps of faithfulness,
4. Trying to walk in the steps of the Saviour, Upward, still upward we'll

Saviour and King; Shaping our lives by his blessed ex-am-ple,
turn from the way; Trusting the arm that is strong to defend us,
mer - cy, and love, Looking to him for - the grace free- ly promised,
fol - low our Guide, When we shall see him, "the King in his beauty."

CHORUS.

Happy, how happy, the songs that we bring. How beautiful to walk in the
Happy, how happy, our praises each day.
Happy, how happy, our journey above.
Happy, how happy, our place at his side.

steps of the Saviour, Stepping in the light, Stepping in the light; How

beautiful to walk in the steps of the Saviour. Led in paths of light.

54 More Room.

E. E. Hewitt.

Jno. R. Sweney.

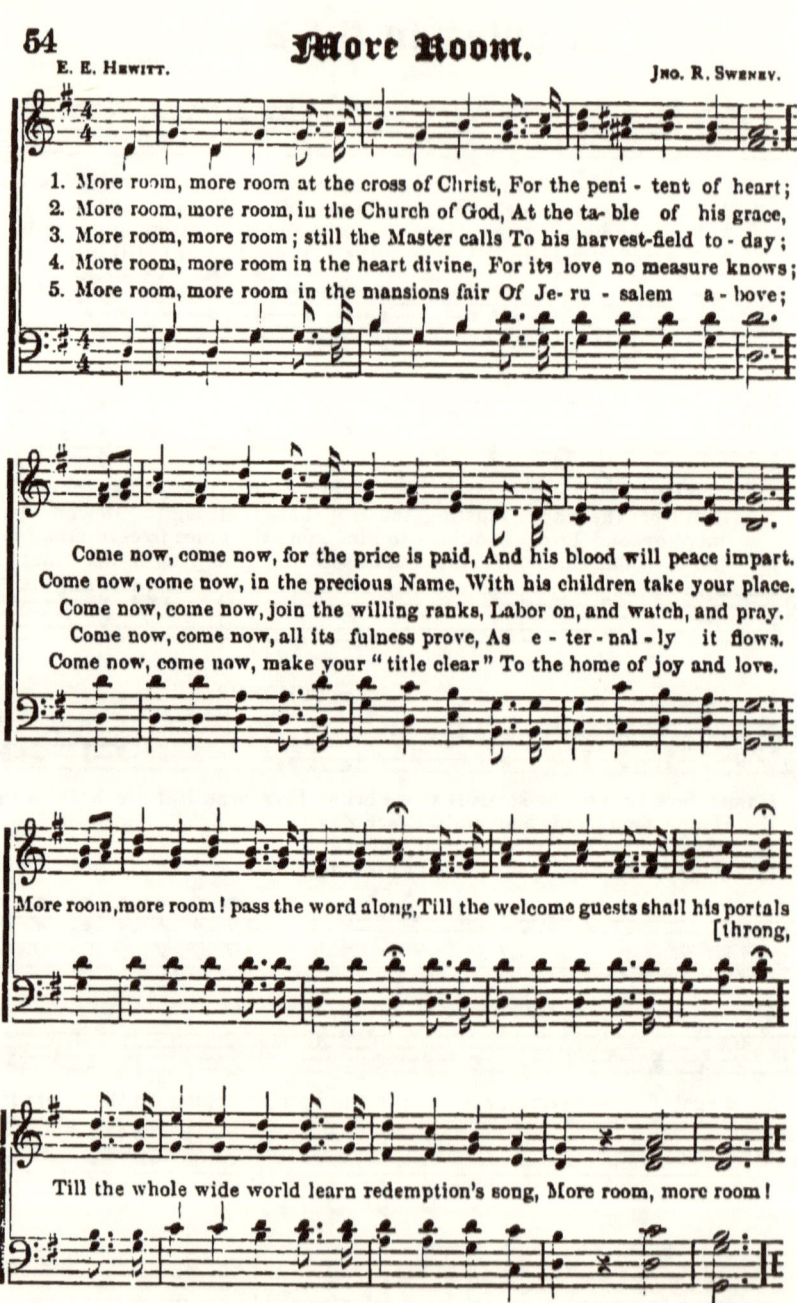

1. More room, more room at the cross of Christ, For the peni - tent of heart;
2. More room, more room, in the Church of God, At the ta- ble of his grace,
3. More room, more room; still the Master calls To his harvest-field to - day;
4. More room, more room in the heart divine, For its love no measure knows;
5. More room, more room in the mansions fair Of Je - ru - salem a - bove;

Come now, come now, for the price is paid, And his blood will peace impart.
Come now, come now, in the precious Name, With his children take your place.
Come now, come now, join the willing ranks, Labor on, and watch, and pray.
Come now, come now, all its fulness prove, As e - ter - nal - ly it flows.
Come now, come now, make your "title clear" To the home of joy and love.

More room, more room! pass the word along, Till the welcome guests shall his portals [throng,

Till the whole wide world learn redemption's song, More room, more room!

Though Your Sins be as Scarlet.

"Though your sins be as scarlet, they shall be as white as snow "—Isaiah I, 18.

FANNY J. CROSBY.

W. H. DOANE. By per.

DUET. *Gently.*

|1st. |2nd.

1. "Tho' your sins be as scarlet, They shall be as white as snow ; as snow ;
2. Hear the voice that entreats you, Oh, return ye unto God ! to God !
3. He'll forgive your transgressions, And remember them no more ; no more ;

QUARTET.

Tho' they be red . . . . like crimson, They shall be as wool ;"
He is of great . . . compassion, And of wondrous love ;
"Look un- to me, . . . ye people," Saith the Lord your God ;

Tho' they be red

DUET. p

QUARTET. f

"Tho' your sins be as scarlet, Tho' your sins be as scarlet,
Hear the voice that entreats you, Hear the voice that entreats you,
He'll forgive your transgressions, He'll forgive your transgressions,

p ritard.

They shall be as white as snow, They shall be as white as snow."
Oh, return ye un - to God! Oh, return ye un - to God!
And remem - ber them no more, And remem -ber them no more.

Blessed Redeemer.

Abbie Mills. H. L. Gilmour.

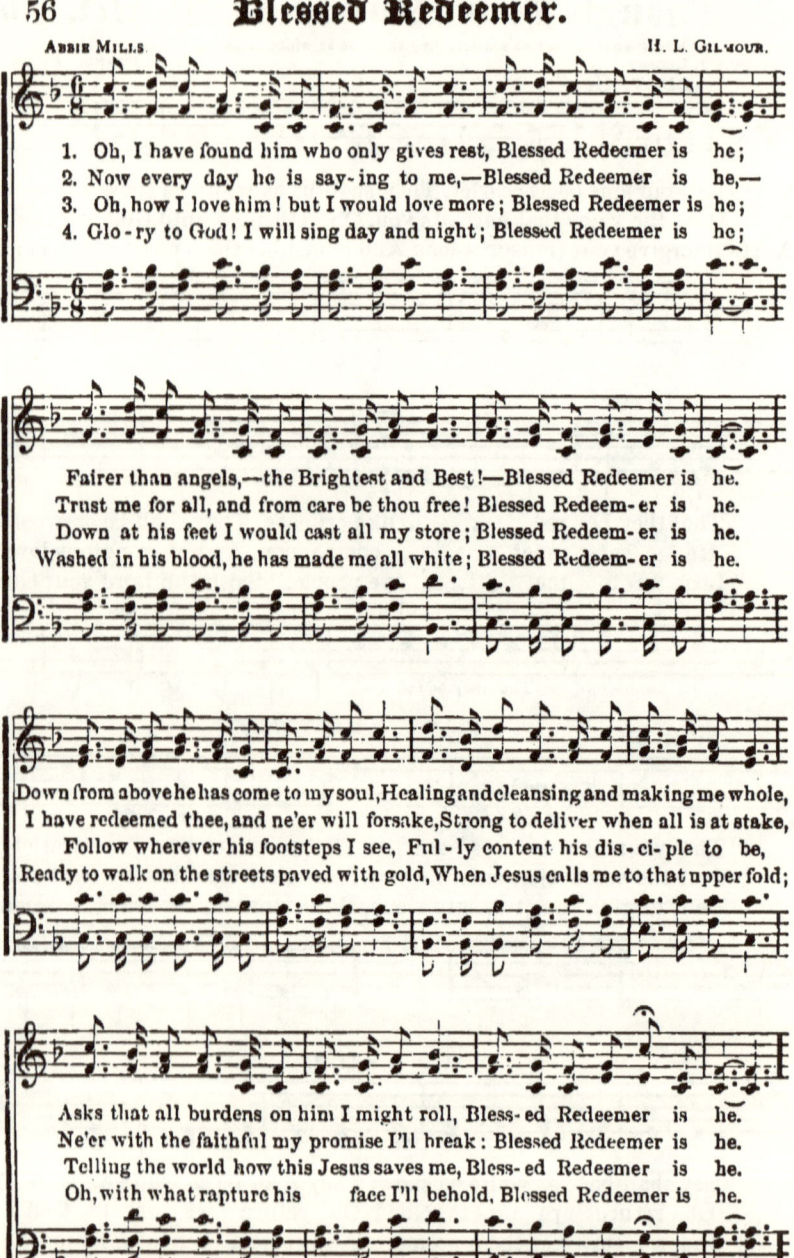

1. Oh, I have found him who only gives rest, Blessed Redeemer is he;
2. Now every day he is say-ing to me,—Blessed Redeemer is he,—
3. Oh, how I love him! but I would love more; Blessed Redeemer is he;
4. Glo-ry to God! I will sing day and night; Blessed Redeemer is he;

Fairer than angels,—the Brightest and Best!—Blessed Redeemer is he.
Trust me for all, and from care be thou free! Blessed Redeem-er is he.
Down at his feet I would cast all my store; Blessed Redeem-er is he.
Washed in his blood, he has made me all white; Blessed Redeem-er is he.

Down from above he has come to my soul, Healing and cleansing and making me whole,
I have redeemed thee, and ne'er will forsake, Strong to deliver when all is at stake,
Follow wherever his footsteps I see, Ful-ly content his dis-ci-ple to be,
Ready to walk on the streets paved with gold, When Jesus calls me to that upper fold;

Asks that all burdens on him I might roll, Bless-ed Redeemer is he.
Ne'er with the faithful my promise I'll break: Blessed Redeemer is he.
Telling the world how this Jesus saves me, Bless-ed Redeemer is he.
Oh, with what rapture his face I'll behold, Blessed Redeemer is he.

CHORUS.

Blessed Redeemer once dying for me, Loving the sinner, oh, how could it be!

Love—it was wonderful!—love set me free; Oh, what a blessed Redeemer is he!

The Golden Key.

"Prayer is the key to unlock the door, and the bolt to shut in the night."

JNO. R. SWENEY.

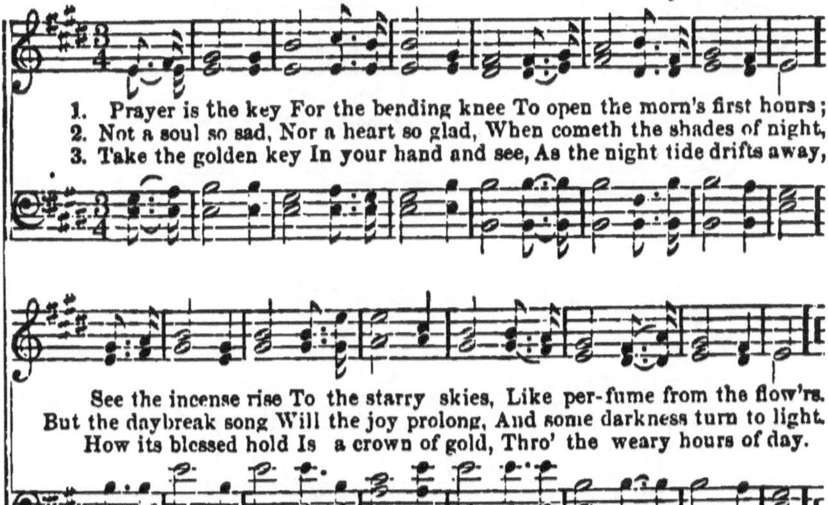

1. Prayer is the key For the bending knee To open the morn's first hours;
2. Not a soul so sad, Nor a heart so glad, When cometh the shades of night,
3. Take the golden key In your hand and see, As the night tide drifts away,

See the incense rise To the starry skies, Like per-fume from the flow'rs.
But the daybreak song Will the joy prolong, And some darkness turn to light.
How its blessed hold Is a crown of gold, Thro' the weary hours of day.

4 When the shadows fall,
  And the vesper call
Is sobbing its low refrain,
  'Tis a garland sweet
  To the toil dent feet,
And an antidote for pain

5 Soon the year's dark door
  Shall be shut no more:
Life's tears shall be wiped away,
  As the pearl gates swing,
  And the gold harps ring,
And the sun unsheathe for aye.

The King of Glory.

E. A. BARNES.　　　" Who is this King of Glory ? " Ps. xxiv. 10.　　　JNO. R. SWENEY.

1. There is a King of Glory, Upon his shining throne, And words cannot be
2. He reigns in all his beauty, The King of joys divine, And where, amid the
3. There is a King of Glo-ry, Within his city bright, And all the blessed

given here, His glory to make known ; In his e-ternal kingdom All
courts of life, The blessed ev-er shine ; In all his many mansions There
sing his praise, Rejoicing in his sight ; The King awaits our coming,—The

shadows disappear, And we shall yet behold the King, If we are faithful here.
is no sigh or tear, And we shall yet behold the King, If we are faithful here.
day is drawing near, When we shall all behold the King, If we are faithful here.

CHORUS.

Who is this King of Glory ? Who is this King of Glory ? 'Tis Je-sus ! 'tis

Jesus ! who reigns a - bove : Who is this king of Glo-ry ? Who is this

King of Glo- ry? 'Tis Je - sus! 'tis Je - sus! who reigns a - bove.

The Lord is my Shepherd.

JAMES MONTGOMERY. Psalm xxiii. Arr. from KOSCHAT.
Note. The melody is in the tenor part.

1. The Lord is my Shepherd, no want shall I know; I feed in green pastures,
2. Thro' the valley and shadow of death tho' I stray, Since thou art my guardian,

safe fold- ed I rest; He leadeth my soul where the still waters flow,
no ev - il I fear; Thy rod shall defend me, thy staff be my stay;

Restores me when wand'ring, redeems when oppressed, Restores me when
No harm can be - fall, with my Comfort-er near, No harm can be-

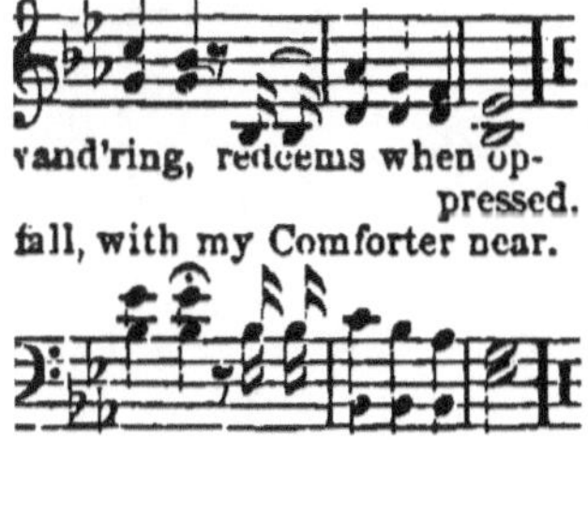

vand'ring, redeems when oppressed.
fall, with my Comforter near.

3 In the midst of affliction my table is spread;
With blessings unmeasured my cup runneth o'er;
With perfume and oil thou anointest my head;
O what shall I ask of thy providence more?

4 Let goodness and mercy, my bountiful God,
Still follow my steps till I meet thee above;
I seek—by the path which my forefathers trod,
Through the land of their sojourn—thy kingdom
of love.

He Hideth my Soul.

FANNY J. CROSBY.

WM. J. KIRKPATRICK.

Allegretto.

1. A wonderful Saviour is Je-sus my Lord, A wonderful Saviour to
2. A wonderful Saviour is Je-sus my Lord, He taketh my burden a-
3. With numberless blessings each moment he crowns, And fill'd with his fulness di-
4. When clothed in his brightness transported I rise To meet him in clouds of the

me, He hideth my soul in the cleft of the rock, Where rivers of
way, He holdeth me up, and I shall not be moved, He giveth me
vine, I sing in my rapture, oh, glo-ry to God For such a Re-
sky, His perfect salvation, his wonderful love, I'll shout with the

CHORUS.

pleasure I see. He hideth my soul in the cleft of the rock, That
strength as my day.
deemer as mine!
millions on high.

shadows a dry, thirsty land; He hid-eth my life in the depths of his

love, And covers me there with his hand, And covers me there with his hand

To Save a Poor Sinner.

Rev. John O. Foster, A. M. Grace I. Foster.

1. I'll sing of the sto-ry, how Je-sus from glo-ry Has saved a poor
2. His glo-ry im-mortal bright o-ver the por-tal, Has banished the
3. Tho' seasons of error, and moments of ter-ror, Like billows of
4. My peace like a riv-er flows onward for-ev-er, A tide to e-

sinner like me; That all who believe him, and all who receive him, His
gloom from the grave; The Lord has ascended, the darkness is ended, And
sorrow may roll; In Christ I'm confiding, in him I am hiding, With
terni-ty's sea; To swell the old story with voices in glory, He

CHORUS.

blessed sal-vation may see. Then sing the glad chorus, His
now he is mighty to save.
safe-ty and rest to my soul.
saved a poor sinner like me.

banner is o'er us, His mercy is boundless and free. From heaven de-

ri.

scended, His love is extended, To save a poor sinner like me.

62 Hear the Gentle, Kindly Word.

E. E. Hewitt.   Wm. J. Kirkpatrick.

1. Hear the gentle, kindly word, "Come to me, come to me,"
2. Weary-hearted, hear him say, "Come to me, come to me,"
3. 'Tis a word of hope and cheer? "Come to me, come to me,"
4. He will draw us nearer still, "Come to me, come to me,"

Sweeter welcome nev- er heard, "Come to me, come to me,"
Bring your sin, your grief, to - day, "Come to me, come to me,"
Can we doubt him? can we fear? "Come to me, come to me,"
With his grace our spirits fill, "Come to me, come to me,"

'Tis the blessed Saviour's call, Off'ring life and peace to all,
Glad-ly make his will your choice, He will make your soul rejoice,
At his feet our hearts we lay, When his bidding we o - bey,
Soon we'll leave the shores of time, From a fair- er, brighter clime

And his tones like dewdrops fall, "Come to me, come to me."
'Tis the Burden-bearer's voice, "Come to me, come to me."
Calling us from sin a - way, "Come to me, come to me."
Comes again that voice sub-lime, "Come to me, come to me."

Coming Home.

Rev. J. P. Dimmitt. W. J. Kirkpatrick.

1. We have wandered far a-way from our Father's home, In the
2. We are coming now by faith, by the Spir-it led, We are
3. We have kindred gone be-fore, to the heavenly home, And they

dark and dreary paths of sin; But we hear our Saviour's voice calling
coming with our hearts to thee; We are trusting in the blood that for
draw us by the chords of love; They are calling us to-day, calling

us to come, And at once a better life be-gin. We are coming home,
us was shed, And the Holy Spirit sets us free.
us to come To the happy, happy home above. coming,

REFRAIN.

We are coming home, coming home to-day; We have
coming, coming, to-day,

heard thy loving voice, Blessed Saviour, and rejoice; We are coming home to-day.

Have You Heard?

H. L. G.

H. L. Gilmour.

1. Have you heard, when sad and weary Je- sus sat on Jacob's well, How a
2. Have you heard, he fed five thousand, With five loaves, two fishes small, Which he
3. Have you heard, that in the garden Jesus sweat great drops of blood? His di-

woman came for water, And the sto- ry he did tell Of the well of liv-ing
brake to his di- sciples, And they gave to one and all? Do you know he still is
sciples all forsook him, When he prayed unto his God? But the cup did not pass

water, Springing ever, flowing free?—Whosoever thirsts may have it, Sinner,
feeding Hungry souls who to him come? Do you know he still is leading Willing
from him, For on Calvary he died, Where his blood flow'd out for sinners, As the

CHORUS.

come, it is for thee. The old, old sto-ry ev-er new, The
feet to heaven and home?
soldiers pierced his side.

ev- er new,

old, old sto-ry grand and true. Tell it out for God's own
grand and true,

glo- ry, 'Tis the same old Gospel story, Of a free and full sal - va - tion.

4 Have you heard he broke death's fetters
   As he rose from Joseph's grave;
For no Roman seal, or soldiers,
   Could prevent the plan to save.

And to-day he reigns in glory,
   Borne by cloud to native sky,
Hear, oh, hear the " old, old story,"
   Sinner, turn: why will you die.

On the Way.

LIZZIE EDWARDS.   JNO. R. SWENEY.

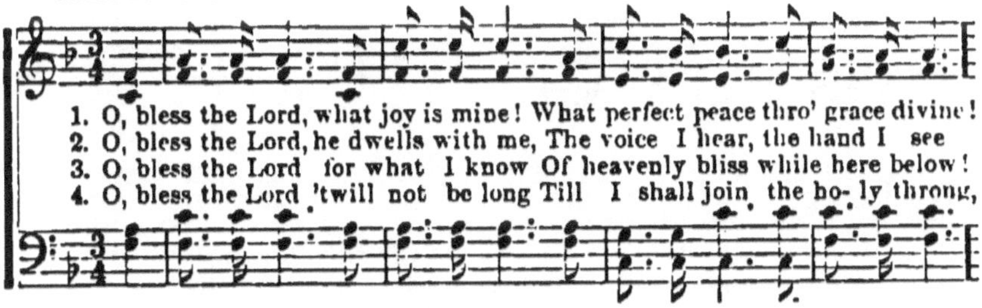

1. O, bless the Lord, what joy is mine! What perfect peace thro' grace divine!
2. O, bless the Lord, he dwells with me, The voice I hear, the hand I see
3. O, bless the Lord for what I know Of heavenly bliss while here below!
4. O, bless the Lord 'twill not be long Till I shall join the ho- ly throng,

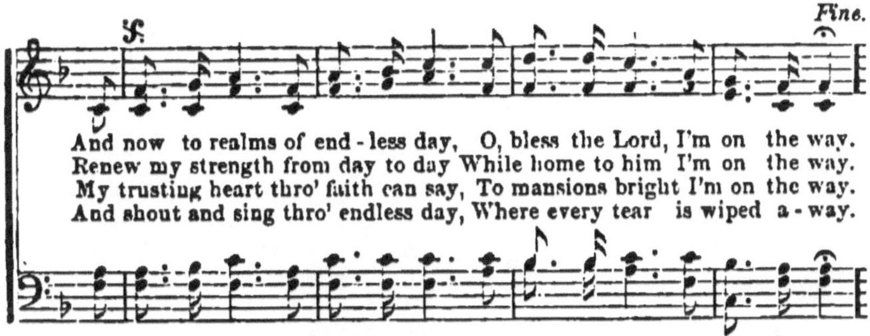

Fine.

And now to realms of end - less day, O, bless the Lord, I'm on the way.
Renew my strength from day to day While home to him I'm on the way.
My trusting heart thro' faith can say, To mansions bright I'm on the way.
And shout and sing thro' endless day, Where every tear is wiped a - way.

D. S.—crown to wear in end - less day, O, bless the Lord, I'm on the way.

CHORUS.   *D S.*

I'm on the way, I'm on the way, In vain the world would bid me stay; A

     Sunlit Songs—E

66 Beautiful Robes.

E. E. HEWITT.   WM. J. KIRKPATRICK.

Not too fast.

1. We shall walk with him in white, In that country pure and bright, Where shall
2. We shall walk with him in white, Where faith yields to blissful sight, When the
3. We shall walk with him in white, By the fountains of delight, Where the

enter naught that may defile; Where the day-beam ne'er declines, For the
beauty of the King we   see; Holding converse full and sweet, In a
Lamb his ransomed ones shall lead, For his blood shall wash each stain, Till no

blessed light that shines Is   the glo - ry of   the Saviour's smile.
fel - lowship complete; Waking songs of   ho - ly mel - o - dy.
spot of sin remain, And the soul for - ev - ermore is freed.

CHORUS.

Beau - - tiful robes, . . Beau - - tiful robes, . .
Beautiful robes,   beautiful robes,   Beautiful robes,   beautiful robes,

Beau - - - ti- ful robes   we then   shall   wear, . .
Beau - ti - ful robes   we then shall wear, Beau - ti - ful robes we then shall wear,

Gar - - ments of light, . . . Love - - ly and bright, . .
Garments of light, . . Garments of light, Lovely and bright, . . Lovely and bright,

Walking with Je - sus in white, Beau - ti - ful robes we shall wear.

Only for Thee.

E. E. H.
Slowly.

W. J. K.

1. Lord, keep my inmost heart Only for thee, Choosing the better part, Only for thee.

Thou hast my ransom bought, Now be my life inwrought, Only for thee.
With this constraining thought,

2 Use thou each gift and power,
  Only for thee;
Hallow the passing hour,
  Only for thee.
So shall my joy-filled days,
Spent in thy gracious ways,
Show forth thy matchless praise,
  Only for thee;

3 Uplift my purest love,
  Only for thee,
Drawn to its source above,
  Only for thee.

Through my petitions, still,
Breathing thy holy will,
Thy blessed grace fulfill,
  Only for thee.

4 Saviour, thy gold refine,
  Only for thee;
Thy beauty in me shine,
  Only for thee:
Then, when thou giv'st the crown,
At thy dear feet laid down
All glory and renown,
  Only for thee.

Come Over.

 F. A. B.

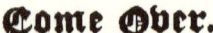 F. A. BLACKMER.

1. Come o- ver, lost one, come O - ver the line to-day, Where Jesus
2. On - ly a step to God, One step to cross the line; Hast-en, O
3. Moment of priceless worth, When God has drawn so near; His wondrous
4. Dare not this call refuse, When du - ty is so plain; The Spir- it
5. Lost one, this call to you May be the ver - y last! Haste! ere for-

CHORUS.

bids you stand : Oh, come a- way.   Come o - ver, oh, come o- ver, Come
dy - ing one, Touch the Divine!
ten- ner-ness, Sin- ner, re- vere.
long denied Comes not a- gain.
ev - er- more Your day be past.

over the line to-day; And heav'n delight, while men invite, And angels seem to

say, Come o - ver, oh, come o - ver, Come o - ver the line to- day;

rit.

To Je - sus bow, He calls you now, Come over the line to - day.

Who will be Waiting?

L. H. Edmunds.

Wm. J. Kirkpatrick.

Slowly.

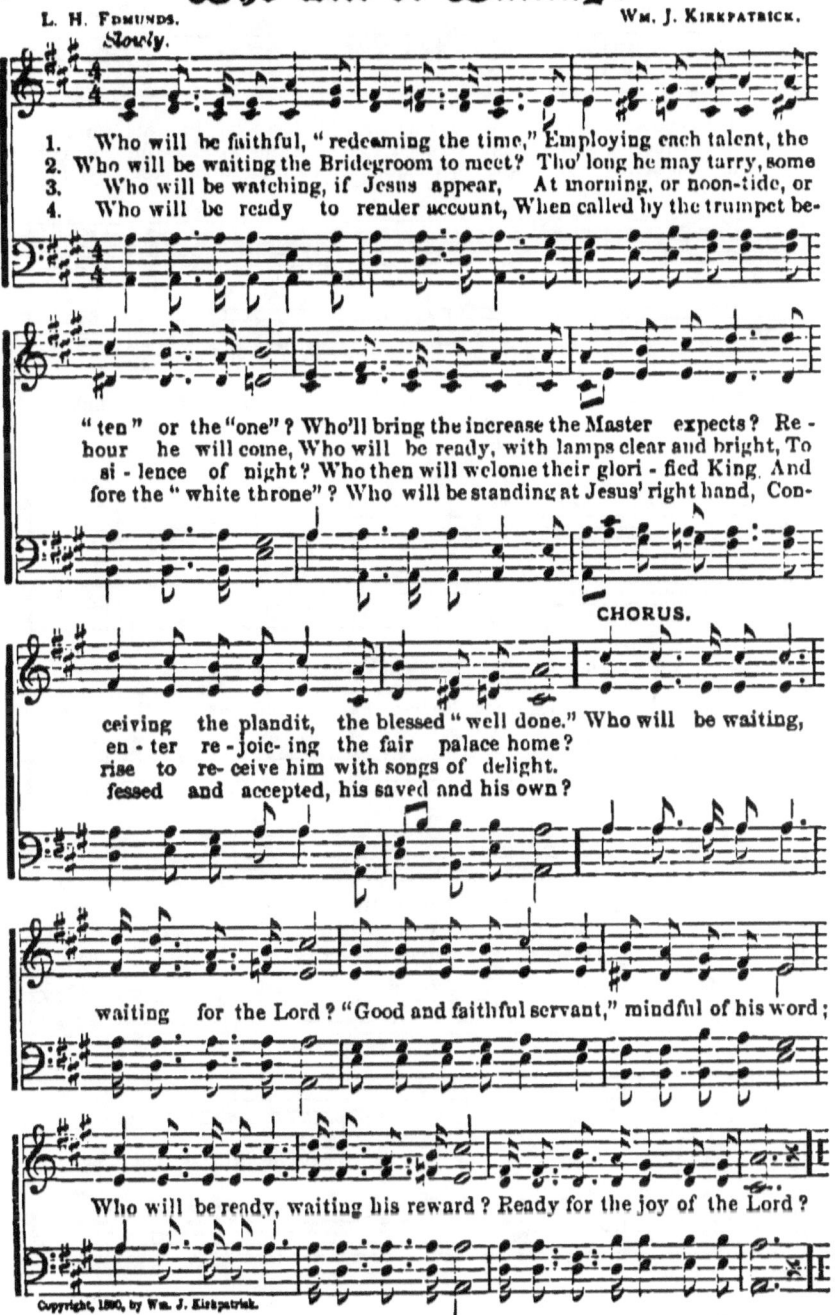

1. Who will be faithful, "redeeming the time," Employing each talent, the
2. Who will be waiting the Bridegroom to meet? Tho' long he may tarry, some
3. Who will be watching, if Jesus appear, At morning, or noon-tide, or
4. Who will be ready to render account, When called by the trumpet be-

"ten" or the "one"? Who'll bring the increase the Master expects? Re-
hour he will come, Who will be ready, with lamps clear and bright, To
si - lence of night? Who then will welcome their glori - fied King, And
fore the "white throne"? Who will be standing at Jesus' right hand, Con-

CHORUS.

ceiving the plaudit, the blessed "well done." Who will be waiting,
en - ter re-joic-ing the fair palace home?
rise to re-ceive him with songs of delight.
fessed and accepted, his saved and his own?

waiting for the Lord? "Good and faithful servant," mindful of his word;

Who will be ready, waiting his reward? Ready for the joy of the Lord?

70 **Victory Through Grace.**

SALLIE MARTIN.   JNO. R. SWENEY.

1. Conquering now and to conquer, Rideth a King in his might,
2. Conquering now and to conquer, Who is this wonder-ful King?
3. Conquering now and to conquer, Jesus, thou Ruler of all,

Leading the host of the faithful In-to the midst of the fight;
Whence are the arm-ies he leadeth, While of his glo-ry they sing?
Thrones and their scepters shall perish, Crowns and their splendor shall fall,

See them with courage ad-vancing, Clad in their brilliant ar-ray,
He is our Lord and Redeem-er, Saviour and monarch di-vine,
Yet shall the arm-ies thou leadest, Faithful and true to the last,

Shouting the name of their Leader, Hear them ex-ult-ing-ly say.
They are the stars that for-ev-er Bright in his kingdom will shine.
Find in thy mansions e-ternal Rest, when their warfare is past.

CHORUS.

Not to the strong is the bat-tle, Not to the swift is the race,

Yet to the true and the faithful Vict'ry is promised through grace.

The Lord will Provide.

WM. J. KIRKPATRICK.

1. When crosses are nearest, When losses thou fearest, When friends lov'd the
2. When earthly friends leave thee, When bitter words grieve thee, When lov'd ones de-
3. When hot tears are falling, When troubles appall- ing Seem constantly
4. His grace shall sustain thee, His mercy constrain thee, His goodness main-

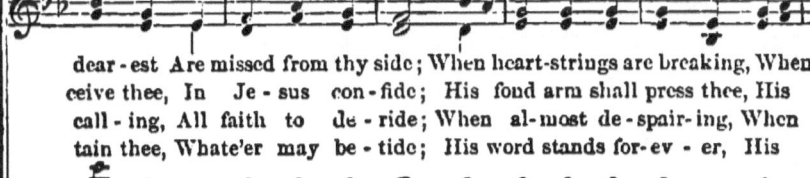

dear - est Are missed from thy side; When heart-strings are breaking, When
ceive thee, In Je - sus con - fide; His fond arm shall press thee, His
call - ing, All faith to de - ride; When al - most de - spair-ing, When
tain thee, Whate'er may be - tide; His word stands for- ev - er, His

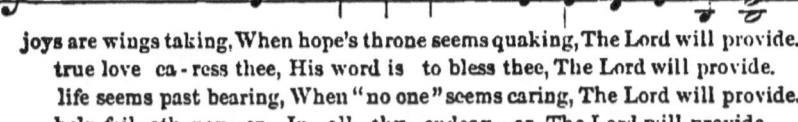

joys are wings taking, When hope's throne seems quaking, The Lord will provide.
true love ca - ress thee, His word is to bless thee, The Lord will provide.
life seems past bearing, When "no one" seems caring, The Lord will provide.
help fail- eth nev - er In all thy endeav - or, The Lord will provide.

All Things in Jesus.

E. E. Hewitt.   *" All things are yours, and ye are Christ's."*   Wm. J. Kirkpatrick.

1. Wonderful promise! all things are mine; Jesus my surety, Saviour divine,
2. Peace that my spirit freshens and calms, Praise and rejoicing, jubilant psalms;
3. Finding the treasures time cannot dim, Joy in his service, likeness to him;
4. All things in Jesus, since he is mine; Light from its fountain, life from
      the vine;

Mine by a cov'nant, order'd and sure, Sign'd by his life-blood, seal'd and secure.
Comfort in sorrow, strength as my day, Wells of salvation cheering the way.
Grace all abounding, fulness of love; Blessings unmeasur'd stream from above.
Only to trust him, only to take Gifts of his purchase, for his dear sake.

CHORUS.

Won - - derful, wonderful promise! Lord, . be it mine; .
Wonderful promise,   wonder- ful promise! Lord, be it mine,   Lord, be it mine;

Glo - - ry and blessing forever, Sav - - iour, be thine.
Glory and blessing   ev - er and ev - er, Saviour be thine, be thine.

JOSEPHINE HINKSON.　　　　　　　　　　　　　　　JNO. R. SWENEY.

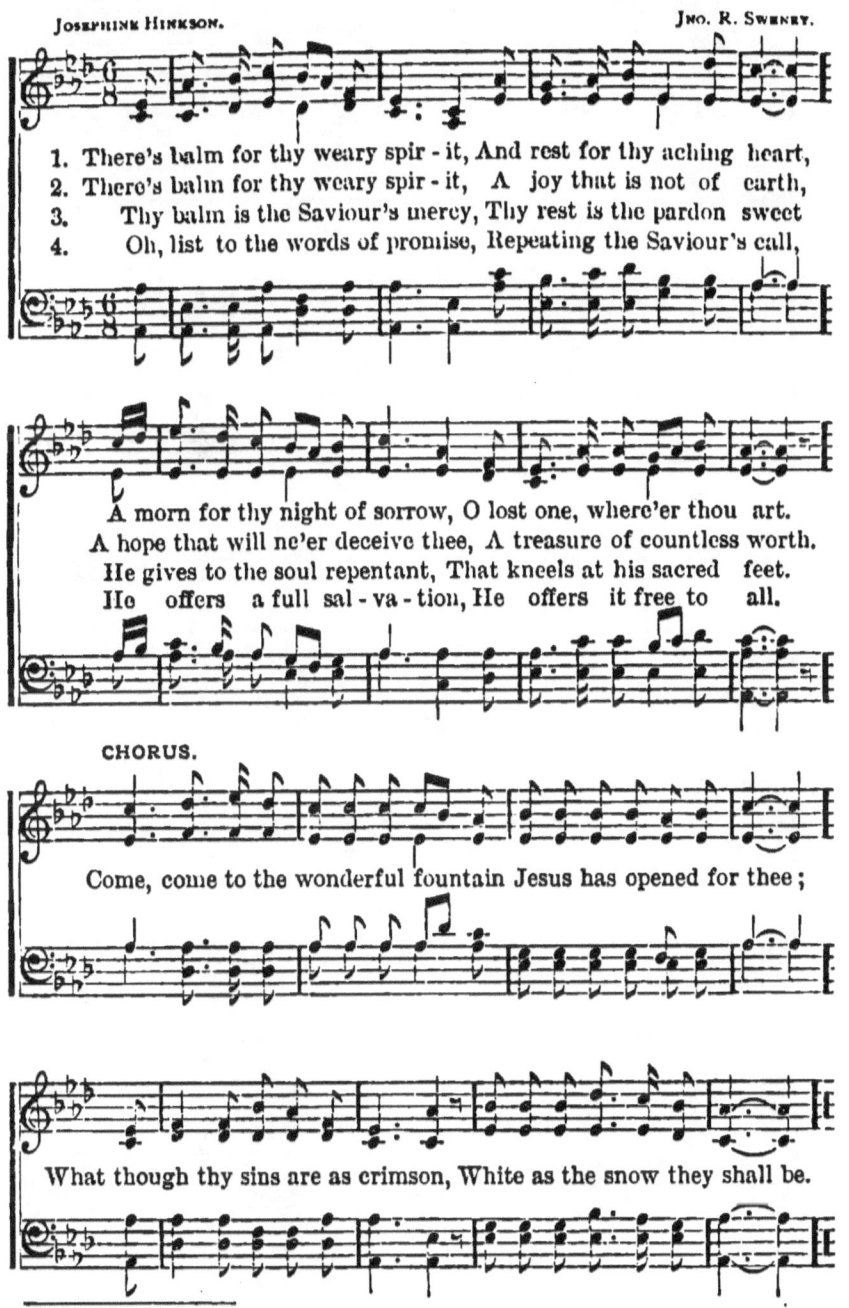

1. There's balm for thy weary spir - it, And rest for thy aching heart,
2. There's balm for thy weary spir - it, A joy that is not of earth,
3. Thy balm is the Saviour's mercy, Thy rest is the pardon sweet
4. Oh, list to the words of promise, Repeating the Saviour's call,

A morn for thy night of sorrow, O lost one, where'er thou art.
A hope that will ne'er deceive thee, A treasure of countless worth.
He gives to the soul repentant, That kneels at his sacred feet.
He offers a full sal - va - tion, He offers it free to all.

CHORUS.

Come, come to the wonderful fountain Jesus has opened for thee;

What though thy sins are as crimson, White as the snow they shall be.

Here and Now.

L. H. Edmunds. Wm. J. Kirkpatrick.

1. On the shining fields of glo-ry They are singing end-less praise,
2. On the shining fields of glo-ry They are singing of the grace
3. From the shining fields of glo-ry Echoes down the blest refrain,

They are telling love's sweet sto-ry, Where the jewelled arch-es blaze;
That hath clothed them in white raiment, Brought them to yon "happy place:"
And my heart, in grateful rapture, Learn's the hal-le-lu-jah strain:

Yet a-mid the heav'nly mu-sic, Je-sus list-ens for the voice
O, that grace my soul is cleansing, Keeps me, saves me all the way,
Sing, O sing, ex-ult-ant spir-its, I will join your band ere long,

Of a contrite, ransomed sinner, Who would fain in him rejoice.
For his pres-ent, sure sal-va-tion I will bless his name to-day.
Then let time be-gin the prelude Of e-ter-ni-ty's grand song.

CHORUS.

I'll not wait, I'll not wait till I pass the pear-ly gate, Till a

crown of life is sparkling on my brow, I will sing of my dear
till it's sparkling on my brow,

Saviour, And his wondrous love and favor, I will praise him here and now.

WM. T. JONES.

Seeking the Lost.

JNO. R. SWENEY.

1. Out on the cold, cold mountain, Out in the darkness deep,
2. Out on the cold, cold mountain, When will you cease to roam?
3. Why will you doubt and linger, Why will you slight his call?
4. Think of his fold so peace-ful, Sheltered and closed and warm,

Go-eth the ten-der Shep-herd, Seek-ing the wand'ring sheep.
O-ver you bends the Shep-herd, Wait-ing to bear you home.
One lit-tle word, if spo-ken, He will forgive you all.
There may you dwell for-ev-er, Safe from the gathering storm.

Come to his arms so gen-tle, Come to his love so true.

CHORUS.

Seek-ing the lost, seek-ing the lost, Seeking, poor soul, for you, for you.

A Shout of Victory.

L. H. Edmunds.   Wm. J. Kirkpatrick.

1. March on, march on, follow the mighty Commander; March on, march on;
2. March on, march on; joyful-ly singing, hosanna; March on, march on;
3. March on, march on; still by his might overcoming; March on, march on;

Jesus our Captain and Lord; March on, march on; see that your steps never
fighting the bat-tle of faith; March on, march on; manfully bearing his
singing his glory and grace; March on, march on; till in the heaven-ly

CHORUS.

fal - ter, March on, march on, heeding his ev - 'ry word. There's a
ban - ner, March on, march on, faithful e'en un - to death.
pal - ace, March on, march on, we shall behold his face.

song, ... that blends with prayer, .. There's a shout ... up-

There's a song,   that blends with prayer,   There's a shout

on the air; ..... 'Tis a song .... of grace so

up-on the air,   'Tis a song

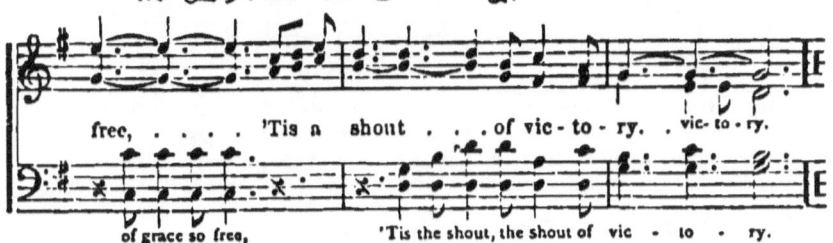

free, ... 'Tis a shout . . .of vic-to-ry. vic-to-ry.

of grace so free, 'Tis the shout, the shout of vic - to - ry.

Vale of Beulah.

E. A. HOFFMAN.

JOSEPH GARRISON.

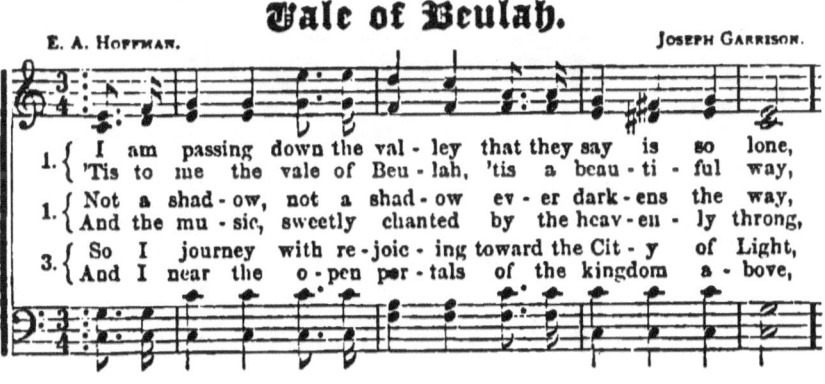

1. { I am passing down the val - ley that they say is so lone,
   { 'Tis to me the vale of Beu - lah, 'tis a beau - ti - ful way,
1. { Not a shad - ow, not a shad - ow ev - er dark - ens the way,
   { And the mu - sic, sweetly chanted by the heav - en - ly throng,
3. { So I journey with re - joic - ing toward the Cit - y of Light,
   { And I near the o - pen por - tals of the kingdom a - bove,

℔ Fine.

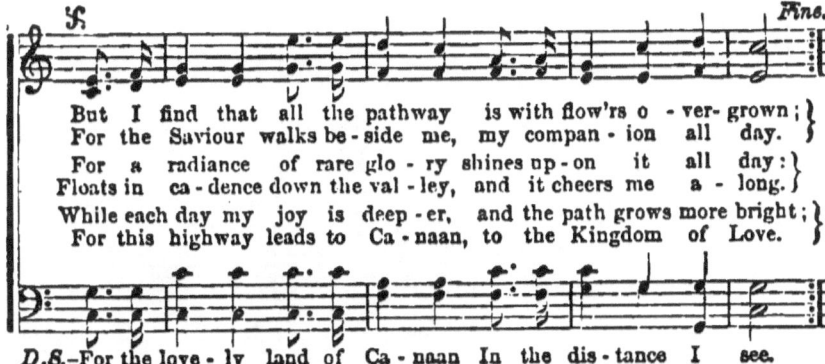

But I find that all the pathway is with flow'rs o - ver-grown; }
For the Saviour walks be - side me, my compan - ion all day. }
For a radiance of rare glo - ry shines up - on it all day: }
Floats in ca - dence down the val - ley, and it cheers me a - long. }
While each day my joy is deep - er, and the path grows more bright; }
For this highway leads to Ca - naan, to the Kingdom of Love. }

D.S.—For the love - ly land of Ca - naan In the dis - tance I see.

CHORUS.

D.S.

Vale of Beulah! Vale of Beulah! Thou art precious to me;

Hosanna in the Highest.

FANNY J. CROSBY.   JNO. R. SWENEY.

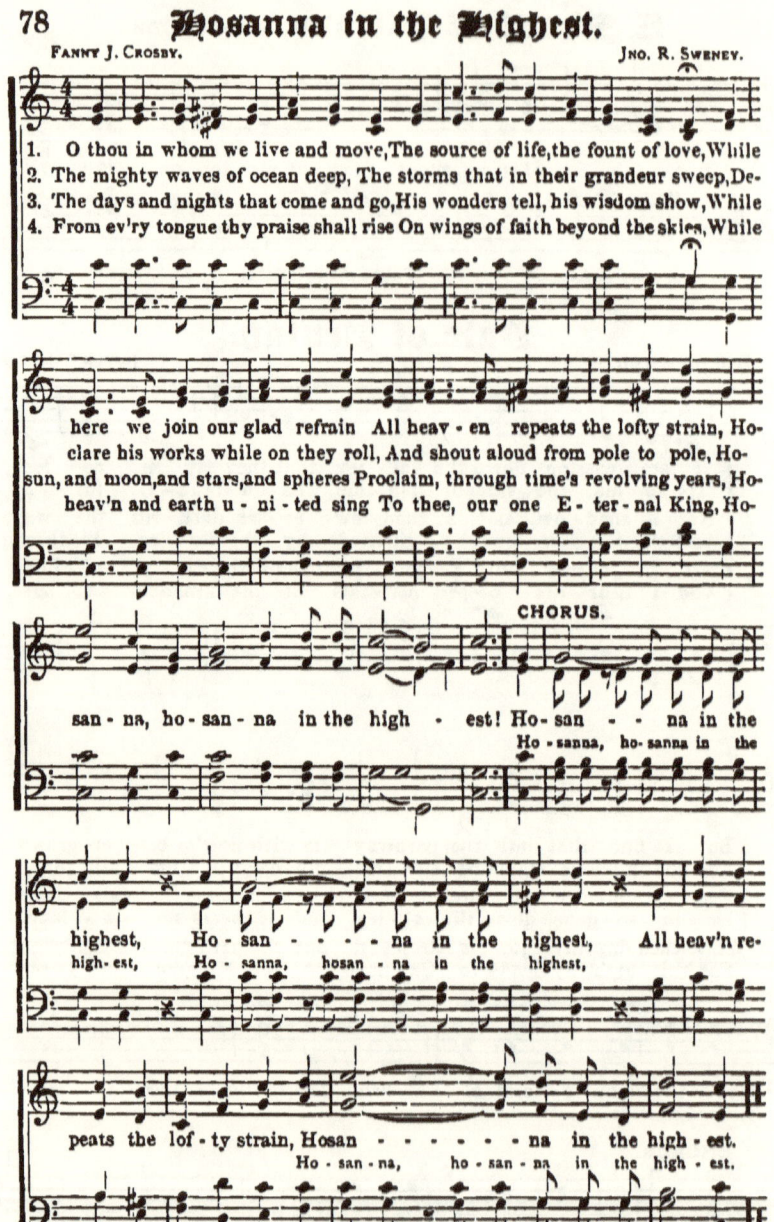

1. O thou in whom we live and move, The source of life, the fount of love, While
2. The mighty waves of ocean deep, The storms that in their grandeur sweep, De-
3. The days and nights that come and go, His wonders tell, his wisdom show, While
4. From ev'ry tongue thy praise shall rise On wings of faith beyond the skies, While

here we join our glad refrain All heav - en repeats the lofty strain, Ho-
clare his works while on they roll, And shout aloud from pole to pole, Ho-
sun, and moon, and stars, and spheres Proclaim, through time's revolving years, Ho-
heav'n and earth u - ni - ted sing To thee, our one E - ter - nal King, Ho-

CHORUS.

san - na, ho - san - na in the high - est! Ho - san - - na in the
Ho - sanna, ho - sanna in the

highest,   Ho - san - - - - na in the highest,   All heav'n re-
high - est,   Ho - sanna,   hosan - na in the highest,

peats the lof - ty strain, Hosan - - - - - - na in the high - est.
Ho - san - na,   ho - san - na in the high - est.

Marching Home Together.

G. W. Collins.   Wm. J. Kirkpatrick.

1. Will you join our hap - py band, Marching home to - geth - er?
2. Strangers here, we seek no place, Marching home to - geth - er!
3. Ev - 'ry day the miles grow less, Marching home to - geth - er!

Trav'ling to the better land, Marching home together? Will you wait with
Ev- 'ry step we learn his grace, Marching home together! Ev'ry need by
As our footsteps onward press, Marching on togeth- er! Even now we

us for him Who will end all sorrow, Gazing past the dark to - day,
him supplied Wakes a note of singing; Ev-'ry sorrow, sanc- ti- fied,
catch a gleam—Hear the chorus swelling! As each wand'rer finds his place

CHORUS.

To heav'ns bright to-morrow? Marching home!   Marching home to-
Praise to him is bringing!   marching home!
In the Father's dwelling.

gether! Heart to heart, and hand in hand, Marching home togeth- er!

Just Ahead.

Edgar Page. Cho. by H. L. G.   H. L. Gilmour.

1. 'Mid the toil and the bat - tle I think of my home, Where the
2. By the bank of life's riv - er our loved we shall greet, With
3. There cher - ubs ef - ful - gent and ser - aphs that blaze May
4. As year af - ter year shall fly swift - ly a - way, And
5. Pre - pare, then, ye faith - ful, to en - ter your land, The

sound of life's conflict can nevermore come, Where the angel of peace spreads his
them shall rejoice in a rapture complete, Shall join in the song that the
join in our anthem of rapturous praise; And the Son that was given the
yet but begun is e - ter - nity's day, While springs of new pleasure de-
mansion prepared by the Saviour's own hand, 'Tis read - y, now waiting, so

wings o'er the scene, And e - ter - ni - ty's sea is all calm and se - rene.
glo - ri - fied sing, While the arches of heav - en shall tremble and ring.
world to redeem, Shall be of our joy - ing and praising the theme.
light - eth the soul, While on - ward, yet on - ward, the ag - es shall roll.
beauteous and fair! Then bind on your san - dals, we soon shall be there.

CHORUS.

Just a - head, just a - head, a - head, I see the pearl - y

gates unfold, And hear the harps of shining gold, Where blood-bought saints the

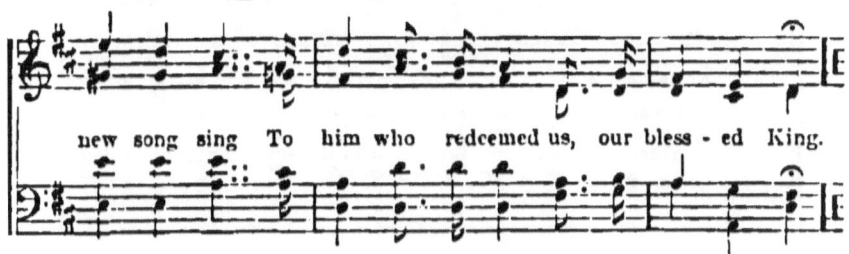

new song sing To him who redeemed us, our bless - ed King.

He Knows it All.

UNKNOWN.

E. S. LORENZ

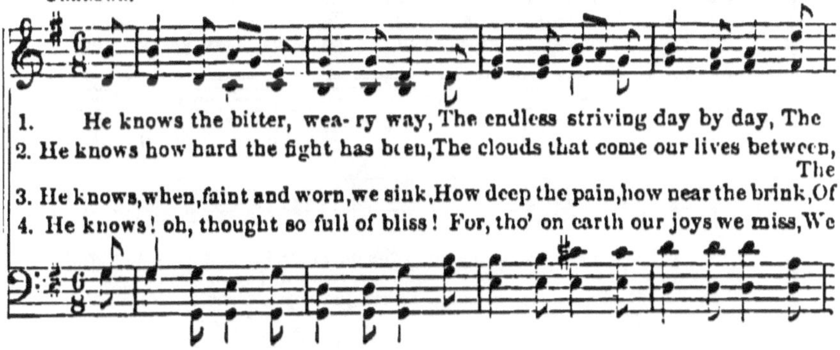

1. He knows the bitter, wea - ry way, The endless striving day by day, The
2. He knows how hard the fight has been, The clouds that come our lives between, The
3. He knows, when, faint and worn, we sink, How deep the pain, how near the brink, Of
4. He knows! oh, thought so full of bliss! For, tho' on earth our joys we miss, We

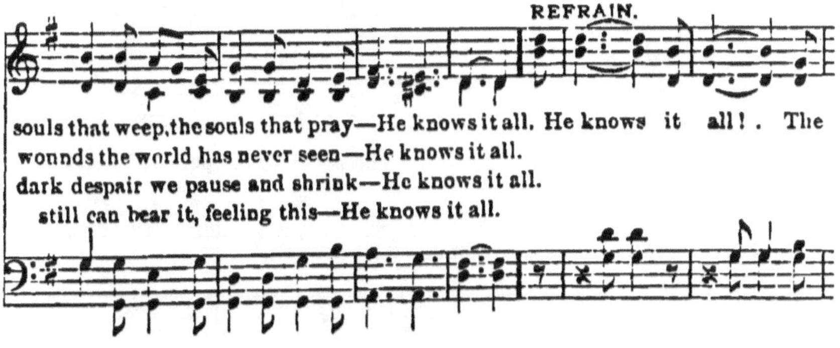

REFRAIN.

souls that weep, the souls that pray—He knows it all. He knows it all! . The
wounds the world has never seen—He knows it all.
dark despair we pause and shrink—He knows it all.
still can bear it, feeling this—He knows it all.

bitter, wea - ry way; O souls that weep, O souls that pray, He knows it all !

He knows, he knows it all !

Light that is in Jesus.

E. A. BARNES.   WM. J. KIRKPATRICK.

1. Light that is in Je - sus, Full of grace and love; Faith its rays re-
2. Light that is in Je - sus, Life in ev - 'ry ray: And with light a-
3. Light that is in Je - sus, Brighter than the sun, Type of coming

veal - ing, Com - ing from a - bove. As we have the gos - pel,
round us, Sin will hide a - way. We have peace and safe - ty,
glo - ry, When our course is run. Let us keep his precepts:

So we have the light, Light amid the darkness, Shining pure and bright.
When we walk in light: For it guides us onward, In the ways of right.
Let us do the right: Singing, as we journey, Je - sus is the light.

CHORUS.

Oh, 'tis shin - ing for all, . . . Bless - ed light, pure and bright,
for all,

Light that is dwelling in Je - sus, Blessed, blessed, light.

Thinking of Home.

Words from Rutherford's "Garden of Spices." Rev. W. A. Spencer.

1. I've been thinking of home, of my Fa - ther's house, Where the ma - ny man - sions be, Of the ci - ty whose streets are paved with gold, Of its jas - per walls so fair to behold, Which the righteous a - lone can see, Which the righteous a - lone can see.

2. I've been thinking of home, where they need not the light Of the sun, nor moon nor star, Of the gates of pearls, not closed by day, For there's no night there, but the weary may Find rest from the world a - far, Find rest from the world a - far.

3. I've been thinking of home, and the loved ones there, Dear friends who have gone be - fore, With whom we walked to the death river-side, And sad - ly thought, as we watched the gate, Of the hap - py days of yore, Of the hap - py days of yore.

4. I've been thinking of home, and my heart is full Of love for the Lamb of God, Who his pre - cious life as a ran - som gave, For a guilt - y world, e'en my soul to save, From the jus - tice - a - veng - ing rod, From the justice - a - veng - ing rod.

5. I've been thinking of home, yes, home, sweet home; Oh, there may we all u - nite With the white-robed throng, and for ev - er raise, To the tri - une God sweetest songs of praise, With glo - ry, and honor and might, With glo - ry and honor and might.

Invocation.

F. G. Burroughs.   "Receive ye the Holy Ghost."—John xx. 22.   H. L. Gilmour.

Prayerfully.

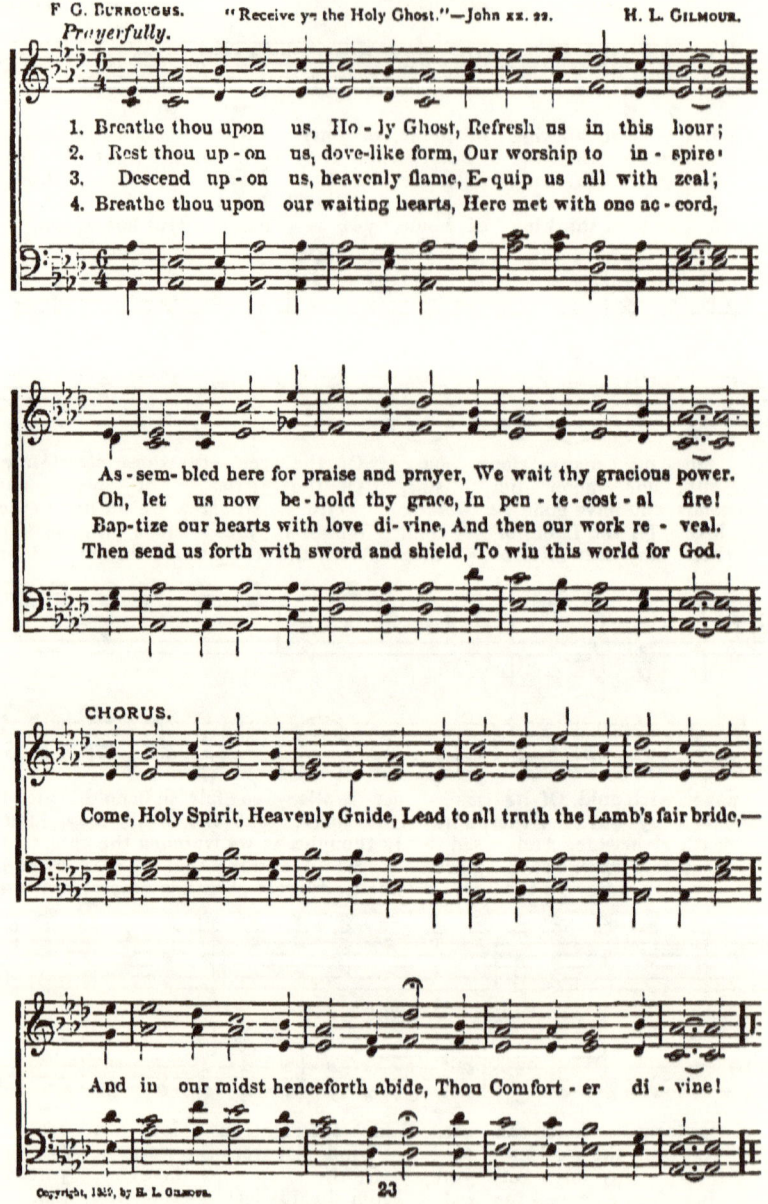

1. Breathe thou upon us, Ho - ly Ghost, Refresh us in this hour;
2. Rest thou up - on us, dove-like form, Our worship to in - spire
3. Descend up - on us, heavenly flame, E - quip us all with zeal;
4. Breathe thou upon our waiting hearts, Here met with one ac - cord;

As - sem - bled here for praise and prayer, We wait thy gracious power.
Oh, let us now be - hold thy grace, In pen - te - cost - al fire!
Bap - tize our hearts with love di - vine, And then our work re - veal.
Then send us forth with sword and shield, To win this world for God.

CHORUS.

Come, Holy Spirit, Heavenly Guide, Lead to all truth the Lamb's fair bride,—

And in our midst henceforth abide, Thou Comfort - er di - vine!

23

Good News of Redemption. 85

Lizzie Edwards.

Jno. R. Sweney.

1. The trump of the gospel is sounding Good news of redemption to-day;
2. The trump of the gospel is sounding, The standard of Jesus unfurled;
3. A balm to the weary is of-fered, A light in the darkness be-hold;
4. Who-ever, with hearty re-pentance, On Jesus our Lord will be-lieve,

Come hither,the lost that have wandered, Oh, come and be saved while you may!
Then rally around it, ye faithful, And shout as ye march thro' the world.
A feast for the hungry is waiting, That welcomes the young and the old.
Shall know the sweet rapture of pardon, And life ev-er-lasting re-ceive.

CHORUS.

The fountain of mercy is free, 'Twas opened for you and for me,

'Tis flowing to-day, Oh,come while you may, The fountain of mercy is free.

What is the Theme?

F. G BURROUGHS.   ADAM GEIBEL.

1. What is the theme of joy   to-day ? Praise to our King, Praise to our King.
2. What does the mountain streamlet say ? Praise ye the Lord, Praise ye the Lord.
3. What is the theme of this glad day ? Praise to our King, Praise to our King.

What is the bur - den of each lay ? Praise, grateful praise to our King;
What hum the bees in meadows gay ? Praise, all ye peo- ple, the Lord ;
This is the bur - den of each lay, Praise, loving praise to our King;

What is the song the glad birds sing ? What are the blossoms offering ? Praise, loving
What do the zephyrs softly croon, Under the rays of the silver moon ? Praise ye the
Swelling the notes the glad birds sing, Joining the flowers' offering, Praise, loving

praise, humble praise, grateful praise To their kind benefactor they raise.
Lord, all ye stars of the night, Praise the Lord for your glorious light.
praise, humble praise, grateful praise To our King and our Saviour we'll raise.

CHORUS.

Let mighty floods now clap their hands; Let little hills a- gain   rejoice;

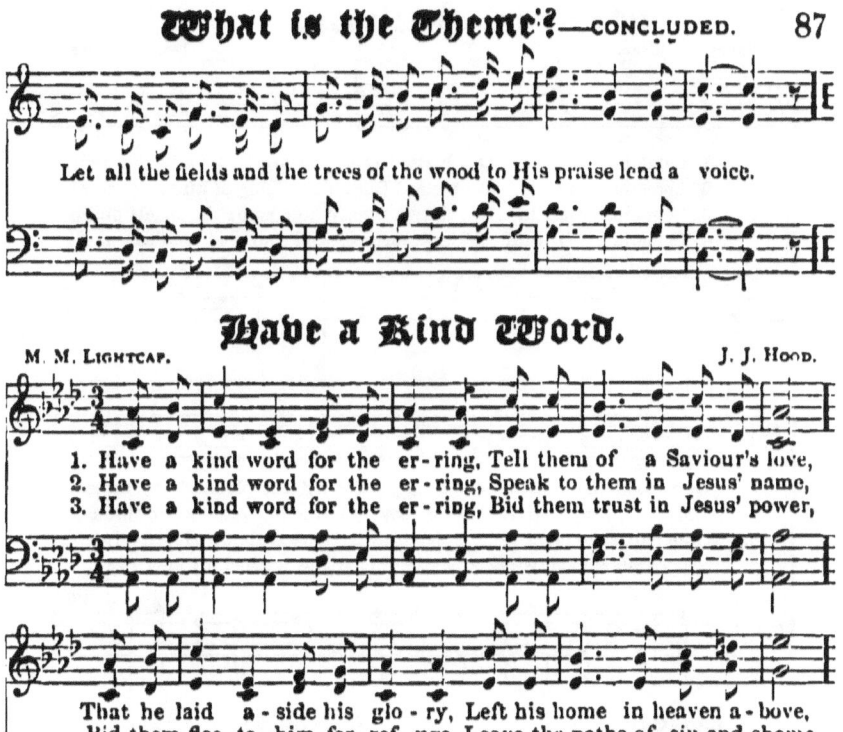

Let all the fields and the trees of the wood to His praise lend a voice.

Have a Kind Word.

M. M. Lightcap.   J. J. Hood.

1. Have a kind word for the er-ring, Tell them of a Saviour's love,
2. Have a kind word for the er-ring, Speak to them in Jesus' name,
3. Have a kind word for the er-ring, Bid them trust in Jesus' power,

That he laid a-side his glo-ry, Left his home in heaven a-bove,
Bid them flee to him for ref-uge, Leave the paths of sin and shame.
Flee to him for help and suc-cor In temp-ta-tion's darkest hour.

Come in, O Blessed One.

Fanny. J. Crosby.   Jno. R. Sweney.

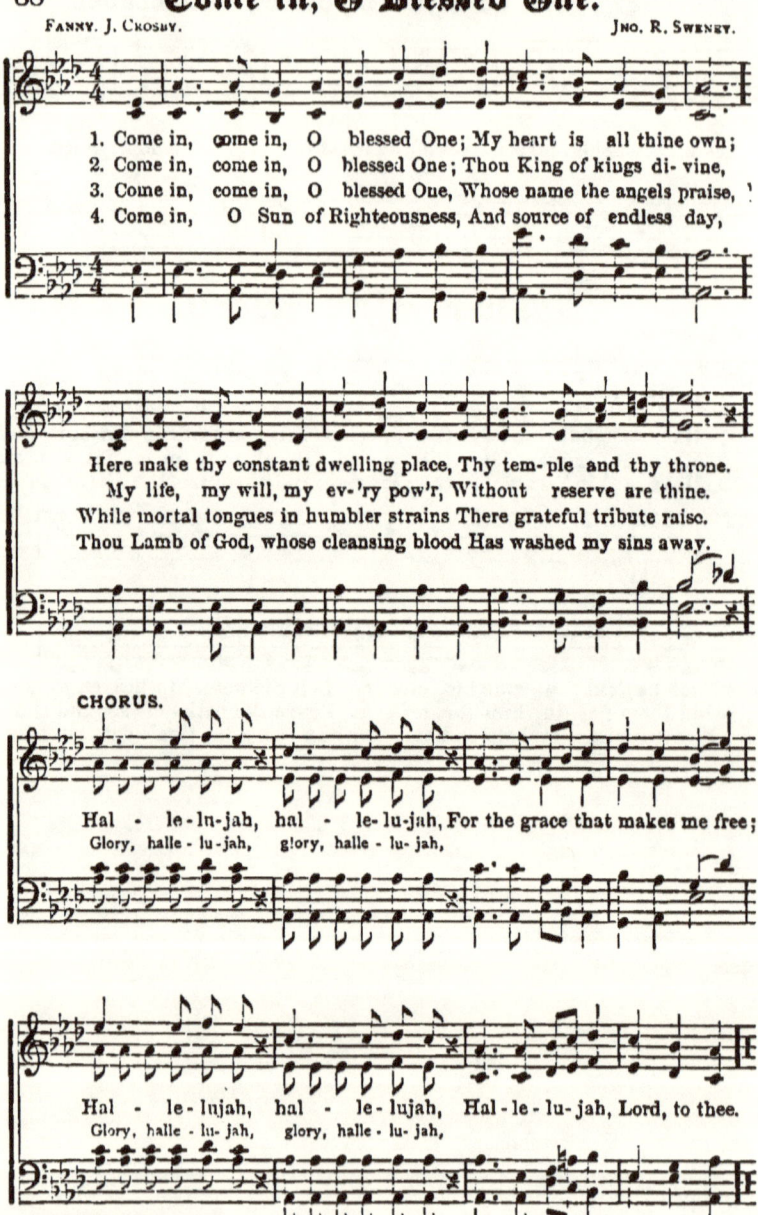

1. Come in, come in, O blessed One; My heart is all thine own;
2. Come in, come in, O blessed One; Thou King of kings di- vine,
3. Come in, come in, O blessed One, Whose name the angels praise,
4. Come in, O Sun of Righteousness, And source of endless day,

Here make thy constant dwelling place, Thy tem-ple and thy throne.
My life, my will, my ev-'ry pow'r, Without reserve are thine.
While mortal tongues in humbler strains There grateful tribute raise.
Thou Lamb of God, whose cleansing blood Has washed my sins away.

CHORUS.

Hal - le-lu-jah, hal - le-lu-jah, For the grace that makes me free;
Glory, halle - lu-jah, glory, halle - lu- jah,

Hal - le-lujah, hal - le- lujah, Hal - le - lu- jah, Lord, to thee.
Glory, halle - lu- jah, glory, halle - lu- jah,

Mrs. R. N. Turner.   Wm. J. Kirkpatrick.

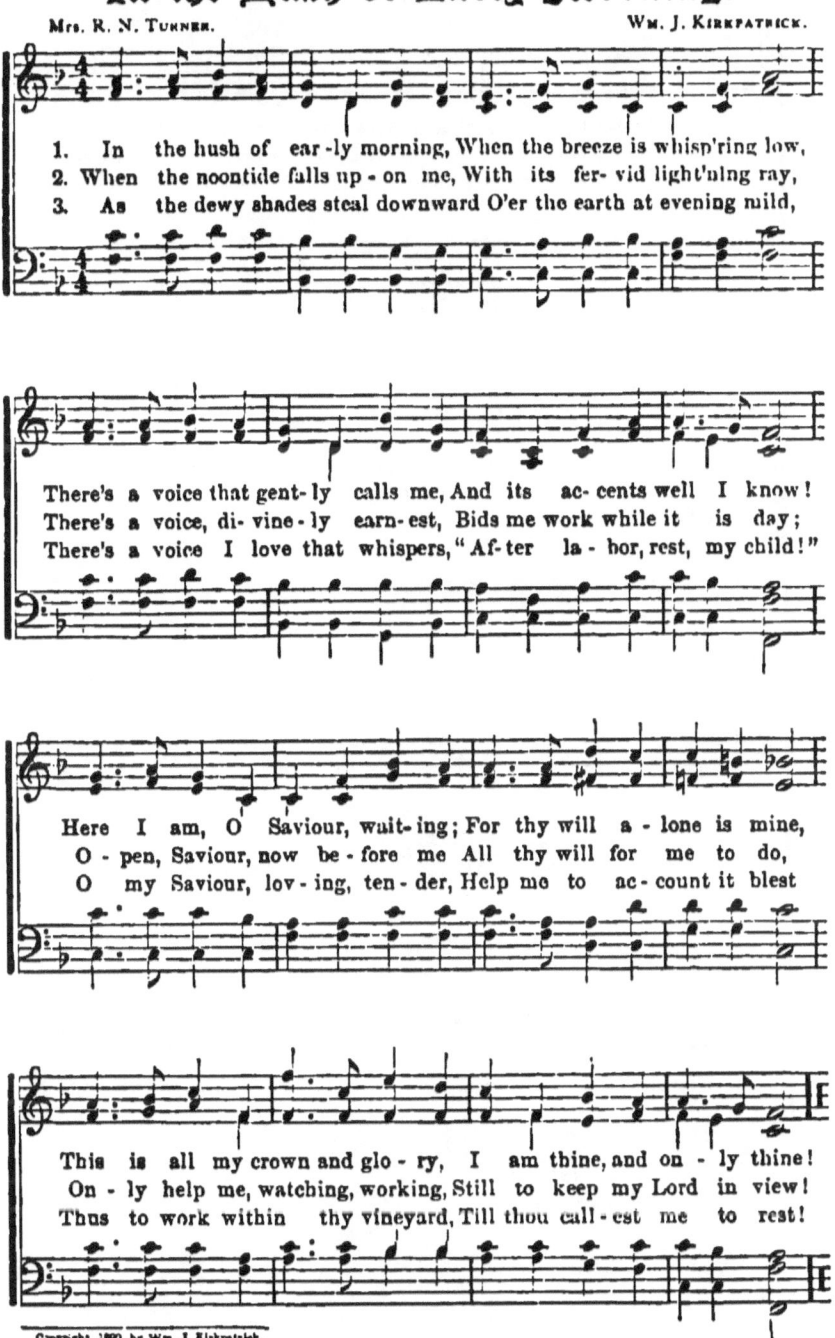

1. In the hush of ear-ly morning, When the breeze is whisp'ring low,
2. When the noontide falls up-on me, With its fer-vid light'ning ray,
3. As the dewy shades steal downward O'er the earth at evening mild,

There's a voice that gent-ly calls me, And its ac-cents well I know!
There's a voice, di-vine-ly earn-est, Bids me work while it is day;
There's a voice I love that whispers, "Af-ter la-bor, rest, my child!"

Here I am, O Saviour, wait-ing; For thy will a-lone is mine,
O-pen, Saviour, now be-fore me All thy will for me to do,
O my Saviour, lov-ing, ten-der, Help me to ac-count it blest

This is all my crown and glo-ry, I am thine, and on-ly thine!
On-ly help me, watching, working, Still to keep my Lord in view!
Thus to work within thy vineyard, Till thou call-est me to rest!

In His Own Appointed Way.

SALLIE E. SMITH.   JNO. R. SWENEY.

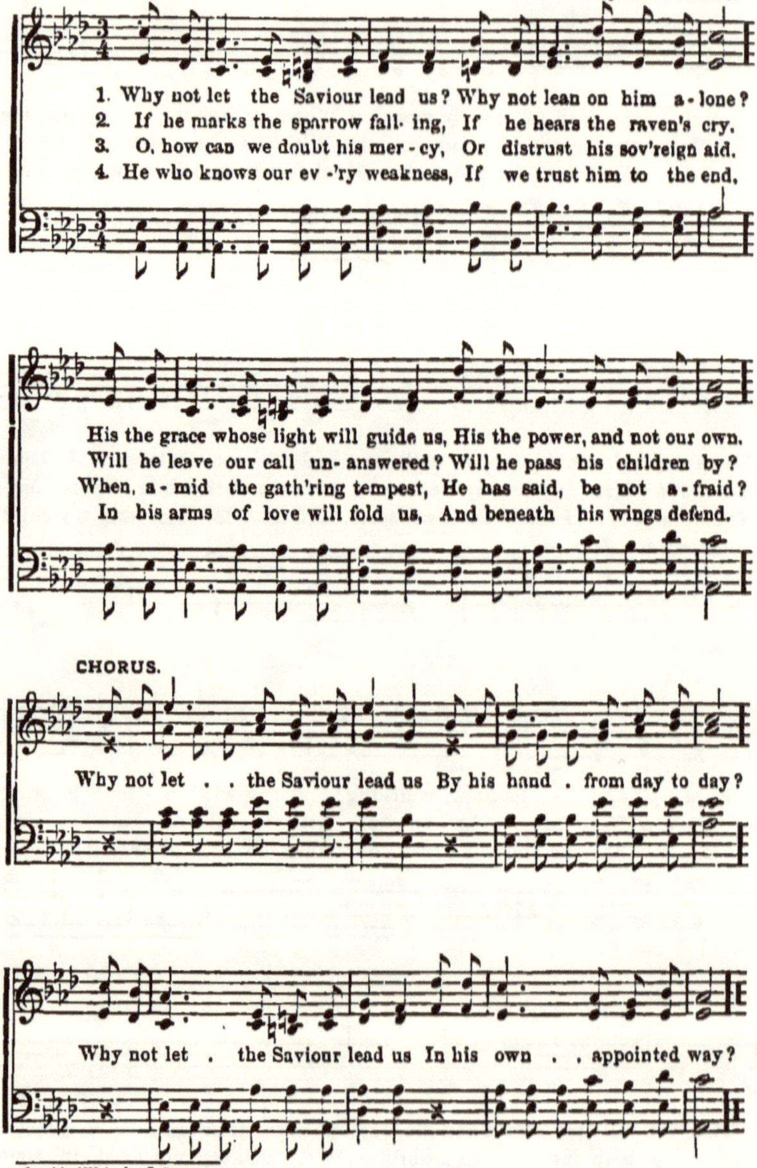

1. Why not let the Saviour lead us? Why not lean on him a-lone?
2. If he marks the sparrow fall-ing, If he hears the raven's cry.
3. O, how can we doubt his mer-cy, Or distrust his sov'reign aid.
4. He who knows our ev-'ry weakness, If we trust him to the end,

His the grace whose light will guide us, His the power, and not our own.
Will he leave our call un-answered? Will he pass his children by?
When, a-mid the gath'ring tempest, He has said, be not a-fraid?
In his arms of love will fold us, And beneath his wings defend.

CHORUS.

Why not let . . the Saviour lead us By his hand . from day to day?

Why not let . the Saviour lead us In his own . . appointed way?

Rise for Jesus.

E. C.

WM. J. KIRKPATRICK.

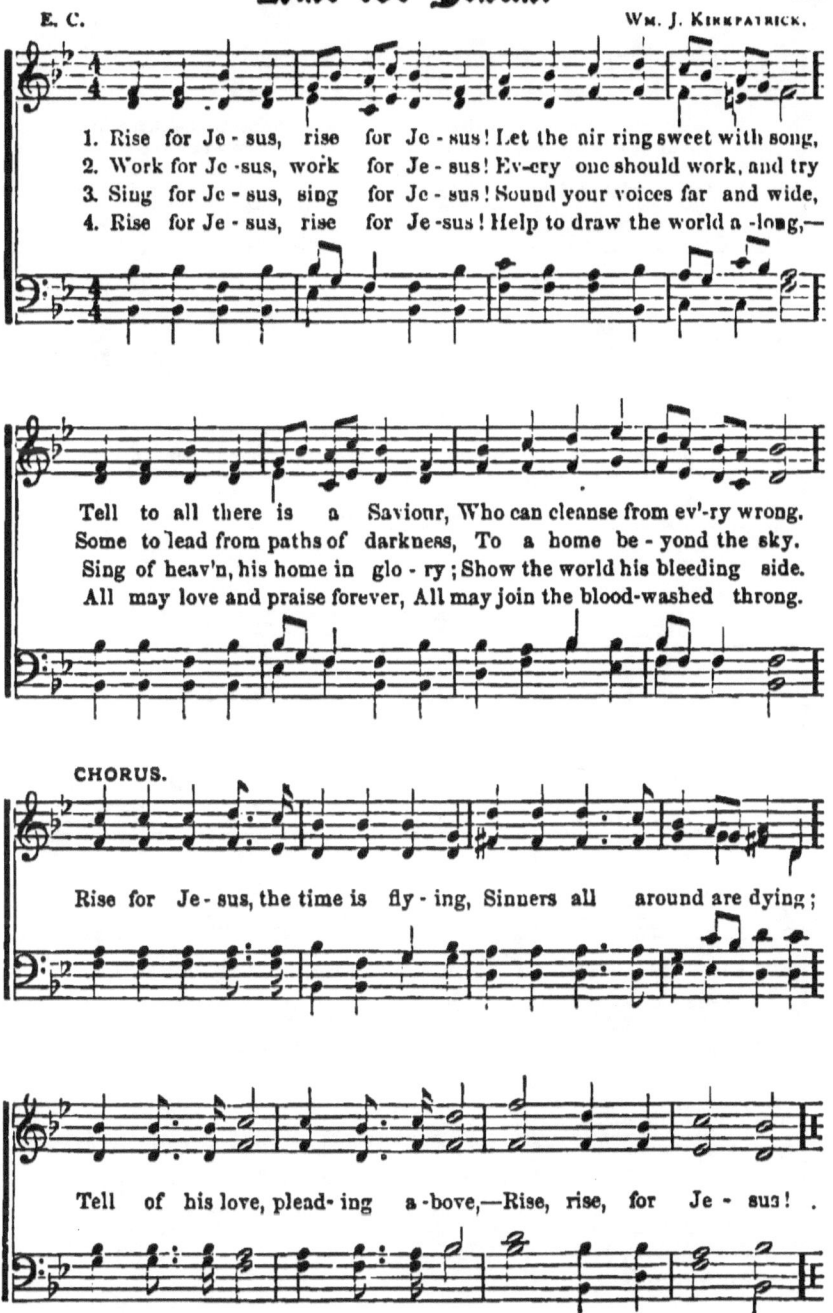

1. Rise for Je-sus, rise for Je-sus! Let the air ring sweet with song,
2. Work for Je-sus, work for Je-sus! Ev-ery one should work, and try
3. Sing for Je-sus, sing for Je-sus! Sound your voices far and wide,
4. Rise for Je-sus, rise for Je-sus! Help to draw the world a-long,—

Tell to all there is a Saviour, Who can cleanse from ev'-ry wrong.
Some to lead from paths of darkness, To a home be-yond the sky.
Sing of heav'n, his home in glo-ry; Show the world his bleeding side.
All may love and praise forever, All may join the blood-washed throng.

CHORUS.

Rise for Je-sus, the time is fly-ing, Sinners all around are dying;

Tell of his love, plead-ing a-bove,—Rise, rise, for Je-sus! .

The Clear Light of Heaven.

F. A. B.

F. A. BLACKMER.

1. In darkness I wandered till Jesus I found, And then, praise his name! And
2. The birds o'er my head seemed to sing a new song, So wondrously sweet, So
3. And now we are walk-ing to-geth-er a-long, My Sa-viour and I, My
4. Oh, wonder-ful Brother, Redeemer and Friend! I love him I know, I

then, praise his name! The clear light of heaven my pathway shone round, And
wondrously sweet; All nature seemed praising in notes loud and long, My
Sa-viour and I; He blesses and leads me with hand kind and strong, And
love him I know; This blessed com-pan-ion-ship, nev-er to end, Grows

CHORUS.

peace to my spir-it there came. And now I'm con-fid-ing, And
Saviour, when first we did meet.
free-ly his grace does sup-ply.
sweet-er as on-ward I go.

sweet-ly a-bid-ing In Je-sus, my Sa-viour, Compan-ion and

Guide: His name I'm confess-ing, He fills me with bless-ing; To

The Clear Light, etc.—CONCLUDED.

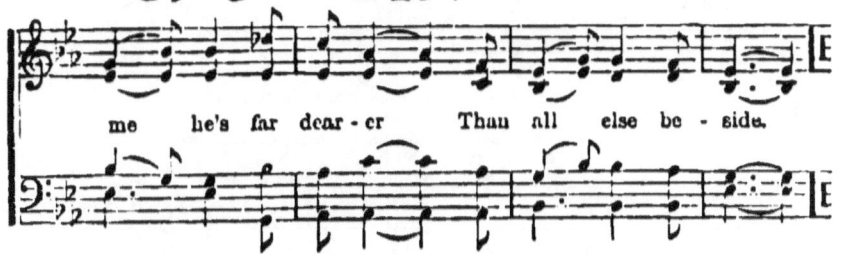

me he's far dear - er Than all else be - side.

It Fills My Heart with Joy.

E. E. Hewitt. Jno. R. Sweney.

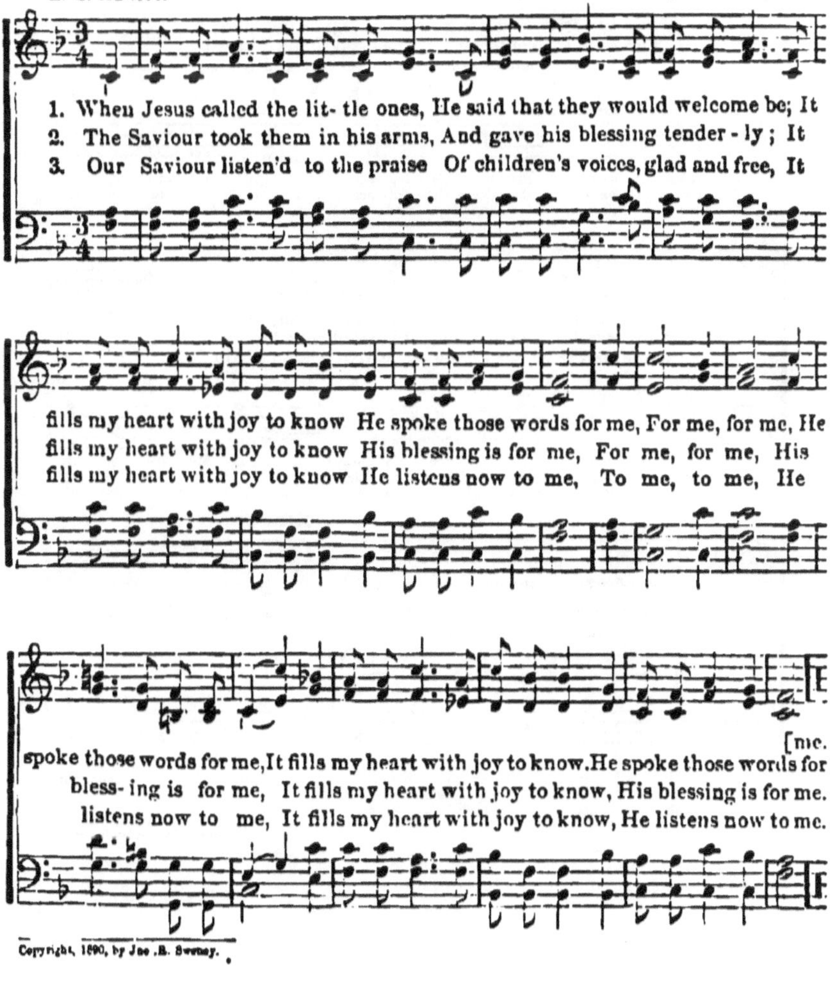
1. When Jesus called the lit- tle ones, He said that they would welcome be; It fills my heart with joy to know He spoke those words for me, For me, for me, He spoke those words for me, It fills my heart with joy to know. He spoke those words for me.
2. The Saviour took them in his arms, And gave his blessing tender - ly; It fills my heart with joy to know His blessing is for me, For me, for me, His bless- ing is for me, It fills my heart with joy to know, His blessing is for me.
3. Our Saviour listen'd to the praise Of children's voices, glad and free, It fills my heart with joy to know He listens now to me, To me, to me, He listens now to me, It fills my heart with joy to know, He listens now to me.

94 Abiding in Jesus.

E. E. Hewitt.　　　　　　　　　　　　　　　　　　　　　Jno. R. Sweney.

1. Abiding in Jesus, what blessing is mine!
2. Abiding in Jesus, no words can express,
3. Abiding in Jesus, his mercies ne'er cease,

1. A-bid-ing in Je - sus, what blessing is mine! . . . For life free-ly
2. A-bid-ing in Je - sus, no words can ex-press . . . The qui-et con-
3. A-bid-ing in Je - sus, his mercies ne'er cease; . . . 'Tis present sal-

For life free-ly flows from the lifegiv-ing vine;
The qui-et contentment, the deep thankfulness;
'Tis present sal-vation, 'tis comfort and peace;

flows . . from . . the life-giv-ing vine; . . . . . More close-ly u-
tent - - ment, . . the deep thankful-ness; . . . . . . "Be care-ful for
va - - tion, . . . 'tis comfort and peace; . . . . . Come, find in this

More closely u-ni-ted to him, be my prayer,　"Much
"Be careful for nothing," his word says to me,　"I'll
Come, find in this Saviour sweet Gil-e-ad's balm,　The

ni - - ted . . to him, be my prayer, ... Much fruit to his
noth - - ing," . his word says to me, ... I'll car-ry thy
Sav - - iour sweet Gil - e - ad's balm, ... The clus-ters of

rit.　　　　　　　　　　　　　　　　　　　　CHORUS.

fruit" to his glory the branch then will bear.　A - bid - - - ing in
carry thy burden; thy helper will be."
clusters of Eshcol, the victor's bright palm.

glo - - - ry the branch then will bear.
bur - - den; thy helper will be."
Esh - - - col, the victor's bright palm.

A - bid-ing in Je-sus, what

Je - sus, A - bid - - - - ing in Je - - - sus, what

blessing is mine! A - bid - ing in Je - sus, what blessing is mine!

blessing, what blessing, what bless - - - - ing is mine! I'll

what blessing, what blessing is mine! I'll

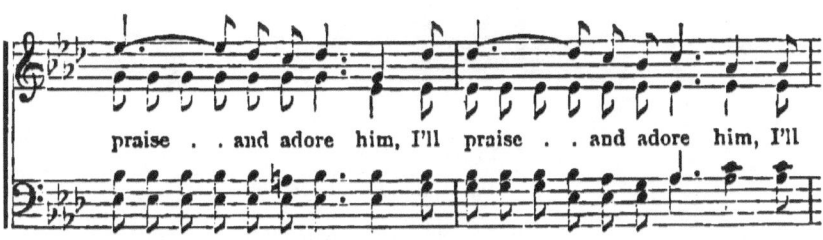

praise . . and adore him, I'll praise . . and adore him, I'll

praise, yes, I'll praise and adore him, I'll praise, yes, I'll praise and adore him, I'll

Our Strength.

James. L. Black.　　　　　　　　　　　　　　Jno. R. Sweney.

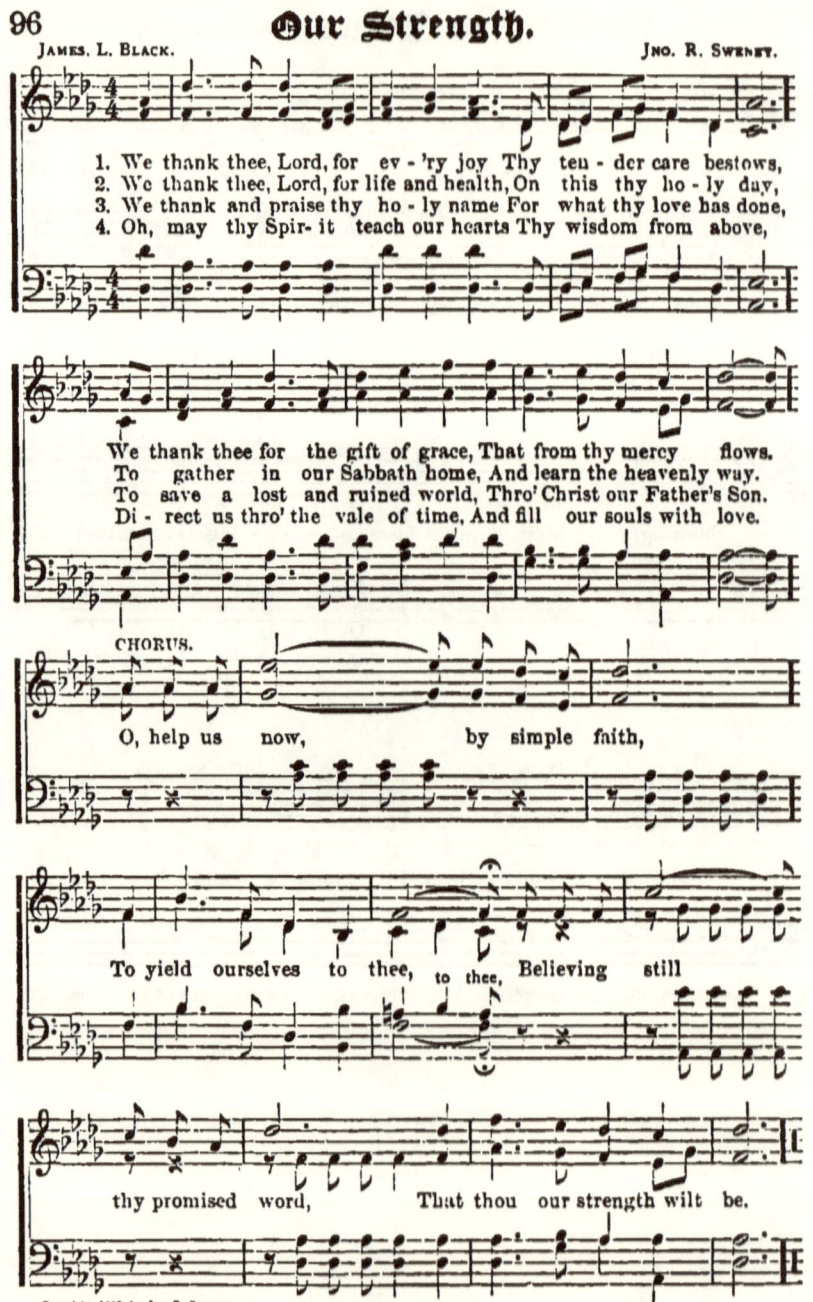

1. We thank thee, Lord, for ev - 'ry joy Thy ten - der care bestows,
2. We thank thee, Lord, for life and health, On this thy ho - ly day,
3. We thank and praise thy ho - ly name For what thy love has done,
4. Oh, may thy Spir- it teach our hearts Thy wisdom from above,

We thank thee for the gift of grace, That from thy mercy flows.
To gather in our Sabbath home, And learn the heavenly way.
To save a lost and ruined world, Thro' Christ our Father's Son.
Di - rect us thro' the vale of time, And fill our souls with love.

CHORUS.

O, help us now, by simple faith,

To yield ourselves to thee, to thee, Believing still

thy promised word, That thou our strength wilt be.

E. E. Hewitt. Wm. J. Kirkpatrick.

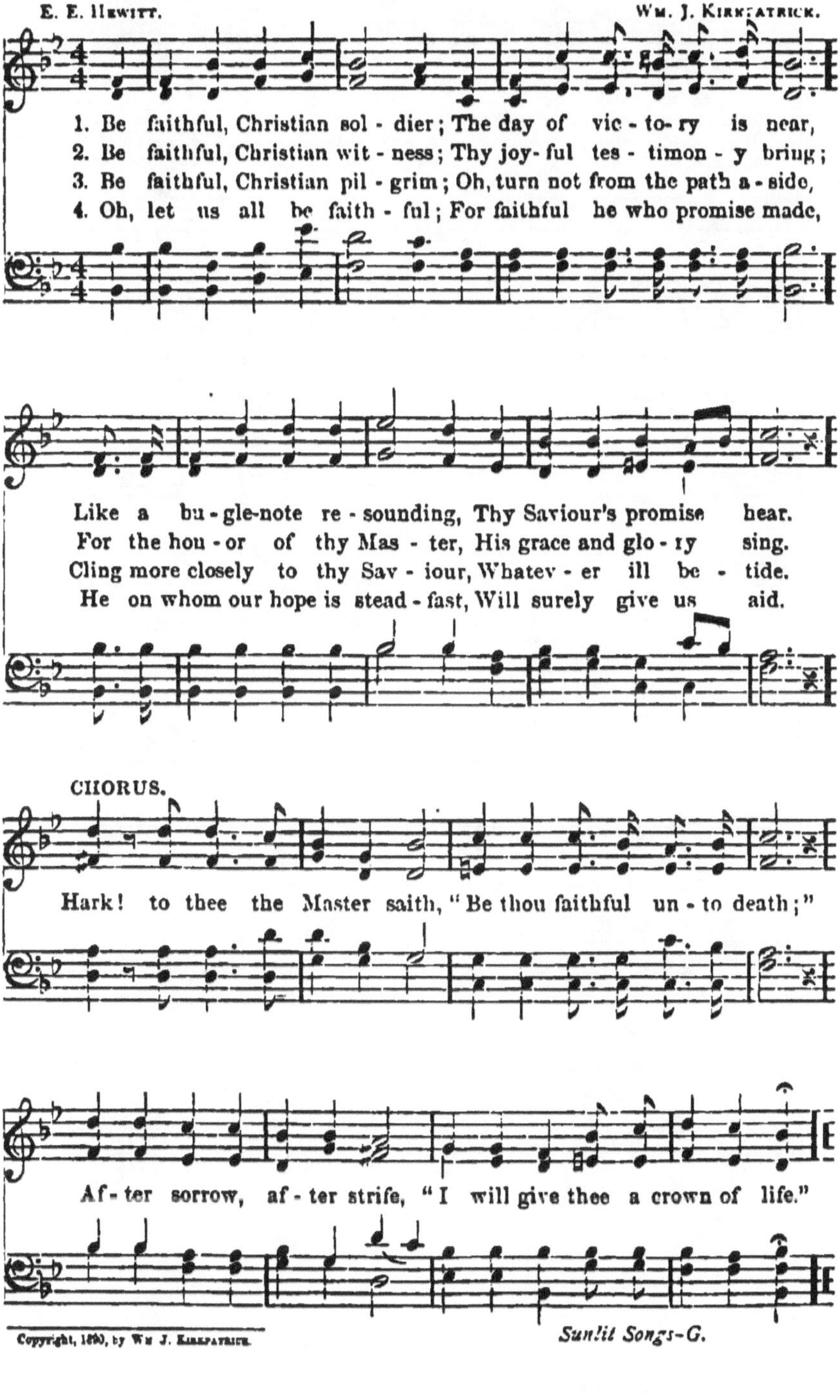

1. Be faithful, Christian sol - dier; The day of vic - to - ry is near,
2. Be faithful, Christian wit - ness; Thy joy- ful tes - timon - y bring;
3. Be faithful, Christian pil - grim; Oh, turn not from the path a - side,
4. Oh, let us all be faith - ful; For faithful he who promise made,

Like a bu - gle-note re - sounding, Thy Saviour's promise hear.
For the hon - or of thy Mas - ter, His grace and glo - ry sing.
Cling more closely to thy Sav - iour, Whatev - er ill be - tide.
He on whom our hope is stead - fast, Will surely give us aid.

CHORUS.

Hark! to thee the Master saith, "Be thou faithful un - to death;"

Af - ter sorrow, af - ter strife, "I will give thee a crown of life."

Sunlit Songs–G.

Count it all Joy.

JAMES L. BLACK.   JNO. R. SWENEY.

1. Look up and press onward, O child of the Lord, No home in this
2. Look up and press onward, re-joice ev-ermore; Give thanks for his
3. Look up and press onward, the way may be dark, Thy heart may be
4. Look up and press onward, for strong is his arm, Whose grace like the

wide world for thee; Let faith spread her wings to the palace above, Where
mer-cy, and sing; For out of afflic-tion, if firm be thy trust, Thy
tempted and tried, But why shouldst thou falter, and tremble with fear, With
dew will descend, He crowneth with blessings the loy-al and true, Who

CHORUS.

Je-sus the King thou wilt see.   Count it all joy, count it all joy Tribu-
soul he has promised to bring.
Je-sus so close to thy side?
meek-ly endure to the end.

la-tion for his blessed name to bear,   For re-cor-ded in his

word is the promise of reward,   A crown by and by thou shalt wear.

Blessed Sunshine.

E. E. Hewitt.　　　　　　　　　　　　　Wm. J. Kirkpatrick.

1. See the love-beams shining from the Saviour's face, Wondrous light of
2. Je- sus is our sunshine, Je- sus is our light; With the tuneful
3. "Light of Life," we praise thee, soon the des- ert gloom With o - ter - nal

glo- ry, gen- tle light of grace; See the sunshine streaming from the
morning scat -ter - ing the night; Oh, to spread the gladness, let the
ver- due joy- ful -ly shall bloom; All the world transforming with the

"heal - ing wings," Rays of heaven- ly brightness o'er our path it flings.
day-break in, To the souls now darkened with the clouds of sin.
gos - pel glow,—Bid the na - tions hail thee, thy sal - va - tion know.

CHORUS.

Blessed sun - shine, blessed sun - shine, Blessed sunshine from the cross I see,

Blessed, blessed sunshine, Blessed, blessed sunshine, Blessed sunshine from the cross I see,

Blessed sunshine, blessed sunshine, Shining now for all the world,
Shining now for me.

Blessed, blessed sunshine, Blessed, blessed sunshine, Shining for the world, shining now for me.

"O Yes, it is True."

L. H. Edmunds.

Wm. J. Kirkpatrick.

1. O, is it too good, too good to be true? This won-der-ful
2. O, is it too good, too good to be true? This of-fer of
3. O, is it too good, too good to be true, That Je-sus a-
4. O, is it too good, too good to be true, His might ev-'ry

story of love, That my Saviour came down, from his throne and his crown, To
in-finate grace, Will he keep me each hour, by his Spirit of power, And
bides with me here; That his image so dim shall be made like to him, And
foe will destroy; He will stand by my side to illume Jordan's tide, And

CHORUS. *A little faster.*

lift a poor sinner a - bove. O yes, it is true, praise the
show me the smiles of his face.
bright to his glo-ry ap - pear?
grant me an entrance of joy?

Lord, it is true; The cross of redemption I see; He came in his

love from the mansions a-bove To save a poor sinner like me.

Say, Will You Come?

James L. Black. Jno. R. Sweney.

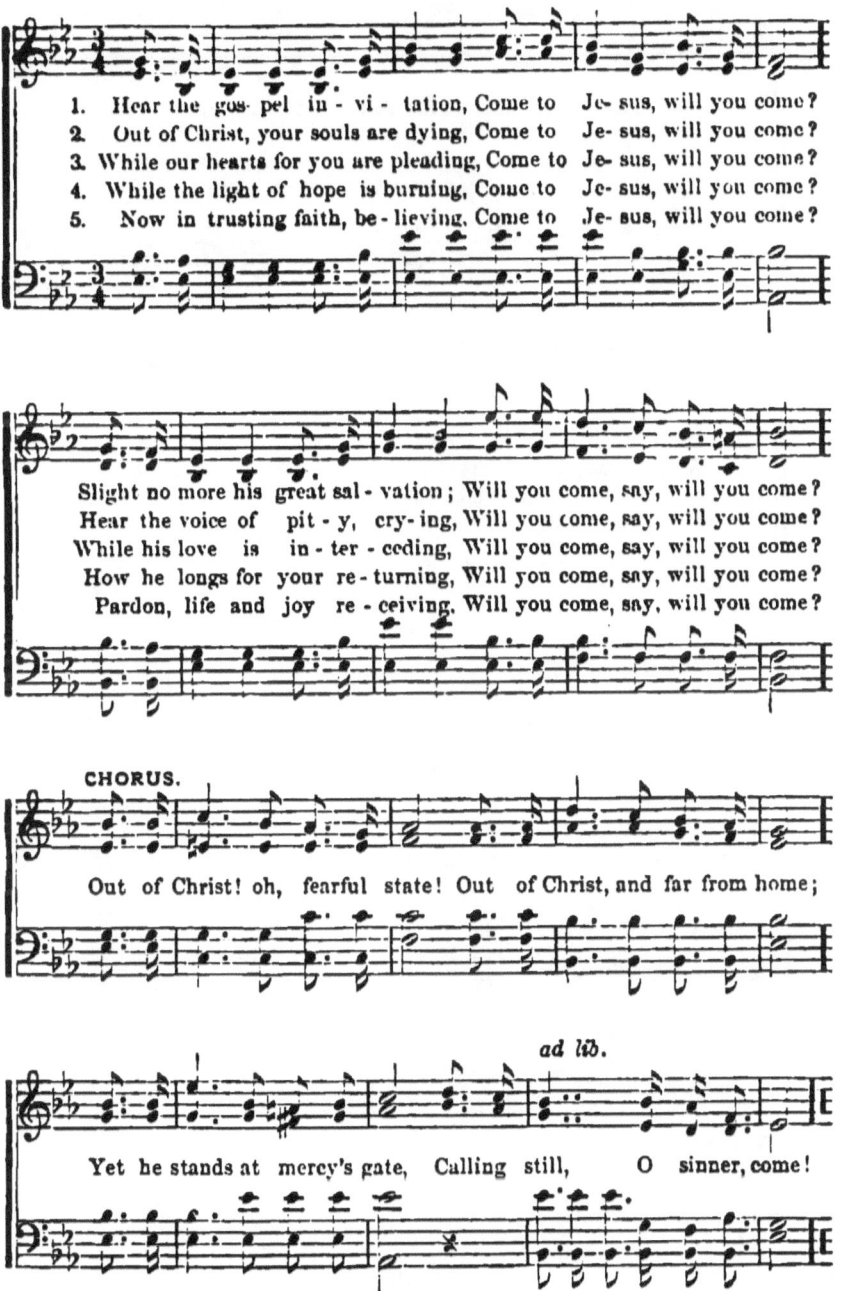

1. Hear the gos-pel in-vi-tation, Come to Je-sus, will you come?
2. Out of Christ, your souls are dying, Come to Je-sus, will you come?
3. While our hearts for you are pleading, Come to Je-sus, will you come?
4. While the light of hope is burning, Come to Je-sus, will you come?
5. Now in trusting faith, be-lieving, Come to Je-sus, will you come?

Slight no more his great sal-vation; Will you come, say, will you come?
Hear the voice of pit-y, cry-ing, Will you come, say, will you come?
While his love is in-ter-ceding, Will you come, say, will you come?
How he longs for your re-turning, Will you come, say, will you come?
Pardon, life and joy re-ceiving, Will you come, say, will you come?

CHORUS.

Out of Christ! oh, fearful state! Out of Christ, and far from home;

ad lib.

Yet he stands at mercy's gate, Calling still, O sinner, come!

O Fly to Him.

FANNY J. CROSBY.

JNO. R. SWENEY.

1. E - ter - ni - ty   is drawing near, O un - convert - ed   soul,
2. E - ter - ni - ty   is drawing near, Yet unprepared art   thou ;
3. E - ter - ni - ty   is drawing near, Fast wanes thy taper light,
4. Oh, slight the Saviour's call no more ; Thou hast no help but he ;

Dost thou not fear the troubled waves That o'er thee soon may roll ?
Alas, what must become of thee Should death o'ertake thee now ?
Oh, think how soon its flick'ring spark May fade in endless night !
And   if thou still his grace refuse Where will thy refuge   be ?

CHORUS.

O   fly to him, the bless-ed One, Who pleads thy cause on high ;

While yet his mer- cy calleth thee, Say. wherefore wilt thou die ?

He Stands at the Open Gate.

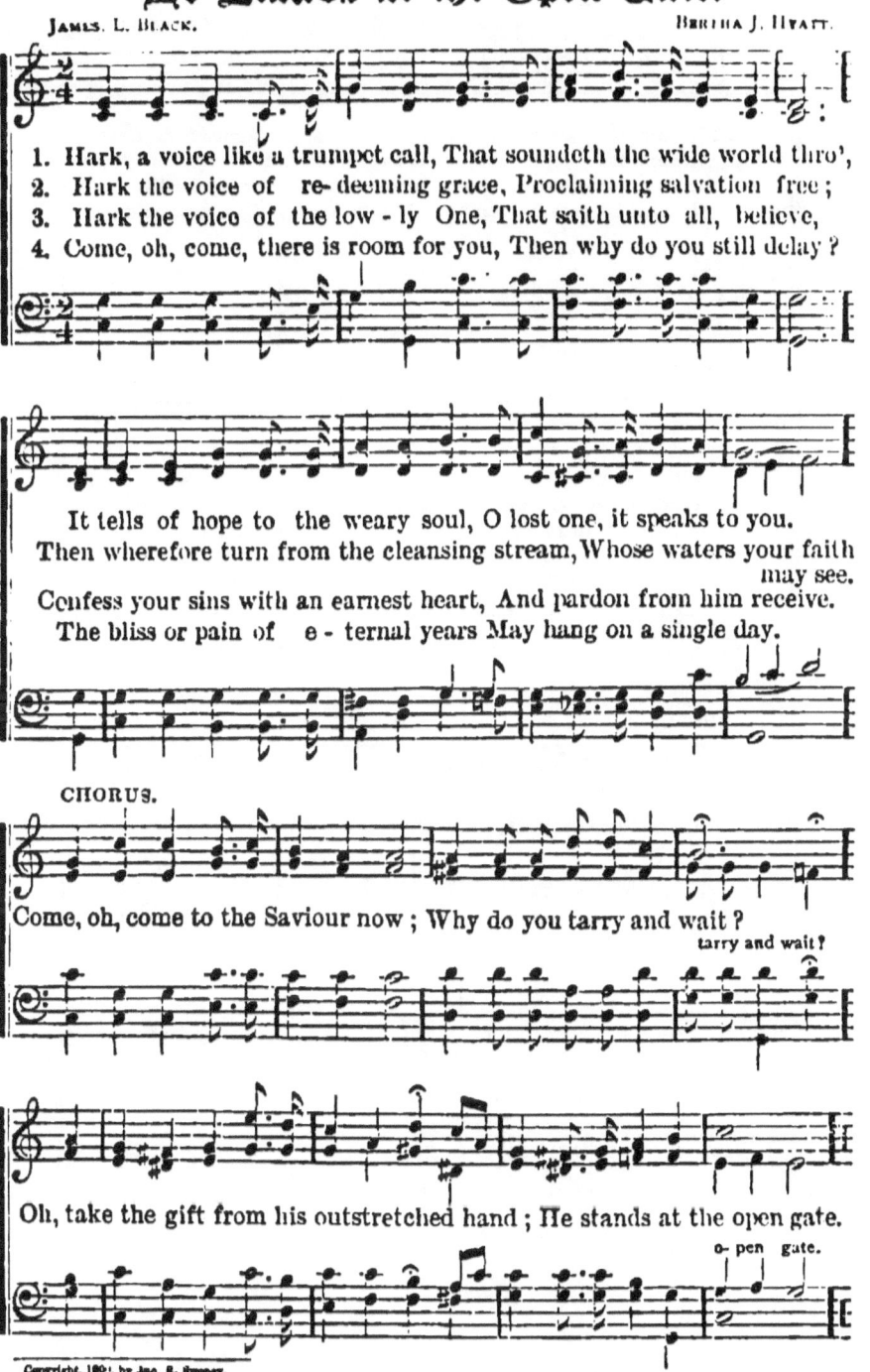

JAMES. L. BLACK.

BERTHA J. HYATT.

1. Hark, a voice like a trumpet call, That soundeth the wide world thro',
2. Hark the voice of re-deeming grace, Proclaiming salvation free;
3. Hark the voice of the low-ly One, That saith unto all, believe,
4. Come, oh, come, there is room for you, Then why do you still delay?

It tells of hope to the weary soul, O lost one, it speaks to you.
Then wherefore turn from the cleansing stream, Whose waters your faith may see.
Confess your sins with an earnest heart, And pardon from him receive.
The bliss or pain of e-ternal years May hang on a single day.

CHORUS.

Come, oh, come to the Saviour now; Why do you tarry and wait?
tarry and wait?

Oh, take the gift from his outstretched hand; He stands at the open gate.
o-pen gate.

Blest are the Poor in Spirit.

FANNY J. CROSBY.   BERTHA J. HYATT.

1. Blest are the poor in spir - it, Who trust in the Saviour's dear name,
2. Blest are the poor in spir - it, The meek and the low- ly in heart,
3. Blest are the poor in spir - it, Who dwell in Imman - u - el's love,
4. We must be poor in spir - it If Je - sus our Lord we would see;

Who live for his hon - or and glo - ry, And seek not for riches or fame.
Who cheerful- ly car - ry their burdens, And rest with the Saviour apart.
Receiv- ing, thro' in - fin - ite mer- cy, A foretaste of glory a - bove.
O Saviour, we pray for the blessing, So graciously promised by thee.

CHORUS.

Blest are the poor in spir - it, Sweet promise our Saviour has given,

Blest are the poor in spir- it, For theirs is the kingdom of heaven.

Copyright, 1890, by Jno. R. Sweney.

A Welcome for All.

Mrs. C. N. Pickop. Wm. J. Kirkpatrick.

1. On the mountain top I'm standing, Glorious prospects there I see,
2. Welcome thro' the blood of Je-sus, And the matchless love of God,
3. All the way has been so pleasant, Peace and plenty day by day,
4. Jesus spreads his bounteous table, Serves with generous, loving hand,
5. Brighten, Lord, the glorious vis-ion Of our future happy home,

Pearl-y gates are thrown wide open, Welcome there for you, for me.
Welcome to the chief of sinners, Who the roy-al road have trod.
Rest from sin, and sweet contentment, Find we in the King's highway.
Sat-is-fies our souls with blessings, Foretaste of the glo-ry land.
'Till we hear the welcome summons, "Child, your Father calls you, come!"

CHORUS.

Wel - come, wel - come, Welcome there for you, for me,
Welcome there, welcome there,

Wel - come, wel - come, Welcome there for you, for me.
Welcome there, welcome there,

What will You do?

F. G. Burroughs.   Adam Geibel.

1. What will you do with the King called Jesus? Many are waiting to
2. What will you do for the King called Jesus, He who for you left his
3. What will you do with the King called Jesus,—Who will submit to his

hear you say,—Some have despised him, rejecting his mercy, What will you
throne above, Here 'mid the low-ly and sin-ful to la-bor, Dail-y un-
gentle sway? Where are the hearts ready now to enthrone him? Who will his

do with your King to-day? What can you witness concerning his goodness,
folding his Father's love. Look on the fields white already to harvest,
kind commands obey? Come with your ointments most costly and precious,

Who died to save you from sin's bitter thrall? Who will declare him the
Who now is willing to toil with the few? What will you do for the
Pour out your gifts at the dear Saviour's feet; Render to him all your

fair - est of thousands? Who now will crown him the Lord of all?
dear Saviour, Jo - sus? Lo, he is waiting, he calls for you!
loy - al de-vo - tion; Seek to ex-alt him by prais-es meet.

RUS. *Voices in unison.*

u do with the King called Jesus? What, oh, what will you do for Jesus?

ts.

o bless all who humbly confess Faith in his blood and righteousness.

At this Welcome Hour.

IRR. WM. J. KIRKPATRICK.

lcome hour of prayer, Lord, we would thy blessing share; Love and joy di-
ly, ho-ly, holy thou! All our pow'rs adoring bow, Peace divine, a
ove will ne'er forget Souls for whom thy bloody sweat Voiced thine agon-

ging Set our heart-bells all a ringing; Ringing praise to Jesus' name,
ure Thou dost give in wond'rous measure Peace the world can never know
When the curse of sin was broken; Still would we thine accents hear,

l evermore the same, Hallelu-jah, halle - lujah, Praise we the Lord.
on only canst bestow, Hallelujah, halle - lujah, Praise we the Lord.
vith you, never fear," Hallelujah, halle - lujah, Praise we the Lord.

WM. J. KIRKPATRICK.

The Beautiful Land.

Fanny J. Crosby   Jno. R. Sweney.

1. We have heard of a land on whose blue, ether skies Not a
2. We have talked of that land when our jour- ney was long, And our
3. We are near - ing that land, we are near - ing the gate To the

cloud for a moment can stay, And it needs not the sun in his
hearts overburdened with care, We have talked of the blest at the
cit - y of jas - per and gold, Where the Saviour to welcome his

splen- dor to rise, For the Lord is the light of its day'; We have
riv - er of song, And how oft we have sighed to be there; And our
children doth wait, And will gath- er them in - to the fold; To the

heard of that land, and its glo - ry we seek, Where the faith-ful with
faith has gone up, like a bird on the wing, To that land on e -
fold of his love, in the mansions a- bove, Where for- ev - er with

The Beautiful Land.—CONCLUDED.

rit.   *a tempo.*

Je - sus shall dwell,   Where the ros - es of youth nev - er
ter - ni - ty's shore,   Where the joy bells of E - den for -
him they shall dwell,   And the eyes that were sad in his

fade from the cheek, And the lips never murmur, farewell.
ev - er shall ring, And the soul shall be wea - ry no more.
smile shall be glad, And the lips never murmur, farewell.

CHORUS.

Beautiful land,   beautiful land,

O - ver the roll - ing sea.(rolling sea.) Beautiful land,   beautiful

land,   When shall   we come to thee?

beautiful land,   When shall we come to thee?

110 Wondrous Glory.

SALLIE M. SMITH. JNO. R. SWENEY.

1. On the mount of wondrous glo - ry, Borne a - loft by faith, we stand,
2. On the mount of wondrous glo - ry, Where so oft 'tis ours to be,
3. On the mount of wondrous glo - ry, Where he bids us come and rest,
4. If on earth our souls are honored With such visions of delight,

While we drink the crystal wa - ters Flowing down from Eden's land.
In the brightness of his presence, Christ our Lord revealed we see.
Je - sus spreads a feast be - fore us, Making each a welcome guest.
Who can tell our heights of rap - ture, When our faith is lost in sight.

CHORUS.

How the heart its toil for-gets, In the
How the heart, its toil forgets,

joy we there behold; In the ful -
In the joy we there behold, there behold, In the

- - ness of his love, That is bet - ter felt than told.
ful - ness of his love, of his love,

Jesus is Leading Me Home.

MARTHA J. LANKTON.   WM. J. KIRKPATRICK.

1. I know I am born of the Spir- it, From death unto life I have passed,
2. I know that his banner is o'er me, His banner of mer-cy and love;
3. I know that my name, tho' unworthy, In life's blessed book he will see;
4. And thus all my conflicts and trials With cheerful submission I bear,

I know with the final - ly faithful My soul shall be gathered at last.
I know that he gives me a foretaste Of joy in the mansions a - bove.
And, oh, when he makes up his jewels, He'll not be unmindful of me.
Be- lieving the palm of the victor In yonder bright world I shall wear.

REFRAIN.

Jesus my Saviour is leading me home, There from his presence I never shall roam;

rit.

Leading me home, leading me home, Jesus my Saviour is leading me home.

Looking unto Jesus.

H. S

H. Sanders. By per.

May be sung as a Solo.

1. I saw an old man bent with years, His locks were snowy white, His
2. I saw the martyr at the stake, And fierce the flames did roar, Yet
3. I saw the soldier on the field Where carnage reigned supreme, And

face was marked with sorrow's tears, And yet his heart was light. I
while his frame with pain did shake, His eye toward heaven did soar. I
yet his courage would not yield, E'en midst the battle's flame. And,

asked him whence his comfort came, And where he found re - lief; He
asked him whence his courage came, And why he had no fear; He
as he torn and bleeding lay, His life-blood gush- ing out, He

said—and ut - t'ring Jesus' name—"He sweetens all my grief."
said—and murm'ring Jesus' name—He's with me ev - en here!
cried—"O Je - sus, come, I pray, Thy love I can - not doubt."

REFRAIN.

Then "looking un - to Je - sus," In sor - row, grief, and pain; His

love, it sweet-ly frees us, We ne'er shall look in vain.

4 I saw a maiden, sweet and fair,
Upon her bed of pain,
And as she lay so helpless there,
She sang a sweet refrain:
'Twas "Jesus loves me, this I know,"—
She sang with heav'nly voice—
Yes, "for the Bible tells me so,"
In Jesus I rejoice.

5 I saw the mother bending o'er
The grave of her loved child,
And tho' her heart with grief was sore,
Yet through her tears she smiled.
By faith she saw her precious flower,
In heaven 'twas blooming fair,
And trusting Jesus' love and power,
She knew she'd meet it there.

6 I saw a Christian hero die,
In far-off pagan land,
And as he on his death-bed lay
I took his fevered hand;
I asked him where his hope was stayed,
And what was his reward:
"I trust in Jesus still," he said,
"My Saviour, and my Lord."

7 O Jesus, Saviour, Brother, Friend,
The Name all names above,
O may thy grace on us descend,
Thy mercy and thy love.
We look to thee in joy, in pain,
And on thee cast our care;
To live for thee is greatest gain,
Thou wilt our sorrows bear.

Responsive Thanksgiving. J. R. S

LEADER.—O give thanks unto the Lord; for he is good:
RESPONSE BY SCHOOL.

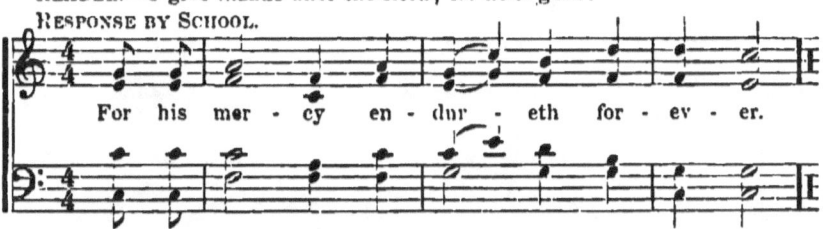

For his mer - cy en - dur - eth for - ev - er.

LEADER.—To him that stretched out the earth above the waters:
RESPONSE.—For his mercy, etc.
LEADER —To him that made great lights:
RESPONSE.—For his mercy, etc.
LEADER.—The sun to rule by day: the moon and stars to rule by night;
RESPONSE.—For his mercy, etc.
LEADER.—To him which led his people through the wilderness:
RESPONSE.—For his mercy, etc.
LEADER.—Who remembered us in our low estate:
RESPONSE.—For his mercy, etc.
LEADER.—And hath redeemed us from our enemies:
RESPONSE.—For his mercy, etc.
LEADER.—Who giveth food to all flesh:
RESPONSE.—For his mercy, etc.
LEADER.—O give thanks unto the God of heaven:
RESPONSE.—For his mercy, etc.

Our Warfare Accomplished.

114

Fanny J. Crosby.

Wm. J. Kirkpatrick.

1. Our warfare will soon be accomplished, Its triumph we soon shall behold,
2. Our warfare will soon be accomplished, Our armor we soon shall resign,
3. Our warfare shall soon be accomplished, The dawn of its ending we see,
4. The Mas-ter our place is preparing, And soon from his lips will be heard

E - ter - ni - ty's vail will be lift - ed, And E- den its beauty un-fold.
And go, with our trophies, to Je - sus, Like stars in his kingdom to shine.
Al - rea - dy our souls are en-rap- tured With visions of what we shall be.
The blessed "Well done, O ye faith- ful, Now enter the joy of your Lord."

CHORUS.

Our warfare will soon be accomplished, Before the white throne we shall stand,

We shall stand.

And sing hal- le - lu- jah for- ever, With harps and with palms in our hands.

We Will.

FANNY J. CROSBY.   JNO. R. SWENEY.

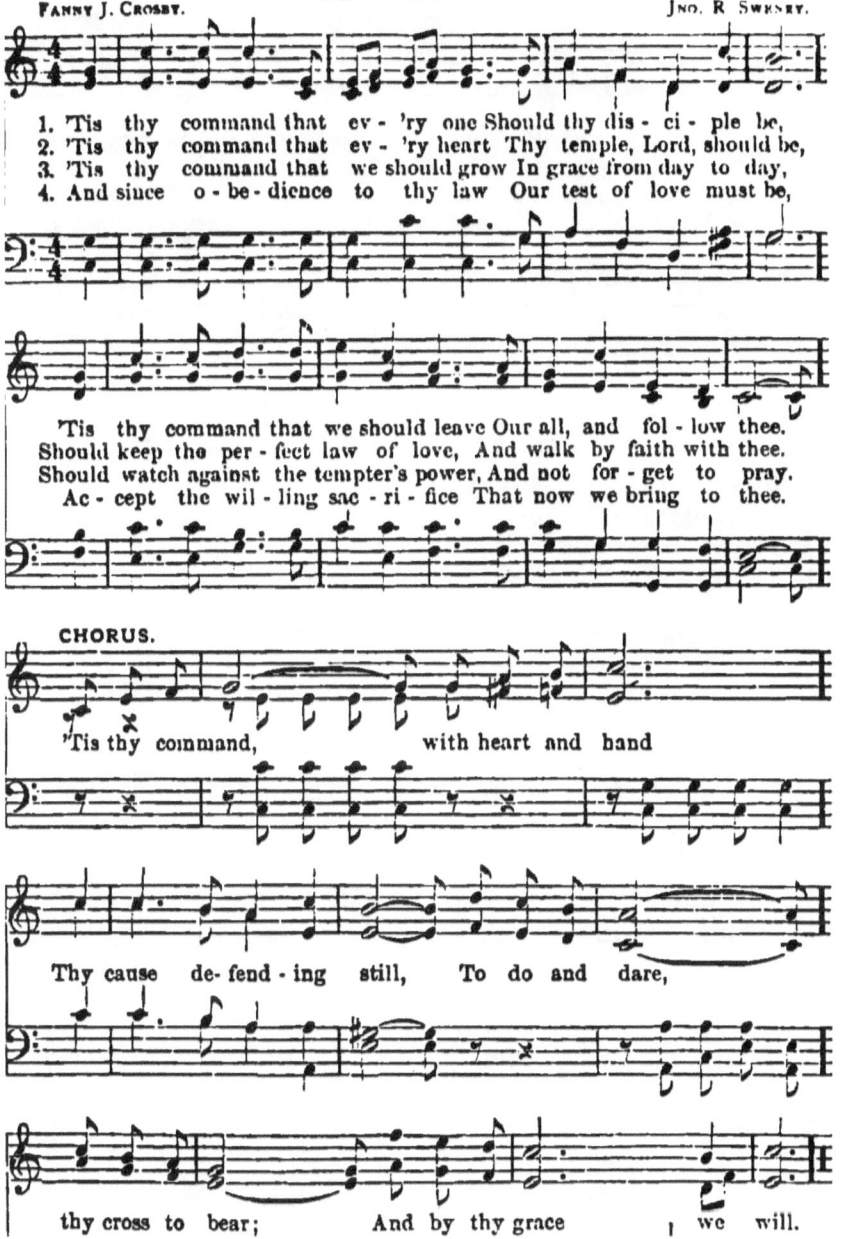

1. 'Tis thy command that ev - 'ry one Should thy dis - ci - ple be,
2. 'Tis thy command that ev - 'ry heart Thy temple, Lord, should be,
3. 'Tis thy command that we should grow In grace from day to day,
4. And since o - be - dience to thy law Our test of love must be,

'Tis thy command that we should leave Our all, and fol - low thee.
Should keep the per - fect law of love, And walk by faith with thee.
Should watch against the tempter's power, And not for - get to pray.
Ac - cept the wil - ling sac - ri - fice That now we bring to thee.

CHORUS.

'Tis thy command,   with heart and hand

Thy cause de- fend - ing still, To do and dare,

thy cross to bear;   And by thy grace   we will.

The Christian Race.

E. E. Hewitt.   Jno. R. Sweney.

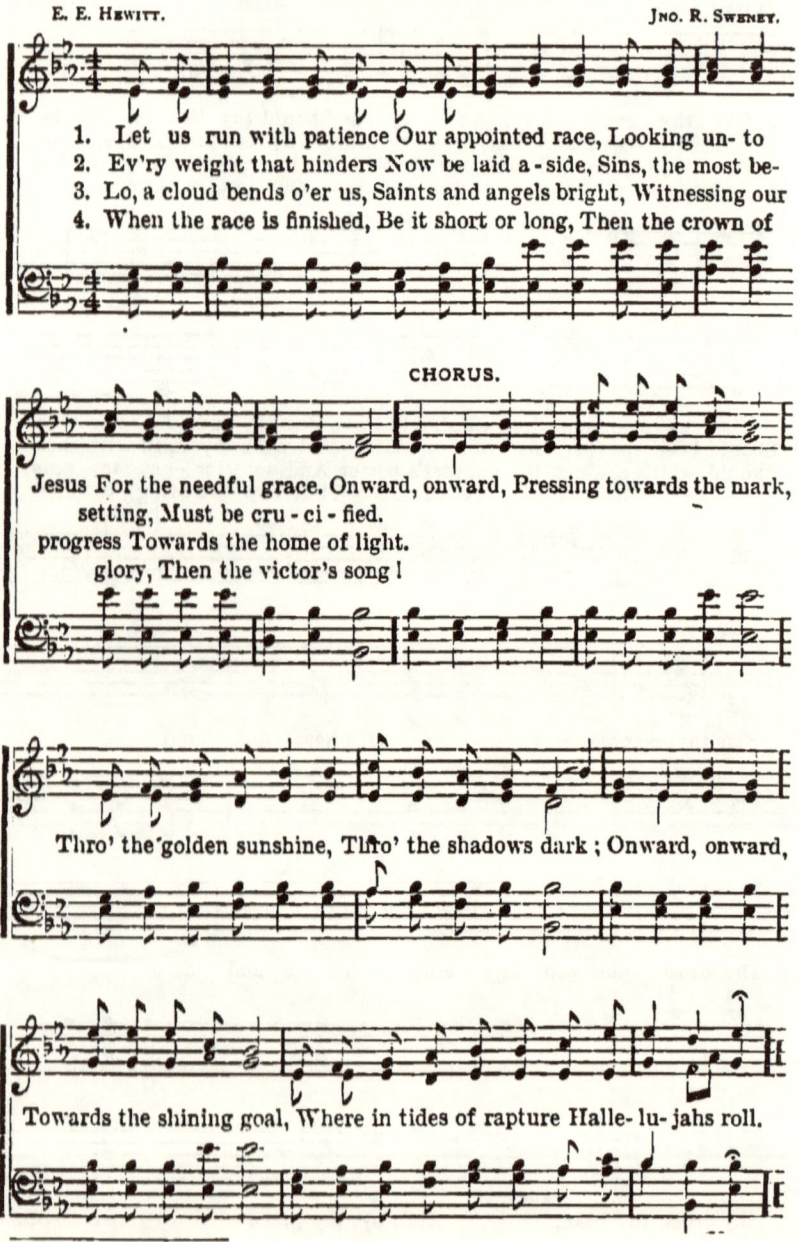

1. Let us run with patience Our appointed race, Looking un- to
2. Ev'ry weight that hinders Now be laid a - side, Sins, the most be-
3. Lo, a cloud bends o'er us, Saints and angels bright, Witnessing our
4. When the race is finished, Be it short or long, Then the crown of

CHORUS.

Jesus For the needful grace. Onward, onward, Pressing towards the mark,
  setting, Must be cru - ci - fied.
progress Towards the home of light.
  glory, Then the victor's song!

Thro' the golden sunshine, Thro' the shadows dark ; Onward, onward,

Towards the shining goal, Where in tides of rapture Halle- lu- jahs roll.

During one of the severe storms that visited Colorado, a young man perished in sight of home. In his bewilderment he passed and repassed his own cottage, to lie down and die almost in range with the "light in the window" which his young wife had placed there to guide him home. All alone she watched the long night through, listening in vain for the footsteps that would come no more; for long before the morning dawned the icy touch of death had stilled that warm, loving heart. The sad death was made still sadder by the fact that he was lost in sight of home.

How many wanderers from the Father's house are lost in sight of home, in the full glare of the Gospel light! They have the open Bible, overflowing with its calls and promises, the faithful warnings from the sacred desk, the manifestations of God's providence, all tending to direct their footsteps heavenward; and yet from all these they turn away, waiting for the more convenient season, and are lost, at last, in sight of the many mansions.—*"Forward."*

H. L. G.   Dr. H. L. GILMOUR.

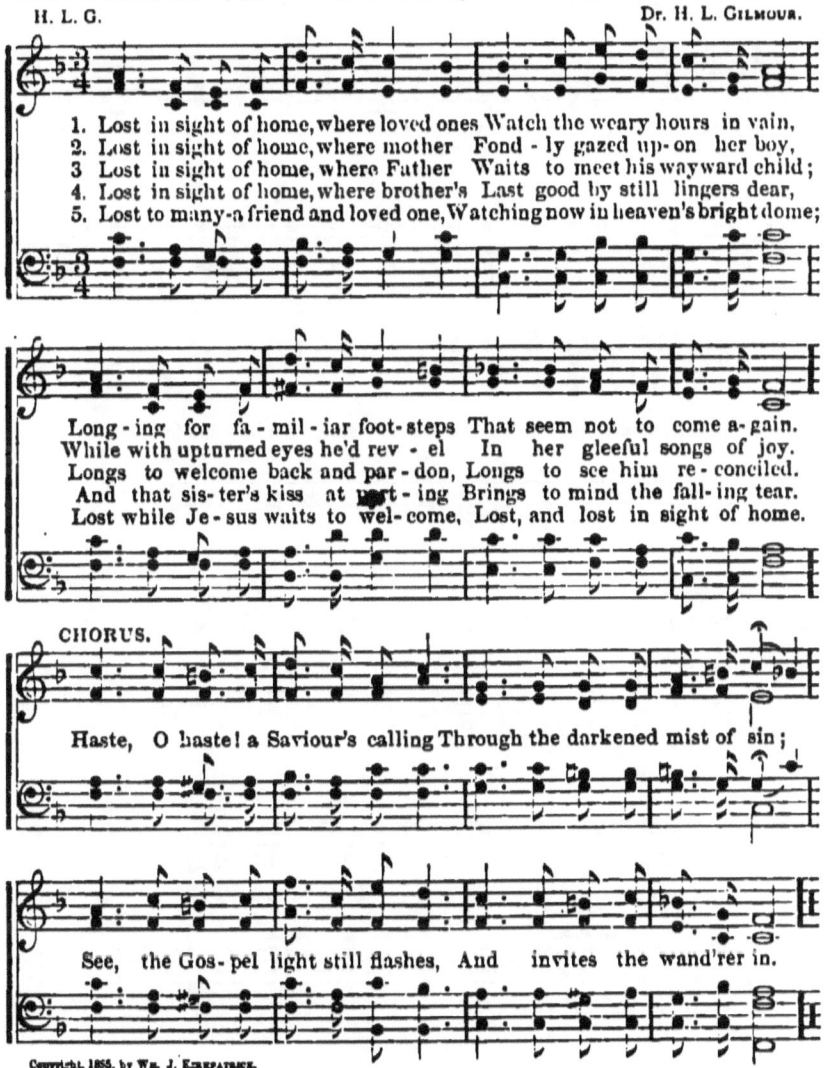

1. Lost in sight of home, where loved ones Watch the weary hours in vain,
2. Lost in sight of home, where mother Fond - ly gazed up-on her boy,
3. Lost in sight of home, where Father Waits to meet his wayward child;
4. Lost in sight of home, where brother's Last good by still lingers dear,
5. Lost to many-a friend and loved one, Watching now in heaven's bright dome;

Long - ing for fa - mil - iar foot-steps That seem not to come a-gain.
While with upturned eyes he'd rev - el In her gleeful songs of joy.
Longs to welcome back and par - don, Longs to see him re - conciled.
And that sis-ter's kiss at part-ing Brings to mind the fall-ing tear.
Lost while Je-sus waits to wel-come, Lost, and lost in sight of home.

CHORUS.

Haste, O haste! a Saviour's calling Through the darkened mist of sin;

See, the Gos-pel light still flashes, And invites the wand'rer in.

Let us Give our Youth to Jesus.

L. H. EDMUNDS.   WM. J. KIRKPATRICK.

DUET OR QUARTET.

1. Let us give our youth to Je - sus, Bring the brightest, sweetest hours,
2. Let us serve our King with gladness, And his wondrous love proclaim,
3. Let us bring our as - pir - a - tions, All that we would be and do,
4. Let us give our youth to Je - sus, Ere the shadows gath-er dim.

Ere the sunbeams lose their spar-kle, Ere the dew has left the flow'rs.
He will bless the lips' "en-deav-or," Bless the deed wrought "in his name."
To the One whose grace can make us No-ble-heart-ed, pure and true.
Hap-py is the life, and bless-ed, Whol-ly yield-ed un-to him.

CHORUS.

While the skies o'erflow With the morning glow, Let us come to Jesus now.

While our hearts are gay, In life's blooming May, Let us come to Jesus now.

Let us come, let us come, Let us come to Je-sus now.!
let us come,   let us come,

Forward.

E. E. Hewitt.  Jno. R. Sweney

1. For- ward, for - ward! all the world for Je - sus; Joy - ful watchword,
2. For- ward, for - ward! on re- mot - est mountains Be the ban - ner
3. For- ward, for - ward! claim the blessed promise, "I am with you
4. For- ward, for - ward! lay up - on his al - tar Love and ser - vice,

bat - tle- cry, and song; He will help us, he will give us wis - dom,
of the cross unfurled; For- ward, for - ward! hear the roy - al bid - ding,
ev - en to the end;" Can we fail when Je - sus is our Lead - er?
heart and hand and pen; His the king- dom, his the power forev - er,

CHORUS.

In his ser- vice he will make us strong. Forward, while his banner to the
Preach my gospel thro' the wide, wide world.
Can we fear with such a might - y Friend?
His the glo - ry ev - er - more, a - men.

breeze we fling; Forward, while his peo- ple will- ing of - f'rings bring.

Till the ransomed nations hallelujah sing; All the world for Christ our King.

Learning of Jesus.

L. H. Edmunds.   W. J. Kirkpatrick.

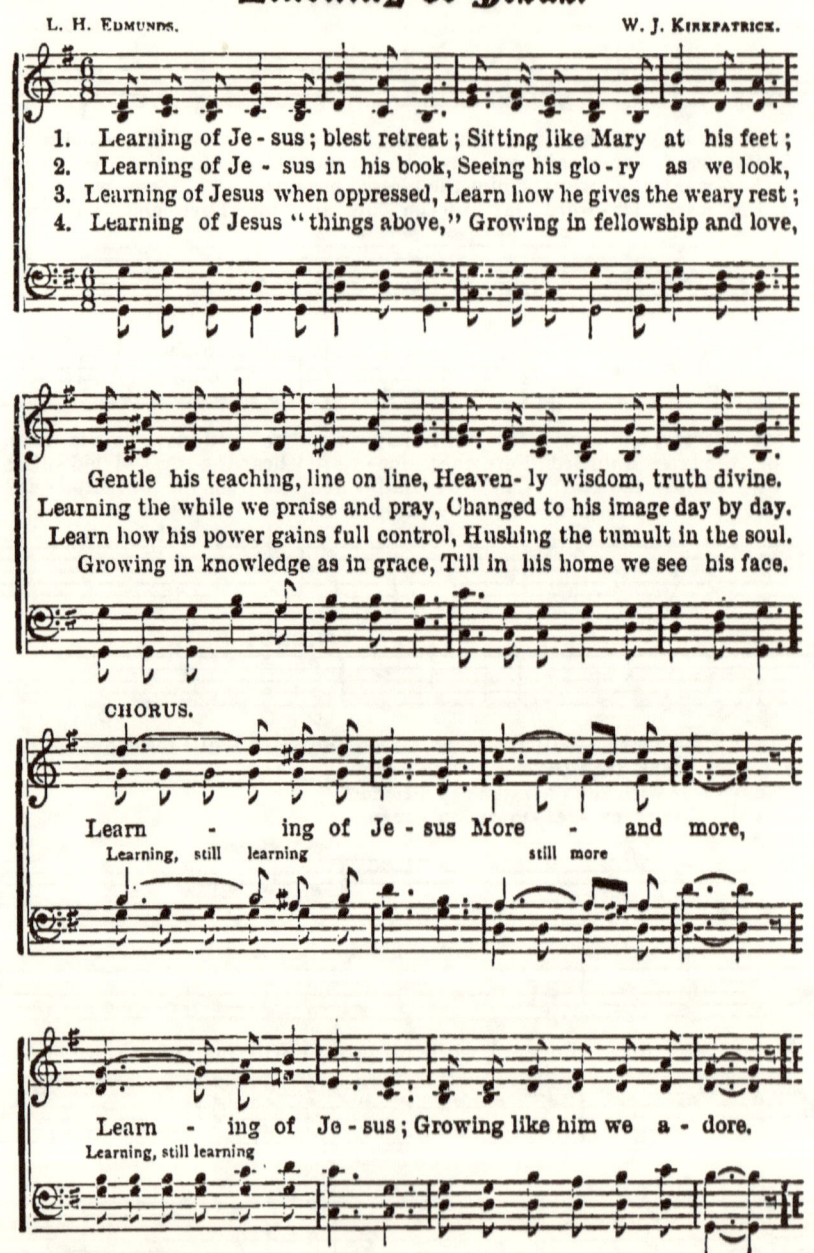

1. Learning of Je - sus; blest retreat; Sitting like Mary at his feet;
2. Learning of Je - sus in his book, Seeing his glo - ry as we look,
3. Learning of Jesus when oppressed, Learn how he gives the weary rest;
4. Learning of Jesus "things above," Growing in fellowship and love,

Gentle his teaching, line on line, Heaven- ly wisdom, truth divine.
Learning the while we praise and pray, Changed to his image day by day.
Learn how his power gains full control, Hushing the tumult in the soul.
Growing in knowledge as in grace, Till in his home we see his face.

CHORUS.

Learn - ing of Je - sus More - and more,
Learning, still learning   still more

Learn - ing of Je - sus; Growing like him we a - dore.
Learning, still learning

He will Hide thee.

James S. Apple.   Jno. R. Sweney.

1. Why art thou fearful, beloved of the Lord? Je - sus will tender- ly
2. Why art thou fearful, when tri - als are deep? Je - sus will tender- ly
3. Why art thou fearful, and where is thy faith? Je - sus will tender- ly
4. Why art thou fearful, he holdeth thy hand? Je - sus will tender- ly

guide thee, Heir to his kingdom, re - mem- ber his word, Safe in the
guide thee, O - ver thy footsteps a watch he will keep, Safe in the
guide thee, Thro' the dark val - ley of shad- ow and death, Still in the
guide thee, Safe till thou en - ter e - ter - ni- ty's land, Safe in the

CHORUS.

Rock he will hide thee. Safe in the Rock when the storm billows roll,
Rock he will hide thee.
Rock he will hide thee.
Rock he will hide thee.

Safe in the Rock he will cov - er thy soul; Be not afraid, O

be not dismayed, Safe in the Rock he will hide thee.

Wanted.

E. F. Hewitt.   Jno. R. Sweney.

1. So great is the work we are giv - en to do, The har - vest is
2. Good men and brave women are wait - ing to go To car - ry the
3. The Fa - ther has promised the king - dom to give To Je - sus, who

ripe, but the la - b'rers are few; The Mas - ter is call - ing for
gos - pel, its life - giv - ing glow; But mon - ey is need - ed to
died that the sin - ner might live; All hon - or and glo - ry 'tis

ad lib.

you and for me; The work needs work - ers; will you be one?
send them, we know; The work needs mon - ey; will you give some?
his to re - ceive; The work needs pray - ing; will you give prayer?

CHORUS.   *rit.*

Wanted: more workers their sheaves to bring;
Wanted: more jewels for Christ our King;

a tempo.

Christ for the world and the world for Christ; Wanted: more voices his glory to sing.

Man the Life Boats.

F. G. BURROUGHS.   H. L. GILMOUR.

1. There are life saving stations a - long the shore, There are life boats al -
2. There are ships slowly sinking beneath the waves, There are thousands of
3. There are pla - ces of rest for each struggling heart, Where no troubled
4. There is life for the dying, there's cordial blest For all who are

slower.   *v'eace.*

read - y to launch; But "Where are the sailors?" sad hearts implore, "Oh,
souls in de - spair: But where is the life boat that quickly braves The
waters o'er- flow; But who will the message of cheer impart, And
fainting and weak; But who'll to the rescue, and no- bly breast All

CHORUS.

where is the crew brave and staunch?" Man the life boats, quick! man the
hea - vi - est seas, tell us, where?
forth to the per - ish - ing go?
billows, the wrecked ones to seek?

life boats, quick! e'er souls are lost; Steer o'er the tempest toss'd main;

man the life boats,

It was Spoken for the Master.

Lizzie Edwards.   Wm. J. Kirkpatrick.

1. It was spok-en for the Mas-ter, Oh, how loving-ly it fell!
2. Oh, we know not when we scatter, Where the precious seed will fall,
3. When our bu-sy toil is o-ver, From the vineyard when we go,

It was uttered in a whis-per, Who had breathed it none could tell.
But we work and trust in Je-sus, For he watcheth o-ver all.
We shall find a store of blessings That on earth we could not know.

It was spok-en for the Mas-ter, On-ly just a lit-tle word,
We may sow be-side the wa-ters Of af-flic-tion, it may be,
We shall wonder at the brightness Of the crowns we then shall wear,

But the chords that long had slumbered, In a grief-worn heart were stirred.
But the fruits of earnest la-bor At the reap-ing we shall see.
But the Lord himself will tell us Why he placed the jewels there.

REFRAIN.

Gentle words of patient kindness, Tho' unheed-ed oft they seem,

To the fold of grace may gather Souls of which we little dream.

The Mercy-seat.

H Stowell.

Chorus by H. L. G.

Dr. H. L. Gilmour.

1. From ev - 'ry storm- y wind that blows, From ev'ry swelling tide of woes,
2. There is a place where Jesus sheds The oil of gladness on our heads;
3. There is a scene where spirits blend, Where friend holds fellowship with friend;

There is a calm, a sure re- treat: 'Tis found beneath the mer- cy-seat.
A place than all besides more sweet: It is the blood-bought mer- cy-seat.
Though sundered far, by faith they meet Around one common mer - cy-seat.

CHORUS.

The mer - cy-seat, the mer - cy-seat, Where weary souls their Saviour meet,

And falling down be- fore his feet, Sal - va- tion flows at the mer- cy-seat.

4 Ah! whither could we flee for aid,
When tempted, desolate, dismayed?
Or how the hosts of hell defeat,
Had suff'ring saints no mercy-seat?

5 There, there on eagle wings we soar,
And sin and sense molest no more; [greet,
And heaven comes down our souls to
While glory crowns the mercy-seat.

126 With Whom We Have to Do.

E. E. Hewitt.   Jno. R. Sweney.

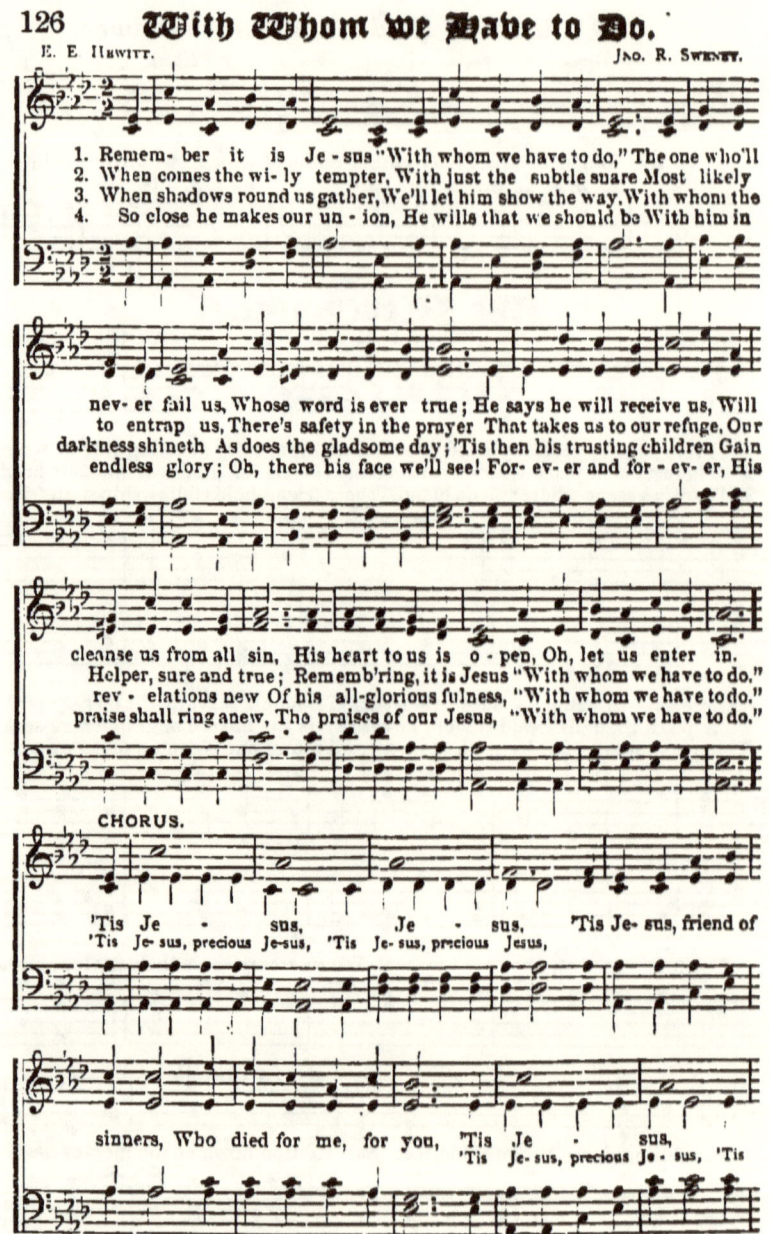

1. Remem-ber it is Je-sus "With whom we have to do," The one who'll
2. When comes the wi-ly tempter, With just the subtle snare Most likely
3. When shadows round us gather, We'll let him show the way, With whom the
4. So close he makes our un-ion, He wills that we should be With him in

nev-er fail us, Whose word is ever true; He says he will receive us, Will
to entrap us, There's safety in the prayer That takes us to our refuge. Our
darkness shineth As does the gladsome day; 'Tis then his trusting children Gain
endless glory; Oh, there his face we'll see! For-ev-er and for-ev-er, His

cleanse us from all sin, His heart to us is o-pen, Oh, let us enter in.
Helper, sure and true; Rememb'ring, it is Jesus "With whom we have to do."
rev-elations new Of his all-glorious fulness, "With whom we have to do."
praise shall ring anew, The praises of our Jesus, "With whom we have to do."

CHORUS.

'Tis Je - sus, Je - sus, 'Tis Je-sus, friend of
'Tis Je-sus, precious Je-sus, 'Tis Je-sus, precious Jesus,

sinners, Who died for me, for you, 'Tis Je - sus,
'Tis Je-sus, precious Je-sus, 'Tis

Je - sus, 'Tis Jesus, Prince and Saviour, "With whom we have to do."
Je - sus, precious Je - sus,

Haste, Return.

MARTHA J. LANKTON. WM. J. KIRKPATRICK.

1. Oh, how long will men refuse Christ, their on - ly hope, to choose?
2. Oh, how long shall mercy cry, Hungry souls, why will ye die?
3. Oh, how long shall love implore, Love the cru - el thorns that bore,
4. Oh, how long shall Je- sus say, Come to me, I am the way;

Fine. CHORUS.

Oh, how long the Spirit plead E'er his tender voice they heed? Haste, return,
Will ye starve and perish here, And your Father's house so near?
Love that came to seek the lost, Love a Saviour's life that cost?
Weary, burden'd souls, opprest, Take my yoke, I'll give you rest.

D.S.—Soon for you 'twill be too late!

D.S.

haste, return; Lest your lamp should cease to burn,—Enter now the narrow gate,

Beautiful Home.

FRANK FOREST.
H. R. PALMER. By per.

1. There is a home e - ter - nal,
2. Flow'rs forev - er are springing
3. Soon shall I join that an - them,

Beau - ti - ful and bright,
In that home so fair,
Far beyond the sky;

Where sweet joys su - per - nal
Thousands of children are sing - ing
Jesus became my ran - som,

Never are dimmed by night;
Praises to Je - sus there;
Why should I fear to die?

White-robed angels are sing - ing
How they swell the glad an - thems
Soon my eyes will behold him

Ev - er around the bright throne;
Ev - er around the bright throne;
Seated up - on the bright throne;

When, Oh, when shall I see thee,
When, Oh, when shall I see thee,
Then, Oh, then shall I see thee,

Beau - ti - ful, beauti - ful home?
Beau - ti - ful, beauti - ful home?
Beau - ti - ful, beauti - ful home!

REFRAIN.

Home, beau- ti - ful home,
Beauti - ful home,

Bright, beau - ti - ful home:
Beauti - ful home;

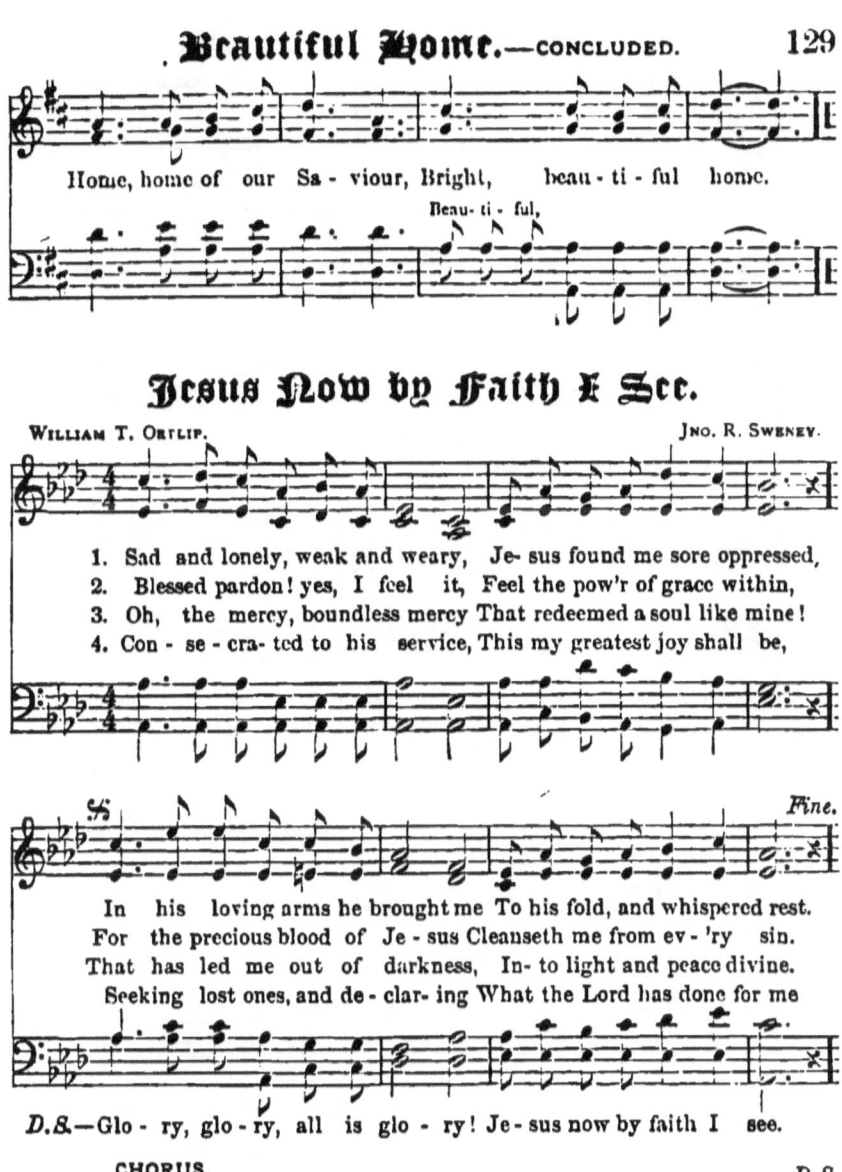

Home, home of our Sa - viour, Bright, beau - ti - ful home.

Beau - ti - ful,

Jesus Now by Faith I See.

WILLIAM T. ORTLIP.   JNO. R. SWENEY.

1. Sad and lonely, weak and weary, Je - sus found me sore oppressed,
2. Blessed pardon! yes, I feel it, Feel the pow'r of grace within,
3. Oh, the mercy, boundless mercy That redeemed a soul like mine!
4. Con - se - cra - ted to his service, This my greatest joy shall be,

Fine.

In his loving arms he brought me To his fold, and whispered rest.
For the precious blood of Je - sus Cleanseth me from ev - 'ry sin.
That has led me out of darkness, In - to light and peace divine.
Seeking lost ones, and de - clar- ing What the Lord has done for me

D.S.—Glo - ry, glo - ry, all is glo - ry! Je - sus now by faith I see.

CHORUS.   D.S.

Glo - ry, glo - ry, all is glo - ry! He reveals himself to me;

Love and Rest at Home.

PRISCILLA J. OWENS.   WM. J. KIRKPATRICK.

1. O pilgrim on life's desert, O wand'rer far astray, Why will you
2. Why wander on in darkness, Amid the storm and cold, While light from
3. Here waters of sal- va- tion Are flowing full and free, The Bread of

toil benighted Along sin's thorny way? The Father's board is spread, Tho
home is shining, To guide you to the fold? Come, leave the bitter past, With
Life is giv- en, Your portion it shall be; O, speed your wearied feet To

feast prepared at home, Here's welcome ready waiting, Why will you longer roam?
all its sins, behind; The Saviour waits to give you A welcome true and kind.
gain this open door; Lay down each heavy burden, And wander never more.

CHORUS.

Come home,   Come home, There's love and rest at home; The
Come home,

Sa - viour now is call - ing: O wand'ring one, come home.

Thou Ridest to Conquer.

James L. Black.   Jno. R. Sweney.

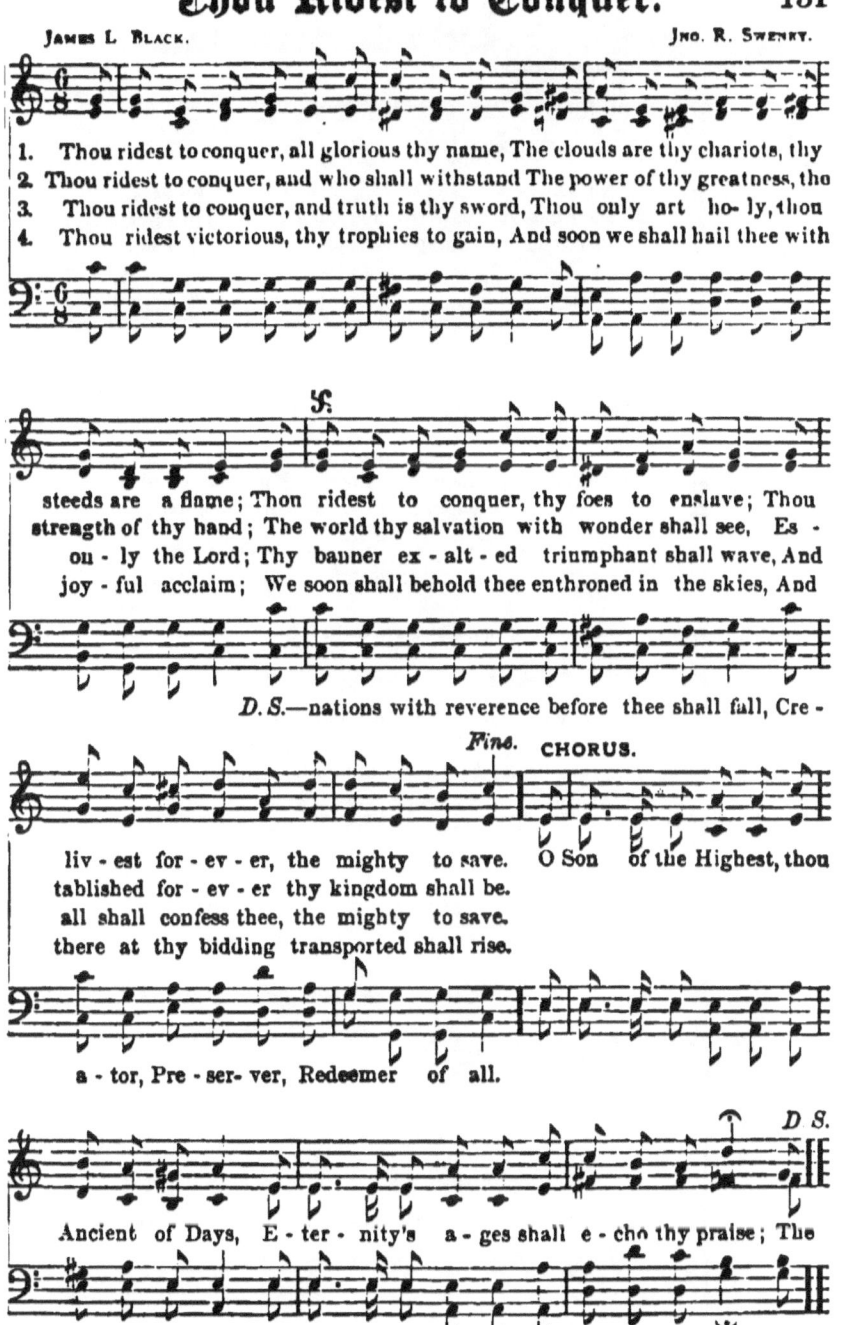

1. Thou ridest to conquer, all glorious thy name, The clouds are thy chariots, thy
2. Thou ridest to conquer, and who shall withstand The power of thy greatness, tho
3. Thou ridest to conquer, and truth is thy sword, Thou only art ho - ly, thou
4. Thou ridest victorious, thy trophies to gain, And soon we shall hail thee with

steeds are a flame; Thou ridest to conquer, thy foes to enslave; Thou
strength of thy hand; The world thy salvation with wonder shall see, Es -
ou - ly the Lord; Thy banner ex - alt - ed triumphant shall wave, And
joy - ful acclaim; We soon shall behold thee enthroned in the skies, And

D. S.—nations with reverence before thee shall fall, Cre -

Fine.   CHORUS.

liv - est for - ev - er, the mighty to save.   O Son of the Highest, thou
tablished for - ev - er thy kingdom shall be.
all shall confess thee, the mighty to save.
there at thy bidding transported shall rise.

a - tor, Pre - ser- ver, Redeemer of all.

D S.

Ancient of Days, E - ter - nity's a - ges shall e - cho thy praise; The

Help Draweth Near.

F. G. BURROUGHS.

Martial style.

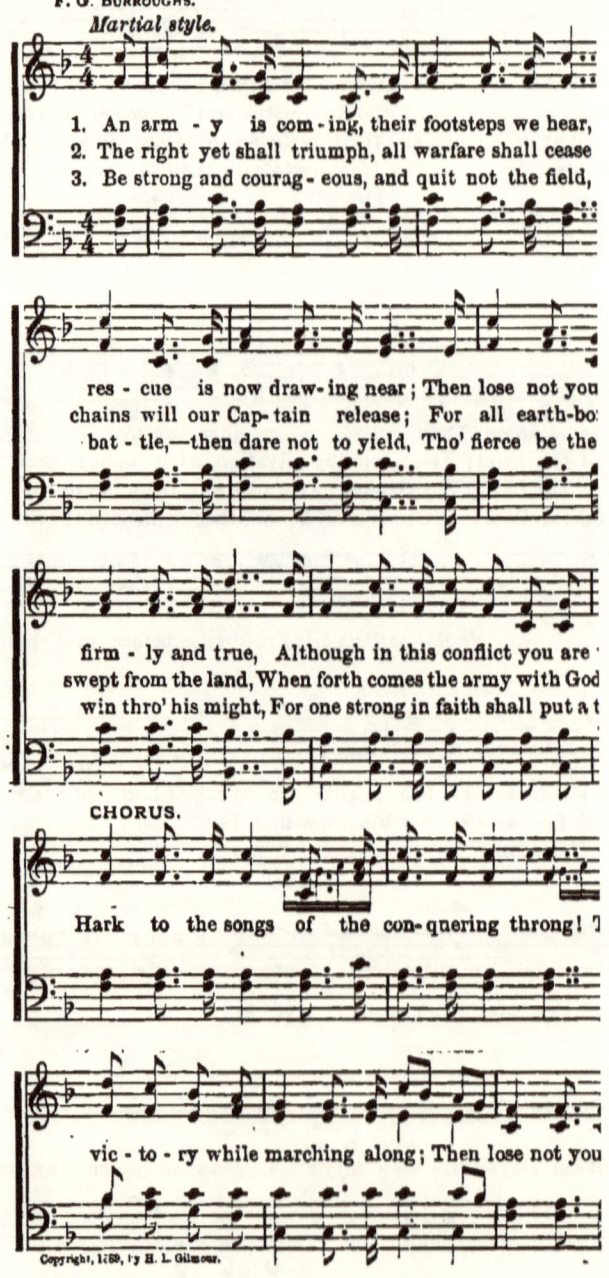

1. An arm - y   is com - ing, their footsteps we hear,
2. The right yet shall triumph, all warfare shall cease
3. Be strong and courag - eous, and quit not the field,

res - cue   is now draw - ing near; Then lose not you
chains will our Cap- tain   release; For all earth-bo:
bat - tle,—then dare not to yield, Tho' fierce be the

firm - ly and true, Although in this conflict you are
swept from the land, When forth comes the army with God
win thro' his might, For one strong in faith shall put a t

CHORUS.

Hark   to the songs of the con - quering throng! 1

vic - to - ry while marching along; Then lose not you

help draweth near: The sound of this army   all God's faithful can hear!

F. G. BURROUGHS.   **The Royal Army.**   ADAM GEIBEL.

1. A sunday school army here gathered are we, To pour forth our carols of
2. A sunday school army u-nited we stand, Tho' part of our host is in
3. A sunday school army undaunted we tread. Still upward and onward by

glad vic - to - ry; To sing as the birds sing their sweet notes of cheer, Un-
Canaan's fair land, They join us   to day in   ascrib - ing all praise To
Christ our King led, To where the ripe fruit of e - ter - ni - ty grows, And

D. S.—banners inscribed with his precepts divine, While
Fine. CHORUS.

mindful of   sorrow, untrammeled by fear. The Lord's royal army is
him who is crowning with goodness our days.
where the pure water   of life's riv - er flows.

in his blest sunlight our strong weapons shine.

The Lamb of God.

134

Fanny J. Crosby.

Jno. R. Sweney.

SOLO.—Alto.

1. O Lamb of God, whose sacred brow Was pierced with thorns for
2. I wan - der up the mountain wild, And trace thy footprints
3. O Lamb of God, what bliss divine My grateful heart has

me, Be - yond the dark forbod - ing clouds My
there, I watch thy form at midnight hour, A -
known When, filled with love thy presence gave, I

faith looks up to thee; I see the path thy wea - ry
lone in si - lent prayer; I stand beside the tranquil
knelt before thy throne; And though in tears I oft have

feet   Through all thy life have trod,   And
deep,   Whose wrath thy will has stayed,   And
past   Be - neath thy chastening rod,   Yet

hear   a voice again repeat,   Behold   the Lamb of God.
hear   the sweet and cheering words,   "'Tis I, be not a- fraid."
still   I heard the voice that said,   Behold   the Lamb of God.

CHORUS.

Be - hold   the Lamb of God,   Be - hold   the Lamb of God,

Be-hold, behold,   Behold, behold,

I hear a voice again repeat Be - hold   the Lamb of God.

Be - hold, behold

Angels Above are Singing.

F. A. S.

FRANCIS A. SIMKINS

1. An - gels a - bove are sing - ing, Heav - en - ly harps are ring - ing,
2. There, where the stars are gleaming, There, where thy smile is beam-ing,
3. Nev - er-more sin nor sigh - ing, Nev - er-more grief nor cry - ing,

Voic - es to me are bring-ing Whis- pers of joy to be;
Sweet-ly my soul is dream-ing, Long- ing thy face to see:
Nev - er-more pain nor dy - ing,— Joy ev - er- more for me:

Oh, to be yon - der, up yon - der, Nev - er, no, nev - er to wan - der,
Ev - er thy pow-er con - fess - ing,—Seeking thy fa - vor and bless-ing,
Praising thee ev-er and ev - er, Leaving thee nev-er, no, nev - er,

Ev - er my heart growing fond- er,—Fond-er, dear Master, of thee.
Still is my soul ev - er press-ing,—Pressing yet near-er to thee.
Dwell-ing in glo - ry for - ev - er,— Ev - er, for - ev - er with thee.

James L. Black.

Jno. R. Sweney.

1. O precious Redeemer, what rapture is mine While here I am singing thy
2. I plunge in the fountain of mercy that flows, And feel the assurance thy
3. Oh, tender compassion, that stoops from above To make a poor sinner a
4. O Jesus my Saviour, when sweetly I rest In yonder bright region, the

goodness divine! All honor and glory, my Saviour, to thee, Thy perfect sal-
promise bestows; The light of thy presence by faith I can see,—Thy perfect sal-
child of thy love, From sin and its bondage forev- er to free A soul that in
home of the blest, I'll join in the chorus whose burden shall be, Thy perfect sal-

CHORUS.

vation a - vaileth for me.   Halle - lujah to thee, my Redeemer, to
vation a - vaileth for me.
darkness has wandered from thee.
vation a - vaileth for me.

Thee! Sal- va - tion is boundless, salvation is   free;   Halle - lujah to

Thee, my Redeemer, to Thee! Thy perfect salvation a - vaileth for me.

Waiting at the Door.

MRS. KATE M. REASONER.   T. C. O'KANE. By per.

1. I am waiting for the Master, Who will bid me rise and come
2. Many-a weary path I've traveled, In the darkest storm and strife,
3. Many friends that traveled with me Reached that portal long a-go;

To the glo-ry of his presence, To the gladness of his home.
Bearing many-a heavy burden,— Oft-en struggling for my life.
One by one they left me battling With the dark and crafty foe.

CHORUS.

They are watch - ing at the portal, They are wait -
They are watching, they are watching at the portal, They are waiting, they are

- ing at the door; Waiting on - ly for my coming,
waiting at the door; Waiting on-ly, waiting on-ly for my coming,

All the loved ones gone before.
All the loved ones, All the loved ones gone before.

4 Yes, their pilgrimage was shorter,
  And their triumphs sooner won
O, how lovingly they'll greet me
  When the toils of life are done.
For they're watching, etc.

5 Yet, O Lord, I wait thy pleasure,
  For thy time and ways are best;
Hear me, Lord, for I am weary;
  O my Father, bid me rest.
They are watching, etc.

E. A. BARNES   We have an advocate with the Father. 1 John II. 1.   JNO. R. SWENEY.

DUET.—Alto and Tenor.

1. He pleads that all who wan- der far May now return and seek his fold;
2. He pleads that all with scar-let sins May now repent, and now be - lieve;
3. He pleads that all as strangers now May know in truth the sinner's friend;
4. He pleads that none may long reject The joy and peace he waits to give;

rit.

He pleads that they in darkness still The light of life may now behold.
He pleads that they who have it not The blessed hope may now receive.
He pleads that they by faith may see That in his name all rich- es blend.
He pleads that none shall perish here, Since he has died that all may live.

CHORUS.

Je - sus pleads,   he pleads for all,   Je - sus
Je - sus pleads,   he pleads for all,

pleads,   he pleads for all,   In realms above, at the

rit.

Fath - er's throne,   He pleads for one and all.
Je - sus pleads   for one and all.

Happy Day of Joy Returning.

Mrs. R. N. Turner. Wm. J. Kirkpatrick.

1. Happy day of joy, returning, Thee we hail, to thee we sing
2. Like the dew, in silence falling While we sleep, at God's command
3. Friends we love we gladly welcome With an ea - ger clasp and true,
4. Peace be with us here assembled, Joy at - tend this pleasant hour,

Festal songs to greet thy coming Thro' the air with gladness ring.
Many mer - cies have descend - ed From the Fa - ther's loving hand.
And we turn with joyful greeting To the fa - ces that are new.
And the God we love uphold us By his gra - cious heavenly power.

CHORUS.

Swell the cho - rus, swell the cho - rus, Swell the chorus loud and deep,
Swell the cho - rus, swell the cho - rus, Swell it loud and deep,

Let it glad - ly onward sweep, Swell the cho - - rus, swell the
Swell the cho - rus,

cho - rus, Ring it sweetly o'er and o'er, As we meet once more.
swell the cho - rus, as we meet once more.

Copyright, 1888, by Wm. J. Kirkpatrick

Singing in the Sunshine.

E. E. Hewitt.   Jno. R. Sweney.

1. Singing in the sunshine of our Father's blessing; Singing in the
2. Singing in the sunshine of the great sal- va- tion, Saving guil- ty
3. Singing in the sunshine of the Ho - ly Spir - it, Blessed light il -

sunshine of his love;   Tho' the shadows gather o'er the misty valley,
sinners, you and me;   Glo - ry be to Je - sus for his "royal bounty,"
luming all the way;   Light of truth most holy, dwelling with the lowly,

CHORUS.

Light is   on the hills above. Trusting o'er and o'er, praising more and more,
Mer - cy   flowing full and free.
Lead us   to the "perfect day."

Singing in the sunshine, praising ev - er more; Trusting o'er and o'er,

Praising more and more, Till we see the glory of the gold - en shore.

The King in His Beauty.

WM. T. JONES.   JNO. R. SWENEY.

DUET.—Alto and Tenor.

1. How lovely are thy dwellings, O Zi-on bright and fair,
2. The promised day is dawning, When all the ran-somed throng
3. Oh, blessed, blessed morning, When, all their per-ils o'er,
4. And still the time draws nearer, Their triumph soon will come,

Unnumbered are the legions Whose harps shall e-cho there.
With joy shall come to Zi-on, And ev-er-last-ing song.
They hear the shout of welcome That greets them from the shore!
And heaven's e-ternal anthems Proclaim the con-querors home.

CHORUS.

The King in his beauty Their rap-tured eyes shall see,

And in his roy-al palace For-ev-er they shall be.

FANNY J. CROSBY.

W. J. KIRKPATRICK.

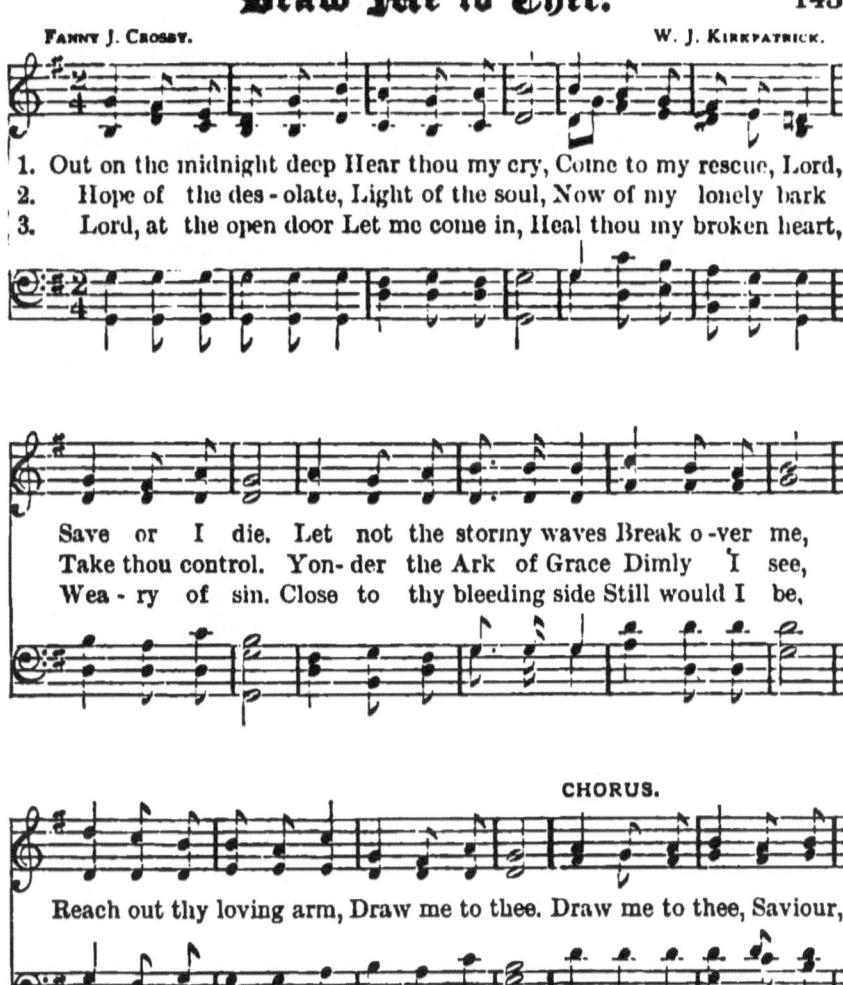

1. Out on the midnight deep Hear thou my cry, Come to my rescue, Lord,
2. Hope of the des-olate, Light of the soul, Now of my lonely bark
3. Lord, at the open door Let me come in, Heal thou my broken heart,

Save or I die. Let not the stormy waves Break o-ver me,
Take thou control. Yon-der the Ark of Grace Dimly I see,
Wea-ry of sin. Close to thy bleeding side Still would I be,

CHORUS.

Reach out thy loving arm, Draw me to thee. Draw me to thee, Saviour,

144 **Ring Out the Hallelujahs.**

Miss Emma M. Johnston.   Wm. J. Kirkpatrick.

1. Sing the song the ransomed sing, Let your hal-le-lujahs ring,
2. Sing the love that set you free; Sing the song of lib-er-ty,
3. Sing the grace that made you whole; Sing the vict'ries of the soul,
4. Sing till heaven shall catch the strain, Hallelu-jah yet a-gain,

Glo-ry to the Lord your King; Ring out the halle-lujahs.
Sing the glo-ry yet to be; Ring out the hal-le-lujahs.
Sing while time shall onward roll; Ring out the hal-le-lujahs.
"Love redeeming" the refrain; Ring out the hal-le-lujahs.

REFRAIN.

Hal-le-lu-jah! . . . . Hal-le-lu-jah! . . . .
Hal-le-lu-jah!   Hal-le-lu-jah!

Glo-ry to our Lord and King; Ring out the halle-lu-jahs.

Tell it to Others.

E. E. Hewitt.

Jno. R. Sweney.

1. Tell it to oth - ers, the story of Je - sus, Your wonderful Saviour con -
2. Tell it to others, there's power in confession; The soul gathers strength with the
3. Tell it to oth - ers; he died to redeem you, He makes intercession a -
4. Tell it to oth - ers, so simply and humbly; Oh, tell it with love in your

fess; So gracious and faithful, so kind and forgiv - ing, So ready to
word; The story grows sweeter; there's joy in the telling, For Christ hath the
bove; Oh, tell of his mer - cy; his grace, all-sufficient; The height and the
heart; Then trustfully pray for the help of his Spir - it, And God will his

CHORUS.

save and to bless. Tell it, oh, tell it, the "good news" from
wit - ness - ing heard.
depth of his love.
bless - ing im - part.

heaven; A message so precious, so true; In mansions of

glo - ry we'll sing the same story, In rapturous strains, ever new.

Sunlit Songs-K

The Beautiful Light.

R. Kelso Carter.

Jno. R. Sweney.

1. Je-sus is the light, the way, We are walking in the light, We are
2. We who know our sins forgiven, We are walking in the light, We are
3. As we journey here be - low, We are walking in the light, We are
4. We will sing his power to save, We are walking in the light, We are

walking in the light; Shining brighter day by day, We are walking in the
walking in the light; Find on earth the joy of heaven, We are walking in the
walking in the light; Oh, what joy and peace we know, We are walking in the
walking in the light; We will triumph o'er the grave, We are walking in the

REFRAIN.

beautiful light of God. We are walk - - ing in the light, We are
Walking in the light, beautiful light of God,

walk - - ing in the light, We are walk - - ing in the
Walking in the light, beau-ti-ful light of God, Walking in the light,

light, ... We are walking in the beauti-ful light of God.
Walk-ing in the light,

Trust and Obey.

Rev. J. H. Sammis.

D. B. Towner.

147

CHORUS.

1. When we walk with the Lord In the light of his word, What a glory he
2. Not a shadow can rise, Not a cloud in the skies, But his smile quickly
3. Not a burden we bear, Not a sorrow we share, But our toil he doth

sheds on our way! While we do his good will, He a-bides with us
drives it a-way; Not a doubt nor a fear, Not a sigh nor a
rich-ly re-pay; Not a grief nor a loss, Not a frown nor a

still, And with all who will trust and o-bey. Trust and o-bey, For there's
tear Can a-bide while we trust and o-bey.
cross, But is blest if we trust and o-bey.

no oth-er way To be hap-py in Je-sus But to trust and o-bey.

4 But we never can prove
The delights of his love
Until all on the altar we lay,
For the favor he shows,
And the joy he bestows,
Are for all who will trust and obey.

6 Then in fellowship sweet
We will sit at his feet,
Or we'll walk by his side in the way;
What he says we will do,
Where he sends we will go,
Never fear, only trust and obey.

148

Onward and Upward.

E. E. Hewitt.

Jno. R. Sweney.

1. Onward still, and upward, Follow ev - ermore Where our mighty
2. Onward, ev - er onward. Thro' the pastures green, Where the streams flow
3. Upward, ev - er upward, T'ward the radiant glow, Far a - bove the

Leader Goes in love before; "Looking unto Je - sus," Reach a helping hand
softly, Under skies serene; Or, if need be, upward, O'er the rocky steep,
valley, Where the mist hangs low; On, with songs of gladness, Till the march shall end,

CHORUS.

To a struggling-neighbor, Helping him to stand. Marching on
Trusting him who guides us, Strong to save and keep. Marching on- ward, marching
Where ten thousand thousand Hallelu- jahs blend.

ward, up - ward, Marching steadi -ly,
onward, on - ward, Up - ward march- ing, up - ward, up- ward,

onward, Je - sus leads the way, Marching on - ward,
onward, march- ing on-ward, on- ward,

up - - ward,
upward, marching upward, upward,
Onward unto glory, To the perfect day.

O Hearts that are Weary.

FANNY J. CROSBY   WM. J. KIRKPATRICK.

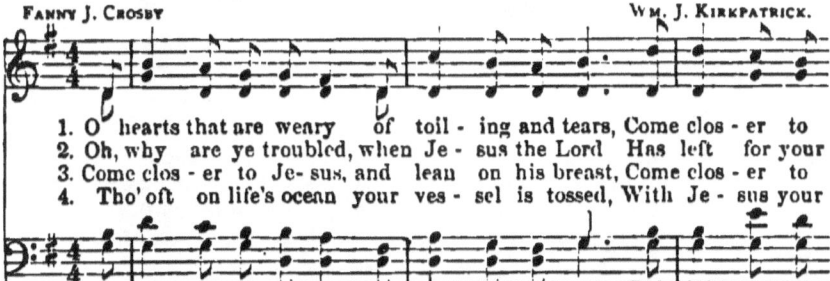

1. O hearts that are weary of toil - ing and tears, Come clos - er to
2. Oh, why are ye troubled, when Je - sus the Lord Has left for your
3. Come clos - er to Je - sus, and lean on his breast, Come clos - er to
4. Tho' oft on life's ocean your ves - sel is tossed, With Je - sus your

CHO.—O hearts that are weary of toil - ing and tears, Come clos - er to

Fine.

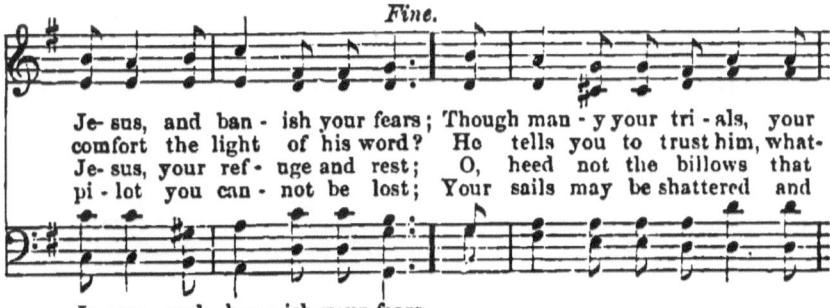

Je - sus, and ban - ish your fears; Though man - y your tri - als, your
comfort the light of his word? He tells you to trust him, what-
Je - sus, your ref - uge and rest; O, heed not the billows that
pi - lot you can - not be lost; Your sails may be shattered and

Je - sus, and ban - ish your fears.

Chorus D. C.

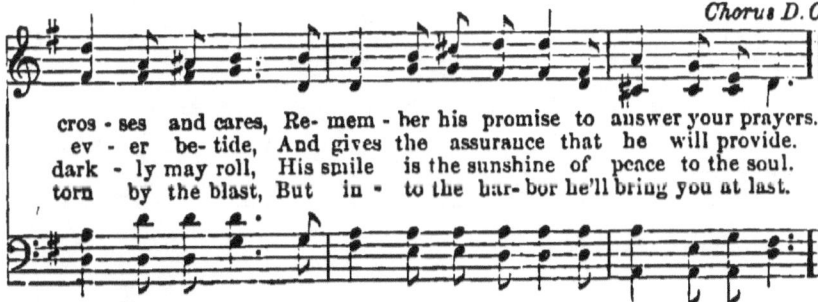

cros - ses and cares, Re - mem - ber his promise to answer your prayers.
ev - er be- tide, And gives the assurance that he will provide.
dark - ly may roll, His smile is the sunshine of peace to the soul.
torn by the blast, But in - to the har - bor he'll bring you at last.

My Native Land.

Rev. E. H. Stokes, D. D.   Wm. J. Kirkpatrick.

1. My native land! my native land! I love thee, O my na- tive land;
2. My native land, home of the free, I love thy songs of lib- er - ty;
3. My native land, in proud delight, I cherish thee, where right is might,
4. My native land! Relig - ion rules! The Bible and the common schools!

Thy valleys and thy no- ble hills, Thy oceans, lakes, and rippling rills;
Thy brilliant banners, floating high, Whose starry folds embrace the sky.
A land redeemed by patriot blood, And guarded by the patriot's God.
Here knowledge is a potent rod, And all are free to worship God.

CHORUS.

My na- tive land, dear native land! I love thee, O my na- tive land!

My na- tive land, dear na- tive land! I love thee, O my na- tive land!

Stand by Your Colors.

F. G. Burroughs.   Thomas O'Neill.

Tempo di marcia.

1. If you are a sol-dier in the ar-my of the Lord, Nev-er be a-
2. If you are a sol-dier, and have on the gir-dle truth, You shall stand be-
3. If you are a sol-dier, you will pa-tiently en-dure All the times of

shamed to battle with the Spir-it's sword; Nev-er be afraid to show the
fore the foe, although you're but a youth; With the breastplate righteousness a
'hardness,' so you may his smile secure; Join-ing in the conflicts, would you

o-ver-coming shield, By your colors nobly stand, the foe will surely yield.
cov-er o'er your heart, Not a wound shall you receive from any fiery dart.
glorious victor be. Stand then by your colors, and the Lord will stand by thee.

CHORUS.

ff
Stand by your col-ors, Nev-er give in, Stand by them boldly, And

you the strife shall win; Stand by your colors, Stand by your colors.

152   # A Beautiful World.

O. Snow.

1. There is a beau - tiful world, Where saints and angels sing;
2. There is a beau - tiful world, Where sorrow nev-er comes;
3. There is a beau - ti-ful world, Unseen to mor-tal sight;
4. There is a beau - ti-ful world, Of harmon-y and love;

A world where peace and pleasure reign, And heav'nly praises ring.
A world where tears shall never fall, In sighing for our home.
And darkness nev - er enters there, That home is fair and bright.
Oh, may we safe - ly enter there, And dwell with God above.

CHORUS.

We'll be there, we'll be there, Palms of vic - t'ry, Crowns of

glo - ry, we shall wear, In that beau - ti -ful land on high.

E. E. HEWITT.   JNO. R. SWENEY.

1. Blessed, blessed Saviour, By thy gentle fav-or Thou hast drawn our
2. In thy love confid-ing, We would trust thy guiding; Trust thy saving
3. Blessed, blessed Saviour, Keep us thine for-ev-er, Help us love and

wayward souls to thee; Thou hast sought and found us, Clasp'd thine arms around us,
might in all our ways; On-ly walk beside us, Needful good provide us,
serve thee more and more; Till we bow before thee, See thee in thy glo-ry,

CHORUS.

Cleansed us from our sins, and set us free.   Praise   to thee, our
Happy then will be our fleeting days.
Join the chorus of the golden shore.   Praise to thee, our Saviour,

Sa - viour;   Grate - ful hearts we bring,
Praise to thee, our Saviour;   Grateful hearts we bring,   Grateful hearts we bring,

While   we tell thy mer - cy,   While thy grace we sing.
While we tell thy mercy,   While we tell thy mercy.

E. E. Hewitt.   Jno. R. Sweney.

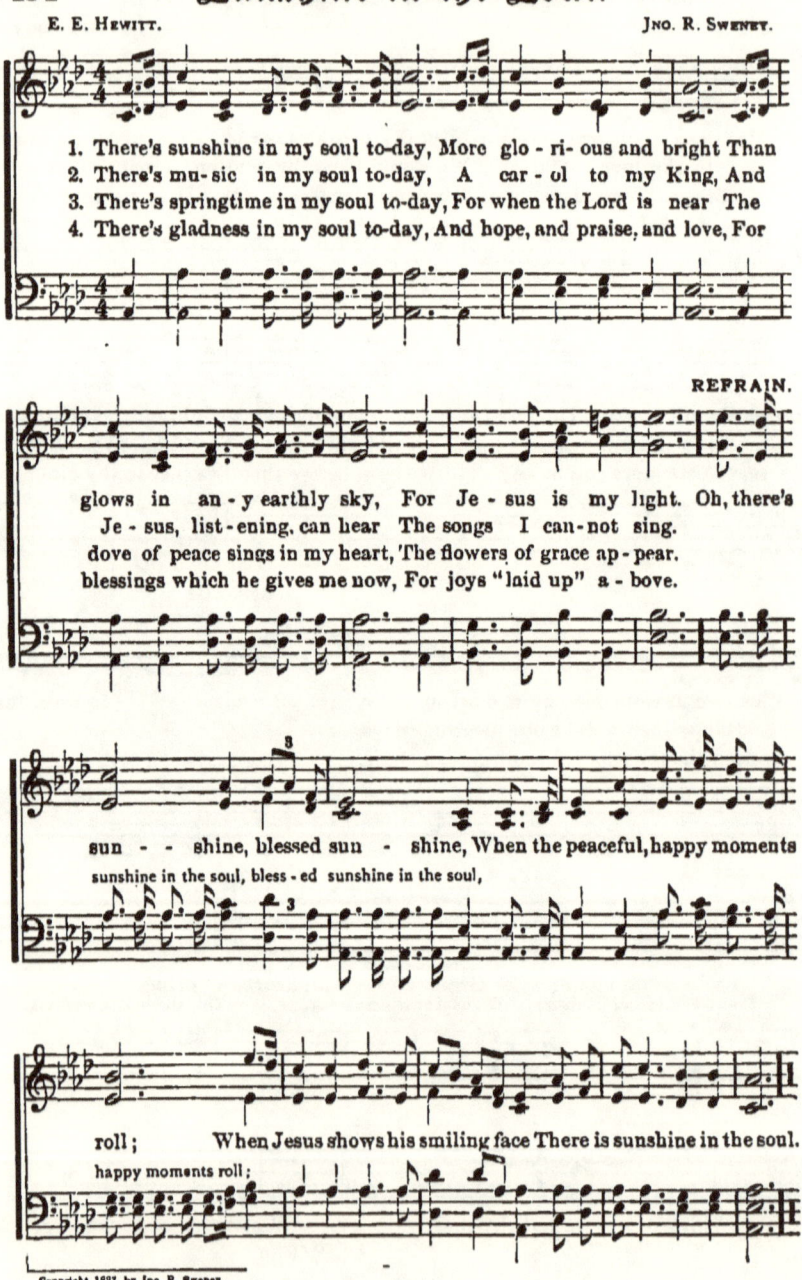

1. There's sunshine in my soul to-day, More glo-ri-ous and bright Than
2. There's mu-sic in my soul to-day, A car-ol to my King, And
3. There's springtime in my soul to-day, For when the Lord is near The
4. There's gladness in my soul to-day, And hope, and praise, and love, For

REFRAIN.

glows in an-y earthly sky, For Je-sus is my light. Oh, there's
Je-sus, list-ening, can hear The songs I can-not sing.
dove of peace sings in my heart, The flowers of grace ap-pear.
blessings which he gives me now, For joys "laid up" a-bove.

sun - - shine, blessed sun - shine, When the peaceful, happy moments
sunshine in the soul, bless-ed sunshine in the soul,

roll;   When Jesus shows his smiling face There is sunshine in the soul.
happy moments roll;

The King is Coming.

Priscilla J. Owens.   Wm. J. Kirkpatrick.

1. Tho' the days be dark and dreary, And the nights be long and weary, Thou must
2. He will aid us in each trouble, For our shame give blessings double, Pain will
3. Let us then be up and doing, Our appointed work pursuing, And our
4. O'er the floods of tribu- lation Roll the anthems of sal- vation, And the

CHORUS. Faster.

faint not, Christian, cheer thee, For the King will come. The King is coming, the
van- ish like a bubble, When the King shall come.
strength each day renewing, From his gracious throne.
Sun of Con- so - lation Gilds the midnight dome.

King is com-ing, The King is com-ing   to call his children home; The

molto rit

King is coming, the King is coming, Coming, coming to claim his own.

156

The Glorious Dawn.

PRISCILLA J. OWENS.   W. J. KIRKPATRICK.

1. Sons of Zi - on, pressing onward, See the cross, your banner, shine,
2. Ev'ry mountain bending lowly Where his herald's feet have trod,
3. All the darkness o - verflowing With the Day-Spring from above,

Je - sus leads his faithful vanguard, Follow him in might divine,
Ev- 'ry val - ley sweet and ho - ly Blossom to the praise of God.
All the i - dols o - verthrowing By his might- y name of Love.

Soon his ho - ly reign shall banish Ev- 'ry chain by er- ror drawn,
All the des - erts' dreary silence Soon shall ech - o with his name ;
Hark : thou wind, that mourning sighest, Let thy weary wailing cease,

And the heathen night shall vanish, And the heathen night shall vanish,
All the mul - ti - tude of islands, All the mul - ti- tude of islands,
Singing "glo- ry in the highest," Singing "glory in the highest,"

And the heathen night shall vanish In the gospel's joyous dawn,
All the mul - ti- tude of islands Shall his sav- ing truth proclaim,
Singing "glo- ry in the highest," For he comes, the Prince of Peace.

CHORUS.

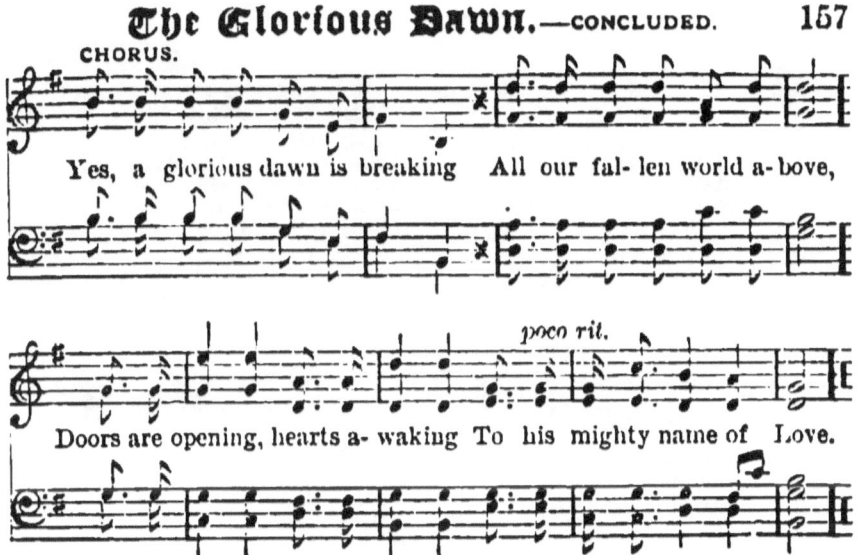

Yes, a glorious dawn is breaking All our fal-len world a-bove,

poco rit.

Doors are opening, hearts a-waking To his mighty name of Love.

I'll Live for Him.

C. R. DUNBAR.

1. My life, my love I give to thee, Thou Lamb of God, who died for me;
2. I now believe thou dost receive, For thou hast died that I might live;
3. Oh, thou who died on Cal-va-ry, To save my soul and make me free,

CHO.—I'll live for him who died for me, How happy then my life shall be!

D.C.

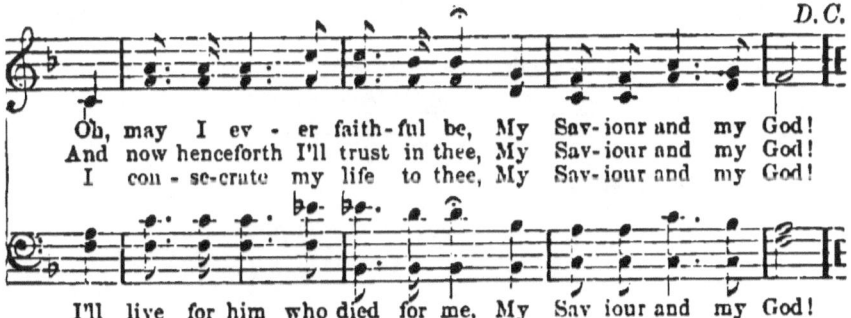

Oh, may I ev-er faith-ful be, My Sav-iour and my God!
And now henceforth I'll trust in thee, My Sav-iour and my God!
I con-se-crate my life to thee, My Sav-iour and my God!

I'll live for him who died for me, My Sav-iour and my God!

The Haven of Rest.

Dr H. L. Gilmour.   Geo. D. Moore.

1. My soul, in sad ex - ile, was out on life's sea, So
2. I yield - ed my - self to his ten - der em - brace, And
3. The song of my soul, since the Lord made me whole, Has
4. How pre - cious the thought that we all may re - cline, Like
5. Oh, come to the Sa - viour, he pa - tient - ly waits To

burdened with sin, and dis - trest,   Till I heard a sweet voice say-ing,
faith tak-ing hold of the word,   My fet-ters fell off, and I
been the OLD STO-RY so blest   Of Je-sus, who'll save who-so-
John the be - lov-ed and blest,   On Jesus' strong arm, where no
save by his power di - vine;   Come, anchor your soul in the

D.S.—The tempest may sweep o'er the

make me your choice; And I en-tered the "Ha - ven of Rest!"
anchored my soul; The ha -ven of rest is my Lord.
ev - er will have A home in the "Ha - ven of Rest!"
tem - pest can harm,— Se - cure in the "Ha - ven of Rest!"
ha - ven of rest, And say, "my Be - lov - ed is mine."

wild, storm-y deep, In Je-sus I'm safe ev - er - more.

CHORUS.   D S.

I've anchored my soul in the haven of rest, I'll sail the wide seas no more;

The Firm Foundation.

GEORGE KEITH.   Tune, PORTUGUESE HYMN.

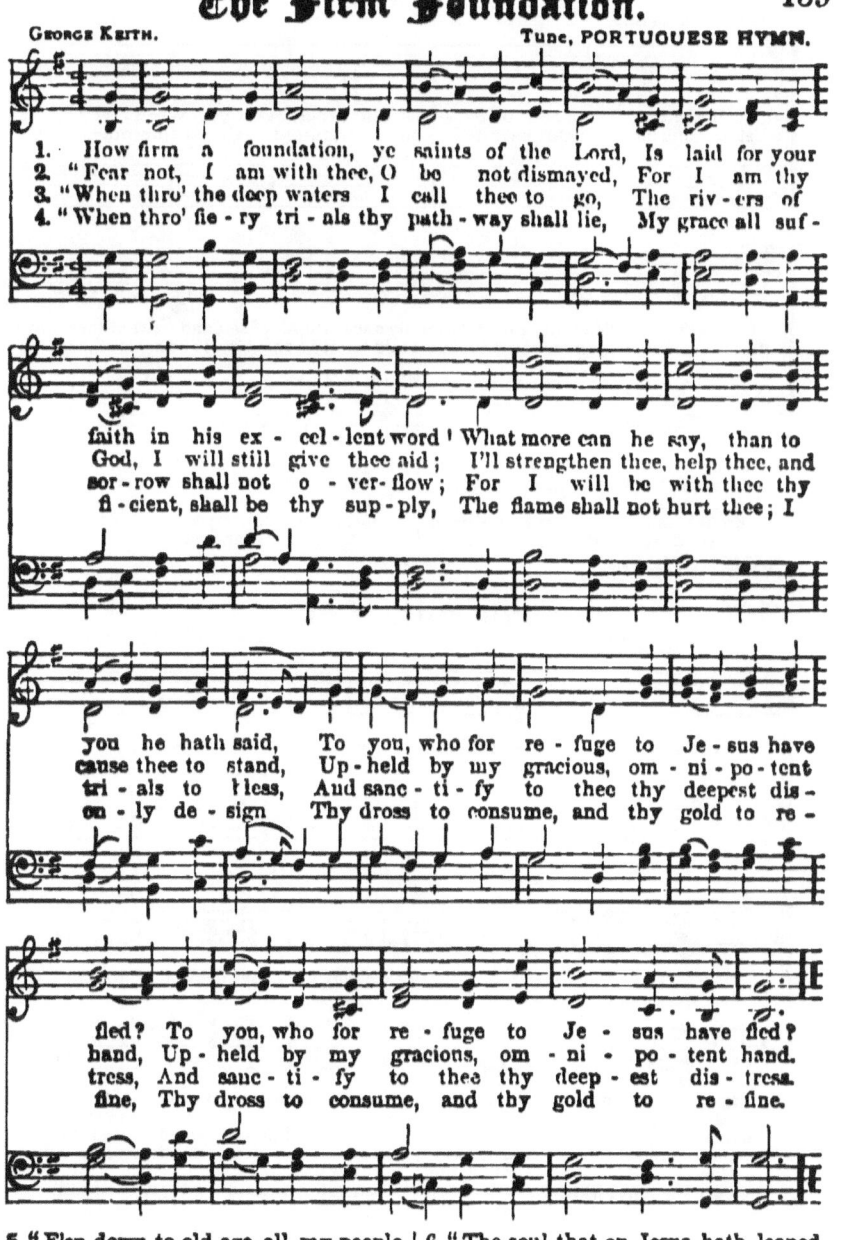

1. How firm a foundation, ye saints of the Lord, Is laid for your
2. "Fear not, I am with thee, O be not dismayed, For I am thy
3. "When thro' the deep waters I call thee to go, The riv-ers of
4. "When thro' fie-ry tri-als thy path-way shall lie, My grace all suf-

faith in his ex - cel-lent word ! What more can he say, than to
God, I will still give thee aid ; I'll strengthen thee, help thee, and
sor-row shall not o - ver-flow ; For I will be with thee thy
fi-cient, shall be thy sup-ply, The flame shall not hurt thee ; I

you he hath said, To you, who for re - fuge to Je - sus have
cause thee to stand, Up-held by my gracious, om - ni-po-tent
tri - als to bless, And sanc - ti - fy to thee thy deepest dis -
on - ly de - sign Thy dross to consume, and thy gold to re -

fled ? To you, who for re - fuge to Je - sus have fled ?
hand, Up - held by my gracious, om - ni - po - tent hand.
tress, And sanc - ti - fy to thee thy deep - est dis - tress.
fine, Thy dross to consume, and thy gold to re - fine.

5 "E'en down to old age all my people shall prove [love;
My sovereign, eternal, unchangeable
And when hoary hairs shall their tem-ples adorn, [be borne.
Like lambs they shall still in my bosom

6 "The soul that on Jesus hath leaned for repose,
I will not, I will not desert to his foes ;
That soul, though all hell should en-deavor to shake,
I'll never, no never, no never forsake!"

160 **The Altered Motto.**

Rev. Theo Monod.   J. G. Robinson.

1. O the bitter ‖ shame and sorrow, ‖ That a time could ‖ ever be, ‖ When I let the ‖
2 Yet he found me, ‖ I beheld him ‖ Bleeding on the ac-‖cursed tree ‖ Heard him pray, for ‖

Saviour's pity ‖ Plead in ‖ vain, and proudly answer'd, All of self and none of thee.
give them, Father, ‖ And my ‖ wistful heart said faintly, Some of self and some of thee.

3 Day by day his ‖ tender mercy, ‖
   Healing, helping, ‖ full and free, ‖
   Sweet, and strong, ‖ and, oh, so patient, ‖
   Brought me ‖ lower while I whispered,
   Less of self and more of thee.

4 Higher than the ‖ highest heaven, ‖
   Deeper than the ‖ deepest sea, ‖
   Lord, thy love ‖ at last has conquer'd, ‖
   Grant me ‖ now my soul's desire,
   None of self and all of thee.

Copyright, 1880, by John J. Hood.

161 **Come unto Me.**

Tune, HENLEY. 11, 10.
S.

1. Come un-to me when shadows darkly gath-er, When the sad heart is

D. S.—Come un-to me, and

Fine.   D. S.

wea-ry and distressed, Seeking for comfort from your heavenly Father,
I will give you rest.

2 Large are the mansions in thy Father's
      dwelling,   [dim ;
   Glad are the homes that sorrows never
   Sweet are the harps in holy music swell-
      ing,   [enly hymn.
   Soft are the tones which raise the heav-

3 There, like an Eden blossoming in glad-
      ness,   [ly pressed :
   Bloom the fair flowers the earth too rude-
   Come unto me, all ye who droop in sad-
      ness,
   Come unto me, and I will give you rest.

P. Doddridge.

Happy Day.

English Melody.

1. { O happy day, that fixed my choice On thee, my Saviour and my God!
Well may this glowing heart rejoice, And tell its raptures all abroad. } Happy

Fine. *D. S.*

day, happy day,
When Jesus washed my sins away! { He taught me how to watch and pray,
And live rejoicing ev'ry day.

2 O happy bond, that seals my vows
 To him who merits all my love!
Let cheerful anthems fill his house,
 While to that sacred shrine I move.

3 'Tis done! the great transaction's done!
 I am my Lord's, and he is mine:
He drew me, and I followed on,
 Charmed to confess that voice divine.

4 Now rest, my long-divided heart;
 Fixed on this blissful center, rest;
Nor ever from thy Lord depart,
 With him of every good possessed.

5 High heav'n that heard the solemn vow,
 That vow renewed shall daily hear,
Till in life's latest hour I bow,
 And bless in death a bond so dear.

163 H E. Blair. ## He Came to Save Me. Wm. J. Kirkpatrick.

1. { When Jesus laid his crown aside, He came to save me;
  When on the cross he bled and died, ... He came to save me.
2. { In my poor heart he deigns to dwell, He came to save me;
  Oh, praise his name, I know it well, ... He came to save me.

REFRAIN.

I'm so glad, I'm so glad, I'm so glad that Jesus came, And grace is free,
He . . . came to save me.

3 With gentle hand he leads me still,
 He came to save me;
And trusting him I fear no ill,
 He came to save me.

4 To him my faith with rapture clings,
 He came to save me;
To him my heart looks up and sings,
 He came to save me.

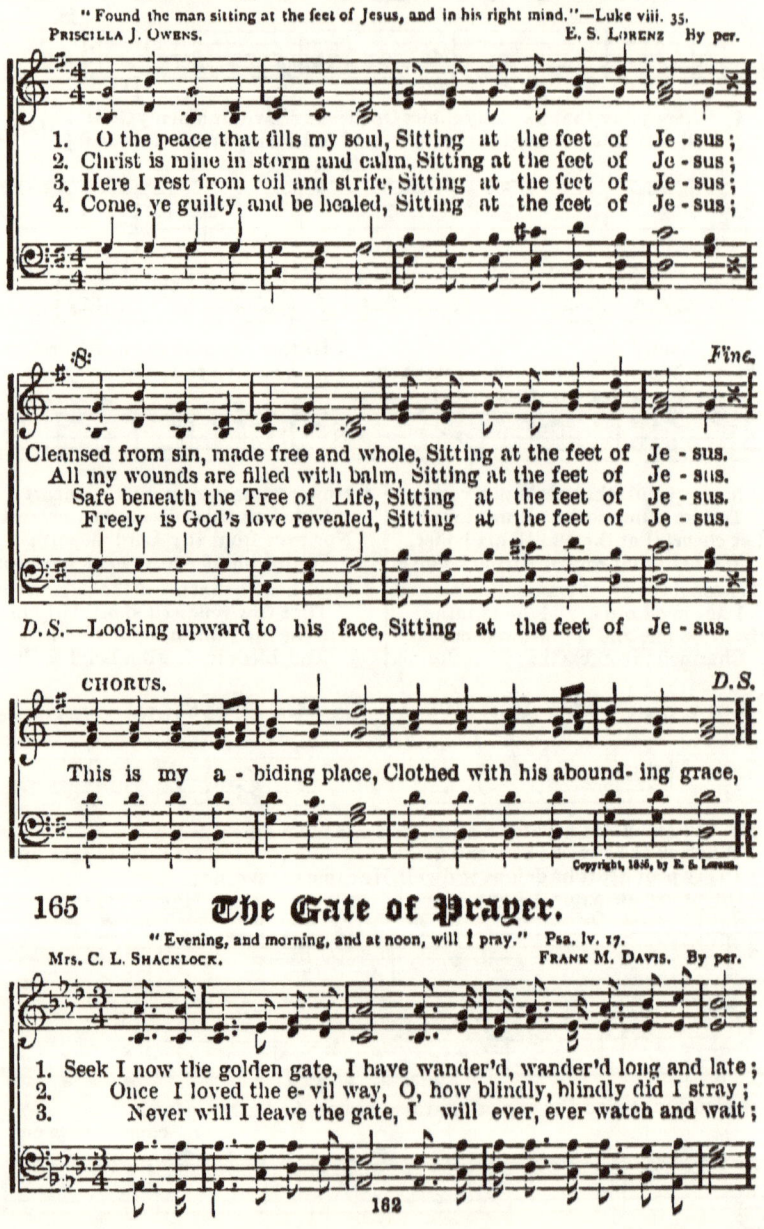

164 Sitting at the Feet of Jesus.

"Found the man sitting at the feet of Jesus, and in his right mind."—Luke viii. 35.

PRISCILLA J. OWENS.   E. S. LORENZ By per.

1. O the peace that fills my soul, Sitting at the feet of Je - sus;
2. Christ is mine in storm and calm, Sitting at the feet of Je - sus;
3. Here I rest from toil and strife, Sitting at the feet of Je - sus;
4. Come, ye guilty, and be healed, Sitting at the feet of Je - sus;

Cleansed from sin, made free and whole, Sitting at the feet of Je - sus.
All my wounds are filled with balm, Sitting at the feet of Je - sus.
Safe beneath the Tree of Life, Sitting at the feet of Je - sus.
Freely is God's love revealed, Sitting at the feet of Je - sus.

D. S.—Looking upward to his face, Sitting at the feet of Je - sus.

CHORUS.   D. S.

This is my a - biding place, Clothed with his abound - ing grace,

Copyright, 1885, by E. S. Lorenz.

165 The Gate of Prayer.

"Evening, and morning, and at noon, will I pray." Psa. lv. 17.

MRS. C. L. SHACKLOCK.   FRANK M. DAVIS. By per.

1. Seek I now the golden gate, I have wander'd, wander'd long and late;
2.   Once I loved the e- vil way, O, how blindly, blindly did I stray;
3.   Never will I leave the gate, I will ever, ever watch and wait;

162

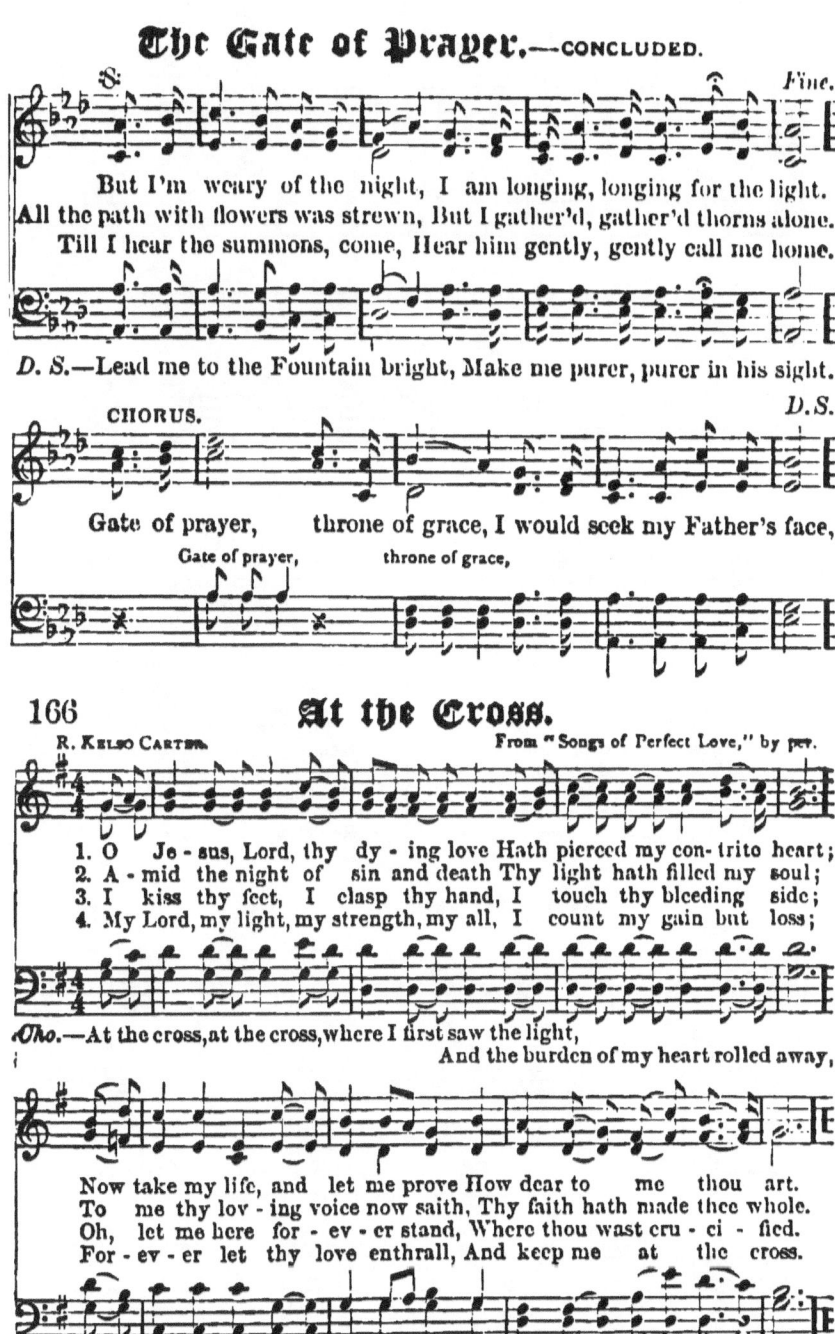

The Gate of Prayer.—CONCLUDED.

Fine.

But I'm weary of the night, I am longing, longing for the light.
All the path with flowers was strewn, But I gather'd, gather'd thorns alone.
Till I hear the summons, come, Hear him gently, gently call me home.

D. S.—Lead me to the Fountain bright, Make me purer, purer in his sight.

D.S.

CHORUS.

Gate of prayer, throne of grace, I would seek my Father's face,
Gate of prayer, throne of grace,

166

At the Cross.

R. Kelso Carter.

From "Songs of Perfect Love," by per.

1. O Je-sus, Lord, thy dy-ing love Hath pierced my con-trite heart;
2. A-mid the night of sin and death Thy light hath filled my soul;
3. I kiss thy feet, I clasp thy hand, I touch thy bleeding side;
4. My Lord, my light, my strength, my all, I count my gain but loss;

Cho.—At the cross, at the cross, where I first saw the light,
And the burden of my heart rolled away,

Now take my life, and let me prove How dear to me thou art.
To me thy lov-ing voice now saith, Thy faith hath made thee whole.
Oh, let me here for-ev-er stand, Where thou wast cru-ci-fied.
For-ev-er let thy love enthrall, And keep me at the cross.

It was there by faith I received my sight, And now I am happy night and day!

Pleyel's Hymn. 7s.

IGNACE PLEYEL.

167 Gracious Spirit, love divine.

1 GRACIOUS Spirit, love divine,
  Let thy light within me shine!
  All my guilty fears remove;
  Fill me with thy heavenly love.

2 Speak thy pardoning grace to me;
  Set the burdened sinner free;
  Lead me to the Lamb of God;
  Wash me in his precious blood.

3 Life and peace to me impart;
  Seal salvation on my heart;
  Breathe thyself into my breast,
  Earnest of immortal rest.

4 Let me never from thee stray;
  Keep me in the narrow way;
  Fill my soul with joy divine;
  Keep me, Lord, forever thine.

168 Holy Ghost, with light divine.

1 HOLY GHOST, with light divine,
  Shine upon this heart of mine;
  Chase the shades of night away,
  Turn my darkness into day.

2 Holy Ghost, with power divine,
  Cleanse this guilty heart of mine;
  Long hath sin, without control,
  Held dominion o'er my soul.

3 Holy Ghost, with joy divine,
  Cheer this saddened heart of mine;
  Bid my many woes depart,
  Heal my wounded, bleeding heart.

4 Holy Spirit, all divine,
  Dwell within this heart of mine;
  Cast down every idol-throne,
  Reign supreme—and reign alone.

Rockingham. L. M.

LOWELL MASON.

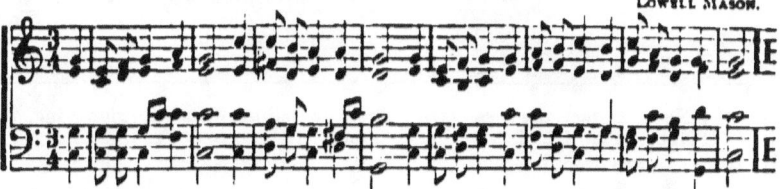

169   Lord, God, the Holy Ghost.

1 LORD, God, the Holy Ghost!
　　In this accepted hour,
　　As on the day of Pentecost,
　　Descend in all thy power.

2 We meet with one accord
　　In our appointed place,
　　And wait the promise of our Lord,—
　　The Spirit of all grace.

3 Like mighty, rushing wind
　　Upon the waves beneath,
　　Move with one impulse every mind;
　　One soul, one feeling breathe.

4 The young, the old, inspire
　　With wisdom from above; [fire,
　　And give us hearts and. tongues of
　　To pray, and praise, and love.

5 Spirit of light! explore,
　　And chase our gloom away,
　　With luster shining more and more,
　　Unto the perfect day.

171   Come, Holy Spirit, come.

1 COME, Holy Spirit, come,
　　With energy divine,
　　And on this poor, benighted soul
　　With beams of mercy shine.

2 From the celestial hills
　　Light, life, and joy dispense;
　　And may I daily, hourly, feel
　　Thy quickening influence.

3 O melt this frozen heart,
　　This stubborn will subdue;
　　Each evil passion overcome,
　　And form me all anew.

4 The profit will be mine,
　　But thine shall be the praise;
　　Cheerful to thee will I devote
　　The remnant of my days.

170   Come, Holy Spirit.

Tune, Rockingham, opposite page.

1 COME, Holy Spirit, raise our songs
　　To reach the wonders of that day,
When, with thy fiery, cloven tongues
Thou didst such glorious scenes display.

2 Lord, we believe to us and ours,
　　The apostolic promise given;
We wait the pentecostal powers,
　　The Holy Ghost sent down from heaven.

3 Assembled here with one accord,
　　Calmly we wait the promised grace,
The purchase of our dying Lord;
　　Come, Holy Ghost, and fill the place.

4 If every one that asks, may find,
　　If still thou dost on sinners fall,
Come as a mighty, rushing wind;
　　Great grace be now upon us all.

5 O leave us not to mourn below,
　　Or long for thy return to pine;
Now, Lord, the Comforter bestow,
　　And fix in us the Guest divine.

172   O Spirit of the Living God.

Tune, Rockingham, opposite page.

1 O SPIRIT of the living God,
　　In all thy plenitude of grace,
Where'er the foot of man hath trod,
　　Descend on our apostate race.

2 Give tongues of fire and hearts of love,
　　To preach the reconciling word;
Give power and unction from above,
　　Where'er the joyful sound is heard.

3 Be darkness, at thy coming, light;
　　Confusion—order, in thy path; [might;
Souls without strength, inspire with
　　Bid mercy triumph over wrath.

4 Baptize the nations; far and nigh
　　The triumphs of the cross record;
The name of Jesus glorify,
　　Till every kindred call him Lord.

173

Now I feel the Sacred Fire.

Arranged by R. KELSO CARTER.

Fine.

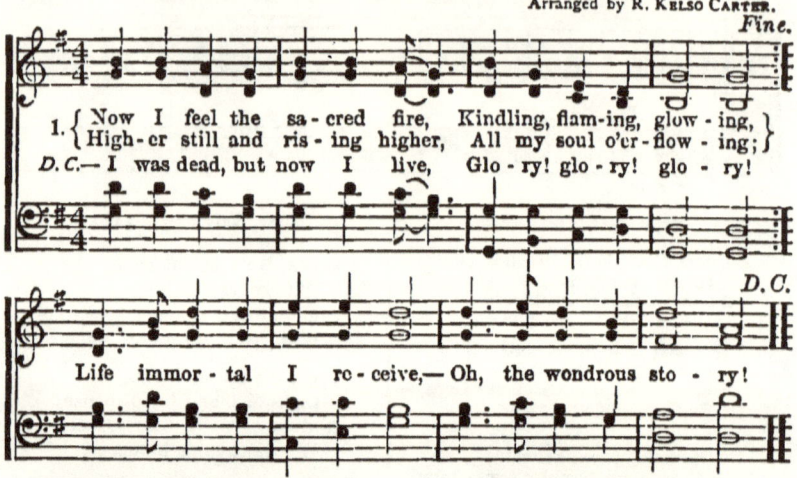

1. { Now I feel the sa-cred fire, Kindling, flam-ing, glow-ing, }
   { High-er still and ris-ing higher, All my soul o'er-flow-ing; }

D.C.— I was dead, but now I live, Glo-ry! glo-ry! glo-ry!

D.C.

Life immor-tal I re-ceive,— Oh, the wondrous sto-ry!

2 Now I am from bondage freed,
  Every bond is riven;
Jesus makes me free indeed,
  Just as free as heaven:
'Tis a glorious liberty—
  Oh, the wondrous story!
I was bound, but now I'm free,
  Glory! glory! glory!

3 Let the testimony roll,
  Roll through every nation;
Witnessing from soul to soul,
  This immense salvation,
Now I know it's full and free;
  Oh, the wondrous story!
For I feel it saving me,
  Glory! glory! glory!

4 Glory be to God on high,
  Glory be to Jesus!
He hath brought salvation nigh,
  From all sin he frees us.
Let the golden harps of God
  Ring the wondrous story;
Let the pilgrim shout aloud,
  Glory! glory! glory!

5 Let the trump of jubilee,
  The glad tidings thunder;
Jesus sets the captives free:
  Bursts their bonds asunder;
Fetters break and dungeons fall,
  Oh, the wondrous story!
This salvation's free to all,
  Glory! glory! glory!

174

Fill Me Now.

Rev. E. H. STOKES, D.D.

JNO. R. SWENEY.

1. Hov-er o'er me, Ho-ly Spir-it; Bathe my trembling heart and brow;
2. Thou can'st fill me, gracious Spir-it, Tho' I can-not tell thee how;
3. I am weakness, full of weakness; At thy sa-cred feet I bow;
4. Cleanse and comfort; bless and save me; Bathe, oh, bathe my heart and brow!

Fill Me Now.—CONCLUDED.

Fine.

Fill me with thy hal - low'd presence, Come, oh, come and fill me now.
But I need thee, great-ly need thee, Come, oh, come and fill me now.
Blest, di- vine, e - ter - nal Spir - it, Fill with power, and fill me now.
Thou art comfort - ing and sav- ing, Thou art sweet - ly fill - ing now.

D.S. Fill me with thy hal-low'd presence,—Come, oh, come and fill me now.

CHORUS.

Fill me now, fill me now, Ho - ly Spir - it, and fill me now;

D.S.

175
BATHURST.

O for that Flame.

Tune, SESSIONS.

1. O for that flame of living fire, Which shone so bright in saints of old;

Which bade their souls to heaven aspire,—Calm in distress, in danger bold.

2 Where is that Spirit, Lord, which dwelt
In Abrah'm's breast, and sealed him
thine?   [melt,
Which made Paul's heart with sorrow
And glow with energy divine?—

3 That Spirit, which from age to age
Proclaimed thy love, and taught thy
Brightened Isaiah's vivid page, [ways?
And breathed in David's hallowed lays?

4 Is not thy grace as mighty now
As when Elijah felt its power;
When glory beamed from Moses' brow,
Or Job endured the trying hour?

5 Remember, Lord, the ancient days;
Renew thy work; thy grace restore,
And while to thee our hearts we raise,
On us thy Holy Spirit pour.

167

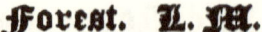

Forest. L. M.

176   O that my load of sin were gone.   L.M.

1 O that my load of sin were gone!
　O that I could at last submit
At Jesus' feet to lay it down—
　To lay my soul at Jesus' feet!

2 Rest for my soul I long to find:
　Saviour of all, if mine thou art,
Give me thy meek and lowly mind,
　And stamp thine image on my heart.

3 Break off the yoke of inbred sin,
　And fully set my spirit free;

I cannot rest till pure within,
　Till I am wholly lost in thee.

4 Fain would I learn of thee, my God,
　Thy light and easy burden prove,
The cross all stained with hallowed blood,
　The labor of thy dying love.

5 I would, but thou must give the power;
　My heart from every sin release;
Bring near, bring near the joyful hour,
　And fill me with thy perfect peace.
　　　　　　　　—CHAS. WESLEY.

177   Lord, I am Thine.   L.M.

1 Lord, I am thine, entirely thine,
　Purchased and saved by blood divine;
With full consent thine would I be,
　And own thy sovereign right in me.

2 Thine would I live, thine would I die;
　Be thine through all eternity;
The vow is past, beyond repeal,
　And now I set the solemn seal.

3 Here, at that cross where flows the blood
　That bought my guilty soul for God,
Thee, my new Master now I call,
　And consecrate to thee my all.

4 Do thou assist a feeble worm
　The great engagement to perform;
Thy grace can full assistance lend,
　And on that grace I dare depend.
　　　　　　　　—SAMUEL DAVIES.

178   I thirst, Thou wounded Lamb of God.   L.M.

1 I thirst, thou wounded Lamb of God,
　To wash me in thy cleansing blood;
To dwell within thy wounds; then pain
　Is sweet, and life or death is gain.

2 Take my poor heart, and let it be
　Forever closed to all but thee:
Seal thou my breast, and let me wear
　That pledge of love forever there.

3 How blest are they who still abide
　Close sheltered in thy bleeding side!
Who thence their life and strength derive,
　And by thee move, and in thee live.

4 What are our works but sin and death,
　Till thou thy quickening Spirit breathe?
Thou giv'st the power thy grace to move;
　O wondrous grace! O wondrous love!

5 How can it be, thou heavenly King,
　That thou shouldst us to glory bring?
Make slaves the partners of thy throne,
　Decked with a never-fading crown?

6 Hence our hearts melt, our eyes o'erflow,
　Our words are lost, nor will we know,
Nor will we think of aught beside,
　"My Lord, my Love is crucified."
　　　　　　　　—NICOLAUS L. ZINZENDORF.

And can it be?

CHARLES WESLEY.

Arranged by WM. G. FISCHER.

Fine.

1. { And can it be that I should gain An int'rest in the Saviour's blood? }
   { Died he for me, who caused his pain? For me, who him to death pursued? }

D.C.—A - mazing love! how can it be, That thou, my Lord, should'st die for me?

D.C.

A - mazing love! how can it be, That thou, my Lord, should'st die for me?

2 'Tis myst'ry all: th' Immortal dies!
  Who can explore his strange design?
In vain the first-born seraph tries
  To sound the depths of love divine.
'Tis mercy all! let earth adore;
Let angel minds inquire no more.

3 He left his Father's throne above;
  (So free, so infinite his grace!)
Emptied himself of all but love,
  And bled for Adam's helpless race.
'Tis mercy all, immense and free,
For, O my God, it found out me!

4 Long my imprisoned spirit lay,
  Fast bound in sin and nature's night;
Thine eye diffused a quickening ray;
  I woke; the dungeon flamed with light;
My chains fell off, my heart was free—
I rose, went forth, and followed thee.

5 No condemnation now I dread;
  Jesus, with all in him, is mine;
Alive in him my living Head,
  And clothed in righteousness divine,
Bold I approach th' eternal throne,
And claim the crown thro' Christ my own.

---

180   The Lord's my Shepherd.

1 The Lord's my Shepherd, I'll not want;
  He makes me down to lie
In pastures green; he leadeth me
  The quiet waters by.

CHO.—His yoke is easy, his burden is
      light,
  I've found it so, I've found it so;
He leadeth me by day and by night
  Where living waters flow.

2 My soul he doth restore again;
  And me to walk doth make
Within the paths of righteousness,
  E'en for his own name's sake

3 Yea, though I walk through death's
      dark vale,
  Yet will I fear no ill;
For thou art with me, and thy rod
  And staff me comfort still.

4 A table thou hast furnished me
  In presence of my foes;
My head thou dost with oil anoint,
  And my cup overflows.

5 Goodness and mercy all my life
  Shall surely follow me;
And in God's house for evermore
  My dwelling-place shall be.
          —FRANCIS ROUS.

Come, Ye Sinners.

JOSEPH HART. Cho. by H. L. G.   Tune, BARTIMEUS. 8,7.

1. Come, ye sin-ners, poor and needy, Weak and wounded, sick and sore;
D. C.—He is a-ble, He is a-ble, He is will-ing: doubt no more;
CHO.—Come to Je-sus, come to Je-sus, Mer-cy's door wide o-pen stands;

D. C.

Je-sus read-y stands to save you, Full of pi-ty, love, and power.
He is a-ble, He is a-ble, He is will-ing: doubt no more.
Lov-ing-ly he waits to welcome; See his beck'ning, wounded hands.

2 Now, ye needy, come and welcome;
  God's free bounty glorify;
True belief and true repentance—
Every grace that brings you nigh—
  Without money,
  Come to Jesus Christ and buy.

3 Let not conscience make you linger,
  Nor of fitness fondly dream;
All the fitness he requireth
Is to feel your need of him.
  This he gives you—
  'Tis the Spirit's glimmering beam.

4 Come, ye weary, heavy laden,
  Bruised and mangled by the fall,
If you tarry till you're better,
You will never come at all.
  Not the righteous—
  Sinners Jesus came to call.

5 Agonizing in the garden
  Your Redeemer prostrate lies;
On the bloody tree behold him,
Hear him cry, before he dies,
  It is finished!—
  Sinners, will not this suffice?

---

182   And can I yet delay!   Tune No. 169.

1 AND can I yet delay
  My little all to give?
To tear my soul from earth away
For Jesus to receive?

2 Nay, but I yield, I yield;
  I can hold out no more:
I sink, by dying love compelled,
And own thee conqueror.

4 Come, and possess me whole,
  Nor hence again remove;
Settle and fix my wavering soul
With all thy weight of love.

3 Though late I all forsake;
  My friends, my all, resign;
Gracious Redeemer, take, oh, take,
And seal me ever thine.

---

183   Lord, I care not for riches.   Key Ab.

1 LORD, I care not for riches,
  Neither silver nor gold;
I would make sure of heaven,
  I would enter the fold;
In the book of thy kingdom,
  With its pages so fair,
Tell me, Jesus, my Saviour,
  Is my name written there?

CHO.—Is my name written there,
  On the page white and fair?
In the book of thy kingdom,
  Is my name written there?

Lord, my sins they are many,
  Like the sands of the sea,

But thy blood, O my Saviour!
  Is sufficient for me;
For thy promise is written,
  In bright letters that glow,
"Though your sins be as scarlet,
  I will make them like snow."

3 Oh! that beautiful city,
  With its mansions of light,
With its glorified beings,
  In pure garments of white;
Where no evil thing cometh,
  To despoil what is fair;
Where the angels are watching,—
  Is my name written there?

Washed White as Snow.

FANNY J. CROSBY.   JNO. R. SWENEY.

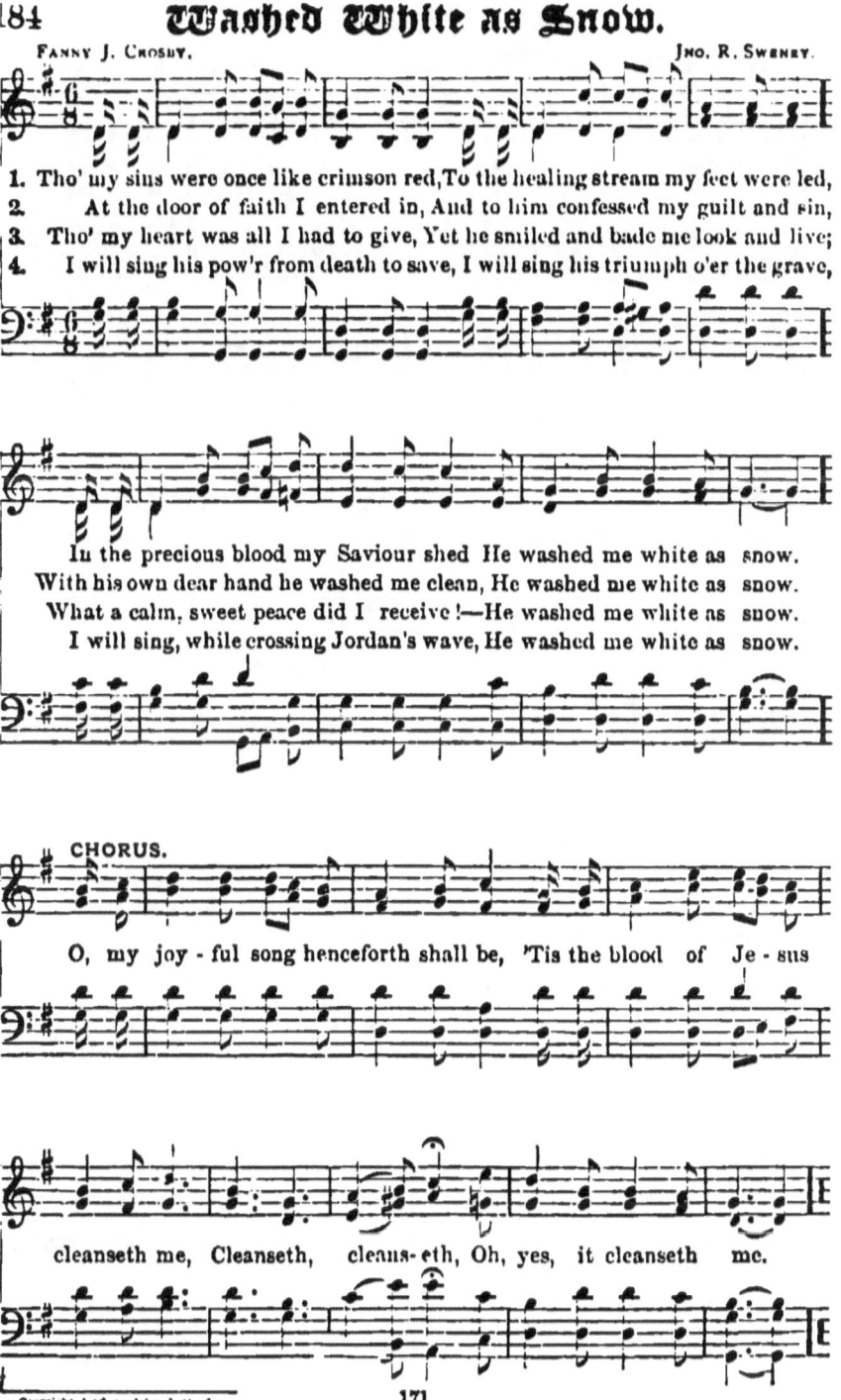

1. Tho' my sins were once like crimson red, To the healing stream my feet were led,
2. At the door of faith I entered in, And to him confessed my guilt and sin,
3. Tho' my heart was all I had to give, Yet he smiled and bade me look and live;
4. I will sing his pow'r from death to save, I will sing his triumph o'er the grave,

In the precious blood my Saviour shed He washed me white as snow.
With his own dear hand he washed me clean, He washed me white as snow.
What a calm, sweet peace did I receive!—He washed me white as snow.
I will sing, while crossing Jordan's wave, He washed me white as snow.

CHORUS.

O, my joy-ful song henceforth shall be, 'Tis the blood of Je-sus

cleanseth me, Cleanseth, cleans-eth, Oh, yes, it cleanseth me.

CHARLES WESLEY.
Cho. by H. L. G.
"Come, for all things are ready."
Luke xiv. 16.
H. L. GILMOUR.

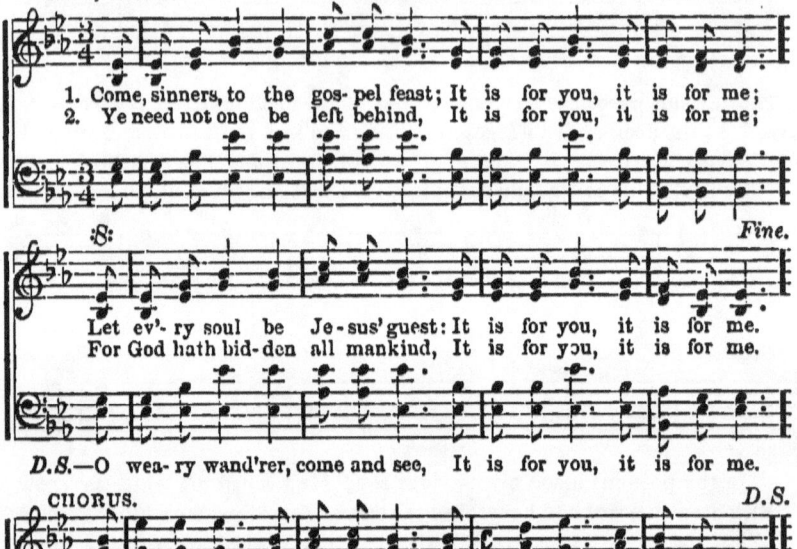

1. Come, sinners, to the gos- pel feast; It is for you, it is for me;
2. Ye need not one be left behind, It is for you, it is for me;

Let ev'- ry soul be Je- sus' guest: It is for you, it is for me.
For God hath bid- den all mankind, It is for you, it is for me.

Fine.

D.S.—O wea- ry wand'rer, come and see, It is for you, it is for me.

CHORUS.   D.S.

Sal- va- tion full, sal - vation free, The price was paid on Calva- ry;

3 Sent by my Lord, on you I call;
  The invitation is to all:

4 Come, all the world! come, sinner, thou!
  All things in Christ are ready now.

5 Come, all ye souls by sin oppressed,
  Ye restless wanderers after rest;

6 Ye poor, and maimed, and halt, and blind
  In Christ a hearty welcome find.

7 My message as from God receive;
  Ye all may come to Christ and live:

8 O let this love your hearts constrain,
  Nor suffer him to die in vain.

9 See him set forth before your eyes,
  That precious, bleeding sacrifice:

10 His offered benefits embrace,
  And freely now be saved by grace.

186   There is a fountain.   Key A.

1 There is a fountain ||: fill'd with blood,:||
  Drawn from Immanuel's veins,
And sinners, plunged ||: beneath that
  Lose all their guilty stains. [flood,:||

CHO.—Oh, glorious fountain!
  Here will I stay,
  And in thee ever
  Wash my sins away.

2 The dying thief ||: rejoiced to see :||
  That fountain in his day,

And there may I, ||: though vile as he,:||
  Wash all my sins away.

3 Thou dying Lamb, ||: thy precious
  Shall never lose its power, [blood:||
Till all the ransomed ||: Church of God:||
  Are saved to sin no more.

4 E'er since by faith ||: I saw the stream :||
  Thy flowing wounds supply,
Redeeming love ||: has been my theme,:||
  And shall be till I die.

187 **The Morning Light.**

SAMUEL F. SMITH.

Tune, WEBB. 7. 6.

Fine.

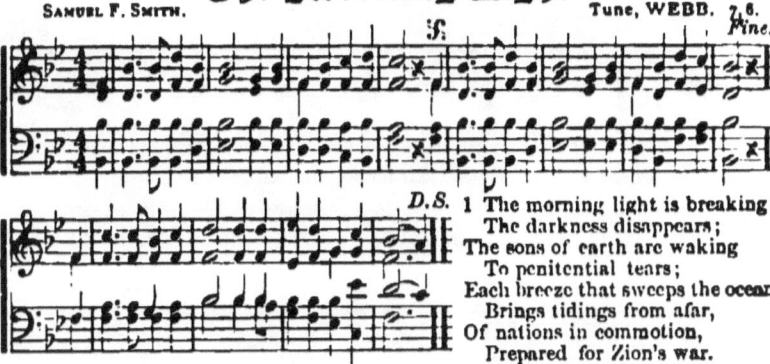

D.S.

1 The morning light is breaking;
The darkness disappears;
The sons of earth are waking
To penitential tears;
Each breeze that sweeps the ocean
Brings tidings from afar,
Of nations in commotion,
Prepared for Zion's war.

2 See heathen nations bending
Before the God we love,
And thousand hearts ascending
In gratitude above;
While sinners, now confessing,
The gospel call obey,
And seek the Saviour's blessing,
A nation in a day.

3 Blest river of salvation,
Pursue thine onward way;
Flow thou to every nation,
Nor in thy richness stay:
Stay not till all the lowly
Triumphant reach their home:
Stay not till all the holy
Proclaim, "The Lord is come!"

188   GEO. DUFFIELD, Jr.   **Stand up, stand up for Jesus.**   Tune above.

1 STAND up, stand up for Jesus,
Ye soldiers of the cross;
Lift high his royal banner,
It must not suffer loss;
From victory unto victory
His army shall he lead
Till every foe is vanquished
And Christ is Lord indeed.

2 Stand up, stand up for Jesus,
The trumpet call obey;
Forth to the mighty conflict,
In this his glorious day:
"Ye that are men, now serve him,"
Against unnumbered foes:
Your courage rise with danger,
And strength to strength oppose.

3 Stand up, stand up for Jesus,
Stand in his strength alone;
The arm of flesh will fail you;
' Ye dare not trust your own:
Put on the gospel armor,
Each piece put on with prayer;
Where duty calls, or danger,
Be never wanting there.

4 Stand up, stand up for Jesus,
The strife will not be long;
This day the noise of battle,
The next the victor's song;
To him that overcometh,
A crown of life shall be;
He with the King of glory
Shall reign eternally.

189   **Work, for the night is coming.**   Key F.

1 WORK, for the night is coming,
Work through the morning hours;
Work, while the dew is sparkling,
Work 'mid springing flowers;
Work, when the day grows brighter,
Work in the glowing sun;
Work, for the night is coming,
When man's work is done.

2 Work, for the night is coming;
Work through the sunny noon;
Fill brightest hours with labor;
Rest comes sure and soon.

Give every flying minute
Something to keep in store;
Work for the night is coming,
When man works no more.

3 Work for the night is coming,
Under the sunset skies;
While their bright tints are glowing,
Work, for daylight flies.
Work till the last beam fadeth,
Fadeth to shine no more;
Work while the night is darkening,
When man's work is o'er.

190

The Hallowed Spot.

Rev. Wm. Hunter, D. D.

Arr. by T. C. O'Kane.

1. { There is a spot to me more dear Than native vale or mountain; }
{ A spot for which affection's tear Springs grateful from its fountain. }

D. S.—where I first my Saviour found, And felt my sins for-giv-en.

'Tis not where kindred souls abound, Tho' that is al-most heaven, But

2 Hard was my toil to reach the shore,
Long tossed upon the ocean:
Above me was the thunder's roar,
Beneath the waves' commotion.
Darkly the pall of night was thrown
Around me, faint with terror;
In that dark hour how did my groan
Ascend for years of error.

3 Sinking and panting as for breath
I knew not help was near me;
I cried, "Oh, save me, Lord, from death,
Immortal Jesus, hear me;

Then quick as thought I felt him mine,
My Saviour stood before me;
I saw his brightness round me shine,
And shouted "Glory, glory,"

4 O sacred hour! O hallowed spot!
Where love divine first found me;
Wherever falls my distant lot
My heart shall linger round thee.
And when from earth I rise, to soar
Up to my home in heaven,
Down will I cast my eyes once more,
Where I was first forgiven.

191   When I Survey the Wondrous Cross. Tune, Rockingham, p. 164.

1 When I survey the wondrous cross,
On which the Prince of Glory died,
My richest gain I count but loss,
And pour contempt on all my pride.

2 Forbid it, Lord, that I should boast,
Save in the death of Christ my God;
All the vain things that charm me most,
I sacrifice them to his blood.

3 See, from his head, his hands, his feet,
Sorrow and love flow mingled down;
Did e'er such love and sorrow meet?
Or thorns compose so rich a crown?

4 Were the whole realm of nature mine,
That were a present far too small;
Love so amazing, so divine,
Demands my soul, my life, my all.
—I. Watts.

192   Glory to His Name.

1 Down at the cross where my Saviour
died,
Down where for cleansing from sin I cried
There to my heart was the blood applied;
Glory to his name.

Cho.—Glory to his name,
Glory to his name,
There to my heart was the blood applied;
Glory to his name.

2 I am so wondrously saved from sin,
Jesus so sweetly abides within;

There at the cross where he took me in;
Glory to his name.

3 Oh, precious fountain, that saves from
I am so glad I have entered in;   [sin,
There Jesus saves me and keeps me clean,
Glory to his name.

4 Come to this fountain, so rich and sweet;
Cast thy poor soul at the Saviour's feet;
Plunge in to-day, and be made complete;
Glory to his name.
—Rev. E. A. Hoffman.

Azmon. C. M.

CARL GOTTHELF GLASER.

193   **Enthroned On High.**

1 ENTHRONED on high, almighty Lord,
   The Holy Ghost send down;
Fulfill in us thy faithful word,
   And all thy mercies crown.

2 Though on our heads no tongues of fire
   Their wondrous powers impart,
Grant, Saviour, what we more desire,—
   Thy Spirit in our heart.

3 Spirit of life, and light, and love,
   Thy heavenly influence give;
Quicken our souls, our guilt remove,
   That we in Christ may live.

4 To our benighted minds reveal
   The glories of his grace,
And bring us where no clouds conceal
   The brightness of his face.

5 His love within us shed abroad,
   Life's ever-springing well;
Till God in us, and we in God,
   In love eternal dwell.
          —THOMAS HAWEIS.

194   **Jesus, thine all-victorious.**

1 JESUS, thine all-victorious love
   Shed in my heart abroad:
Then shall my feet no longer rove,
   Rooted and fixed in God.

2 O that in me the sacred fire
   Might now begin to glow,
Burn up the dross of base desire
   And make the mountains flow!

3 O that it now from heaven might fall,
   And all my sins consume!
Come, Holy Ghost, for thee I call;
   Spirit of burning, come!

4 Refining fire, go through my heart;
   Illuminate my soul;
Scatter thy life through every part,
   And sanctify the whole.

5 My steadfast soul, from falling free,
   Shall then no longer move,
While Christ is all the world to me,
   And all my heart is love.
          —CHAS. WESLEY.

195   **Jesus, My Life.**

1 JESUS, my life, thyself apply,
   Thy Holy Spirit breathe:
My vile affections crucify;
   Conform me to thy death.

2 Conqueror of hell and earth, and sin,
   Still with the rebel strive:
Enter my soul, and work within,
   And kill, and make alive.

3 More of thy life, and more I have,
   As the old Adam dies;
Bury me, Saviour, in thy grave,
   That I with thee may rise.

4 Reign in me, Lord; thy foes control,
   Who would not own thy sway;
Diffuse thine image through my soul;
   Shine to thy perfect day.

5 Satter the last remains of sin,
   And seal me thine abode;
O make me glorious all within,
   A temple built by God!
          —CHAS. WESLEY.

196   **I Worship Thee.**

1 I WORSHIP thee, O Holy Ghost,
   I love to worship thee;
My risen Lord for aye were lost
   But for thy company.

2 I worship thee, O Holy Ghost,
   I love to worship thee; [know'st
I grieved thee long, alas! thou
   It grieves me bitterly,

3 I worship thee, O Holy Ghost,
   I love to worship thee;
Thy patient love, at what a cost
   At last it conqured me!

4 I worship thee, O Holy Ghost,
   I love to worship thee;
With thee each day is Pentecost,
   Each night Nativity,
          —W. F. WARREN.

Jerusalem the Golden.

BERNARD OF CLUNY.   Tr. by J. M. NEALE.   Tune, EWING. 7, 6.

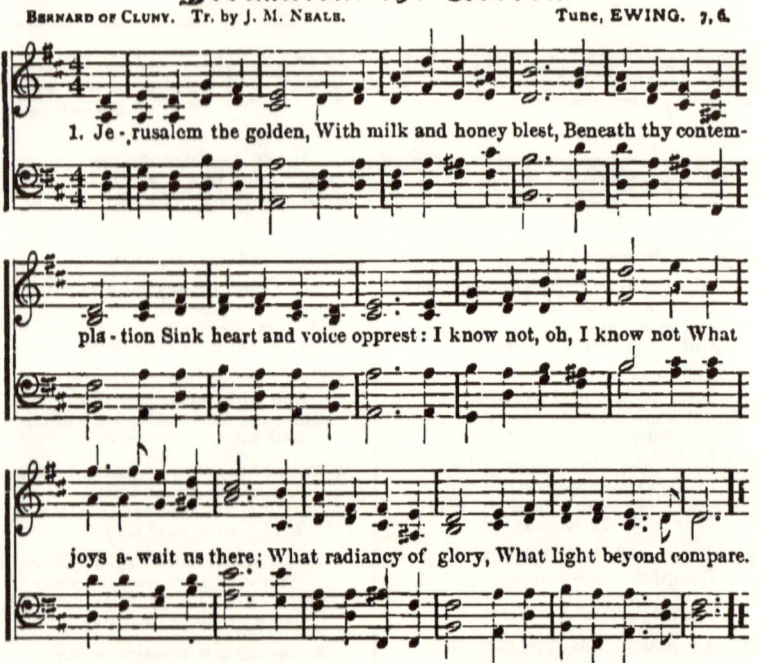

1. Je - rusalem the golden, With milk and honey blest, Beneath thy contem-
pla - tion Sink heart and voice opprest: I know not, oh, I know not What
joys a- wait us there; What radiancy of glory, What light beyond compare.

2 They stand, those halls of Zion,
    All jubilant with song,
And bright with many an angel,
 And all the martyr throng:
The Prince is ever in them,
    The daylight is serene;
The pastures of the blessed
    Are decked in glorious sheen.

3 There is the throne of David;
    And there, from care released,
The song of them that triumph,
    The shout of them that feast;

And they who, with their Leader,
    Have conquered in the fight,
Forever and forever
    Are clad in robes of white.

4 O sweet and blessed country,
    The home of God's elect!
O sweet and blessed country
    That eager hearts expect!
Jesus, in mercy bring us
    To that dear land of rest;
Who art, with God the Father,
    And Spirit, ever blest.

198   Love Divine.

CHARLES WESLEY.   Tune, LOVE DIVINE. 8, 7, d.

1. Love di - vine, all love ex - cel- ling, Joy of heaven, to earth come down!

Love Divine.—CONCLUDED.

Fix in us thy hum-ble dwelling! All thy faith-ful mer-cies crown.

D.S.—Vis-it us with thy sal-va-tion; En-ter ev-'ry trembling heart.

Je-sus, thou art all com-pas-sion, Pure, unbounded love thou art;

2 Breathe, oh, breathe thy loving Spirit
Into every troubled breast!
Let us all in thee inherit,
Let us find that second rest.
Take away our bent to sinning;
Alpha and Omega be;
End of faith, as its beginning,
Set our hearts at liberty.

3 Come, almighty to deliver,
Let us all thy life receive;
Suddenly return, and never,
Never more thy temples leave;

Thee we would be always blessing,
Serve thee as thy hosts above,
Pray, and praise thee without ceasing,
Glory in thy perfect love.

4 Finish then thy new creation;
Pure and spotless let us be;
Let us see thy great salvation,
Perfectly restored in thee:
Changed from glory into glory,
Till in heaven we take our place,
Till we cast our crowns before thee,
Lost in wonder, love, and praise.

199   Num. vi. 24–26.   The Lord Bless Thee.   W. J. K.

A blessing for use in closing Sabbath-school, or other service, in the absence of a minister.

The Lord bless thee, and keep thee: The Lord make his face shine upon thee and be [gracious

unto thee: The Lord lift up his countenance upon thee, and give thee peace. Amen.

200 More Faith in Jesus.

HENRIETTA E. BLAIR.

WM. J. KIRKPATRICK.

1. While struggling thro' this vale of tears I want more faith in Je- sus; A-
2. To war against the foes with-in I want more faith in Je- sus; To
3. To brave the storms that here I meet I want more faith in Je- sus; To
4. I want a faith that works by love, A constant faith in Je - sus; A

D. S.—And

Fine. CHORUS.

mid tempta- tions, cares, and fears, I want more faith in Je - sus. I
rise a - bove the powers of sin I want more faith in Je - sus.
rest con - fid - ing at his feet I want more faith in Je - sus.
faith that mountains can remove, A liv - ing faith in Je - sus.

this my cry, as time rolls by, I want more faith in Je - sus.

D. S.

want more faith, I want more faith, A clearer, brighter, stronger faith in Jesus;

201 Hallelujah! Amen.

HENRIETTA E. BLAIR.

Adapted and arr. by WM. J. KIRKPATRICK.

1. How oft in holy converse With Christ, my Lord, alone, I seem to hear the
2. They pass'd thro' toils and trials. And tho' the strife was long, They share the victor's
3. My soul takes up the chorus, And pressing on my way, Communing still with
4. Thro' grace I soon shall conquer, And reach my home on high; And thro' e - ternal

CHORUS.

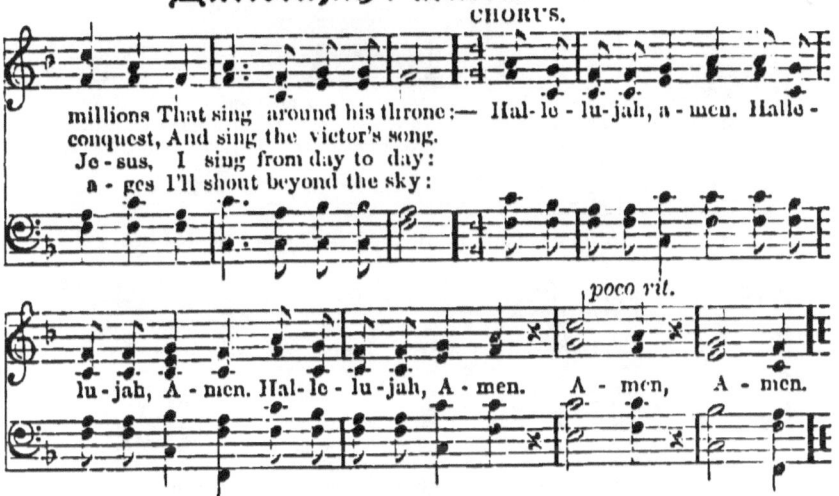

millions That sing around his throne:— Hal-le-lu-jah, a-men. Halle-
conquest, And sing the victor's song.
Je-sus, I sing from day to day:
a-ges I'll shout beyond the sky:

poco rit.

lu-jah, A-men. Hal-le-lu-jah, A-men. A-men, A-men.

202 O Thou in whose.

Tune, MEDITATION. 11,8.

JOSEPH SWAIN.

FREEMAN LEWIS, arr. by HUBERT P. MAIN.

1 O thou in whose presence my soul takes
On whom in affliction I call, [delight,
My comfort by day and my song in the
My hope, my salvation, my all! [night,

2 Where dost thou, dear Shepherd, resort
with thy sheep,
To feed them in pastures of love?
Say, why in the valley of death should I
Or alone in this wilderness rove? [weep,

3 Or why should I wander an alien from
Or cry in the desert for bread? [thee,
Thy foes will rejoice when my sorrows they
And smile at the tears I have shed. [see,

4 Ye daughters of Zion, declare, have you
The star that on Israel shone? [seen
Say if in your tents my Beloved has been,
And where with his flocks he has gone.

5 He looks! and ten thousands of angels
And myriads wait for his word; [rejoice,
He speaks! and eternity, filled with his
Re-echoes the praise of the Lord. [voice,

6 Dear Shepherd, I hear, and will follow
thy call;
I know the sweet sound of thy voice;
Restore and defend me, for thou art my all,
And in thee I will ever rejoice.

The Silver Trumpet-G

203 I am Coming to the Cross.

Rev. Wm. McDonald.   John vi. 37.   Wm. G. Fischer. By per.

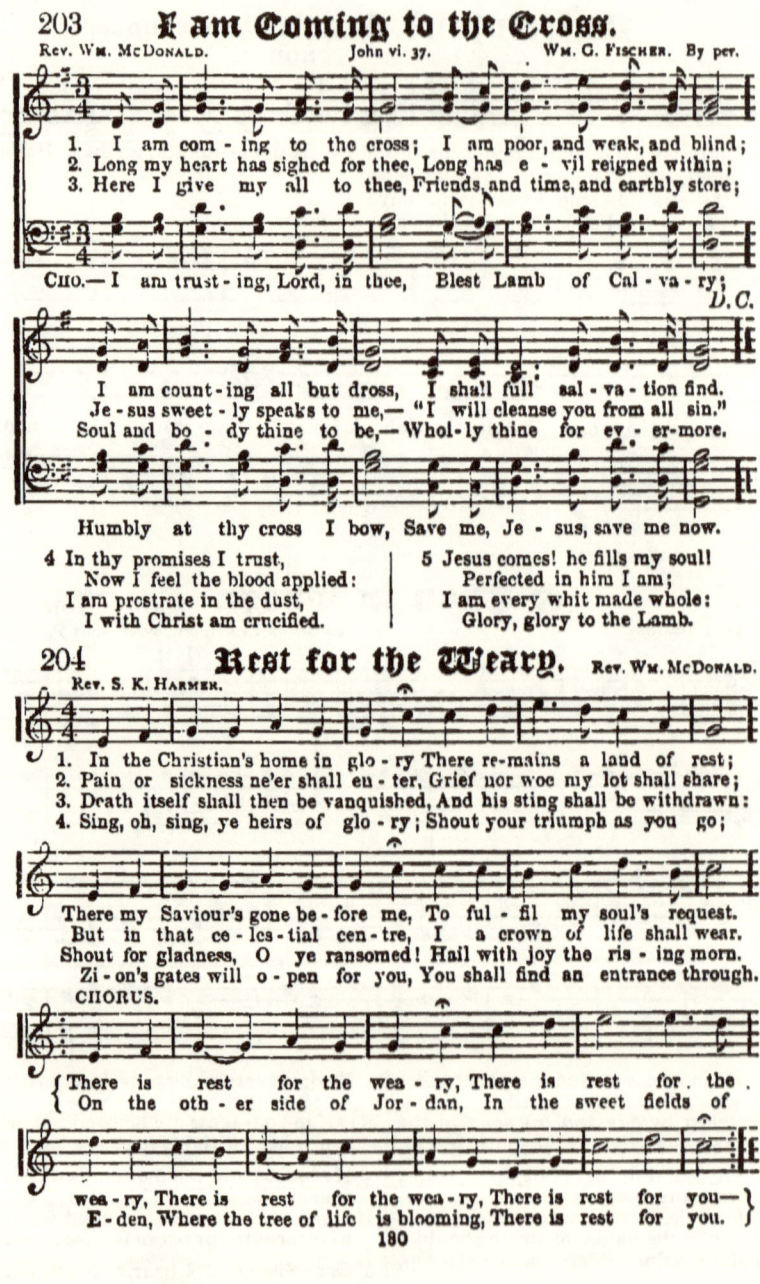

1. I am com - ing to the cross; I am poor, and weak, and blind;
2. Long my heart has sighed for thee, Long has e - vil reigned within;
3. Here I give my all to thee, Friends, and time, and earthly store;

Cho.— I am trust - ing, Lord, in thee, Blest Lamb of Cal - va - ry;

D.C.

I am count - ing all but dross, I shall full sal - va - tion find.
Je - sus sweet - ly speaks to me,— "I will cleanse you from all sin."
Soul and bo - dy thine to be,— Whol - ly thine for ev - er-more.

Humbly at thy cross I bow, Save me, Je - sus, save me now.

4 In thy promises I trust,
   Now I feel the blood applied:
   I am prostrate in the dust,
   I with Christ am crucified.

5 Jesus comes! he fills my soul!
   Perfected in him I am;
   I am every whit made whole:
   Glory, glory to the Lamb.

204 Rest for the Weary.   Rev. Wm. McDonald.

Rev. S. K. Harmer.

1. In the Christian's home in glo - ry There re - mains a land of rest;
2. Pain or sickness ne'er shall en - ter, Grief nor woe my lot shall share;
3. Death itself shall then be vanquished, And his sting shall be withdrawn:
4. Sing, oh, sing, ye heirs of glo - ry; Shout your triumph as you go;

There my Saviour's gone be - fore me, To ful - fil my soul's request.
But in that ce - les - tial cen - tre, I a crown of life shall wear.
Shout for gladness, O ye ransomed! Hail with joy the ris - ing morn.
Zi - on's gates will o - pen for you, You shall find an entrance through.

CHORUS.

There is rest for the wea - ry, There is rest for the
On the oth - er side of Jor - dan, In the sweet fields of

wea - ry, There is rest for the wea - ry, There is rest for you—
E - den, Where the tree of life is blooming, There is rest for you.

180

Onward, Christian Soldiers!

SABINE BARING-GOULD.

Tune, ONWARD. 6, 5.

1. Onward, Christian soldiers! Marching as to war, With the cross of Jesus
2. At the sign of triumph Satan's host doth flee; On, then, Christian soldiers,
3. Like a mighty army Moves the Church of God; Brothers, we are treading

Go-ing on be-fore. Christ, the royal Mas-ter, Leads against the foe;
On to vic-to-ry! Hell's foundations qiv-er At the shout of praise;
Where the saints have trod; We are not di-vid-ed, All one bo-dy we,

CHORUS.

Forward into bat-tle, See, his banners go! Onward, Christian soldiers!
Brothers, lift your voices, Loud your anthems raise.
One in hope and doctrine, One in chari-ty.

Marching as to war, With the cross of Je-sus Going on be-fore.

4 Crowns and thrones may perish,
  Kingdoms rise and wane,
But the Church of Jesus
  Constant will remain;
Gates of hell can never
  'Gainst that Church prevail;
We have Christ's own promise,
  And that cannot fail.

5 Onward, then, ye people!
  Join our happy throng,
Blend with ours your voices
  In the triumph-song;
Glory, laud, and honor
  Unto Christ the King,
This through countless ages
  Men and angels sing.

Zerah. C. M.

206   Come, ye that love.

1 COME, ye that love the Saviour's name,
  And joy to make it known,
The Sovereign of your hearts proclaim,
  And bow before his throne.

2 Behold your Lord, your Master crowned
  With glories all divine;
And tell the wondering nations round
  How bright those glories shine.

3 When, in his earthly courts, we view
  The glories of our King,
We long to love as angels do,
  And wish like them to sing.

4 And shall we long and wish in vain?
  Lord, teach our songs to rise:
Thy love can animate the strain,
  And bid it reach the skies.

207   What glory gilds.

1 WHAT glory gilds the sacred page!
  Majestic, like the sun,
It gives a light to every age;
  It gives, but borrows none.

2 The power that gave it still supplies
  The gracious light and heat;
Its truths upon the nations rise;
  They rise, but never set.

3 Lord, everlasting thanks be thine
  For such a bright display,
As makes a world of darkness shine
  With beams of heavenly day.

4 My soul rejoices to pursue
  The steps of him I love,
Till glory breaks upon my view
  In brighter worlds above.

208   The Prince of Peace.

1 To us a Child of hope is born,
  To us a Son is given;
Him shall the tribes of earth obey,
  Him, all the hosts of heaven.

2 His name shall be the Prince of Peace,
  Forevermore adored;
The Wonderful, the Counselor,
  The great and mighty Lord.

3 His power, increasing, still shall spread;
  His reign no end shall know;
Justice shall guard his throne above,
  And peace abound below.

4 To us a Child of hope is born,
  To us a Son is given;
The Wonderful, the Counselor,
  The mighty Lord of heaven.

209   The joyful sound.

1 SALVATION! O the joyful sound
  What pleasure to our ears!
A sovereign balm for every wound,
  A cordial for our fears.

2 Salvation! let the echo fly
  The spacious earth around,
While all the armies of the sky
  Conspire to raise the sound.

3 Salvation! O thou bleeding Lamb!
  To thee the praise belongs:
Salvation shall inspire our hearts,
  And dwell upon our tongues.

210   Doxology. C. M.

To Father, Son, and Holy Ghost,
  The God whom we adore,
Be glory, as it was, is now,
  And shall be evermore.

211 Precious Friend is Jesus.

JAMES I. BLACK.   JNO. R. SWENEY.

1. Mourner, lay thy brok-en heart At the feet of Je-sus;
2. Art thou vexed with anx-ious care, Leave it all with Je-sus;
3. Lean thy ach-ing head to rest On the arm of Je-sus;
4. Go to Cal-vary's heal-ing stream, On-ly trust in Je-sus,

Fine.

All thou hast, and all thou art, Give them now to Je-sus.
Are thy bur-dens hard to bear, Cast their weight on Je-sus.
Though by sor-row long oppressed, There's a balm in Je-sus.
O'er thy spir-it light will beam, Precious light from Je-sus.

D.S.—Ten-der-ly he cares for thee,—Precious Friend is Je-sus.

CHORUS. | D.S.

Now thy soul at peace may be,— Take the love he of-fers free;

212 I'm Going Home.

WM. HUNTER, D. D.   Arr. by REV. W. McDONALD.

1. { My heav'nly home is bright and fair; Nor pain, nor death can enter there: }
   { Its glitt'ring tow'rs the sun outshine; That heav'nly mansion shall be mine. }

CHO. { I'm go-ing home, I'm going home, I'm go-ing home to die no more! }
     { To die no more, to die no more, I'm go-ing home to die no more! }

2 My Father's house is built on high,
Far, far above the starry sky:
When from this earthly prison free.
That heavenly mansion mine shall be.

3 While here, a stranger far from home,
Affliction's waves may round me foam;
Although like Lazarus, sick and poor,
My heavenly mansion is secure.

4 Let others seek a home below,
Which flames devour, or waves o'er-
Be mine a happier lot to own [flow;
A heavenly mansion near the throne.

5 Then fail this earth, let stars decline,
And sun and moon refuse to shine,
All nature sink and cease to be,
That heavenly mansion stands for me.

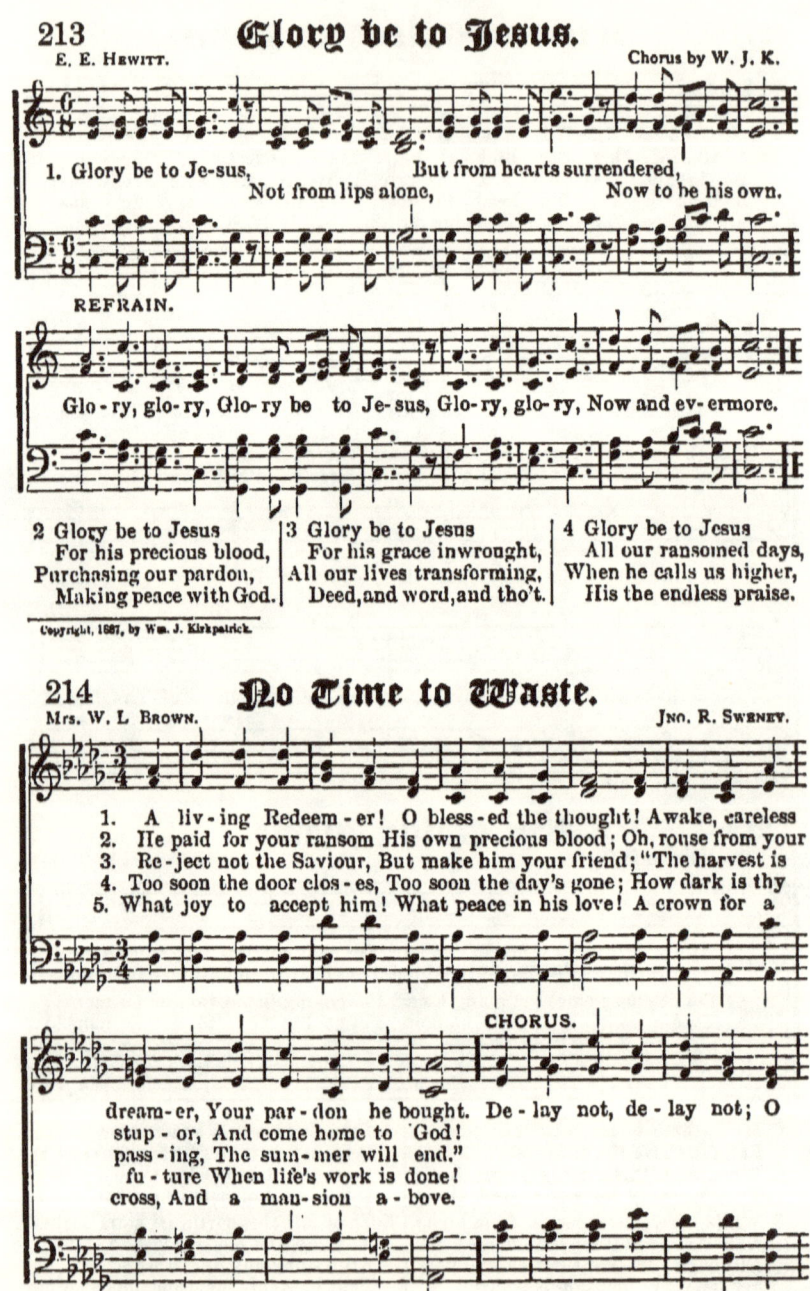

213 **Glory be to Jesus.**

E. E. Hewitt.   Chorus by W. J. K.

1. Glory be to Je-sus,   But from hearts surrendered,
   Not from lips alone,   Now to be his own.

REFRAIN.

Glo-ry, glo-ry, Glo-ry be to Je-sus, Glo-ry, glo-ry, Now and ev-ermore.

2 Glory be to Jesus
  For his precious blood,
  Purchasing our pardon,
  Making peace with God.

3 Glory be to Jesus
  For his grace inwrought,
  All our lives transforming,
  Deed, and word, and tho't.

4 Glory be to Jesus
  All our ransomed days,
  When he calls us higher,
  His the endless praise.

214 **No Time to Waste.**

Mrs. W. L. Brown.   Jno. R. Sweney.

1. A liv-ing Redeem-er! O bless-ed the thought! Awake, careless
2. He paid for your ransom His own precious blood; Oh, rouse from your
3. Re-ject not the Saviour, But make him your friend; "The harvest is
4. Too soon the door clos-es, Too soon the day's gone; How dark is thy
5. What joy to accept him! What peace in his love! A crown for a

CHORUS.

dream-er, Your par-don he bought. De-lay not, de-lay not; O
stup-or, And come home to God!
pass-ing, The sum-mer will end."
fu-ture When life's work is done!
cross, And a man-sion a-bove.

No Time to Waste.—CONCLUDED.

sinner, make haste! The door now stands open,—There's no time to waste.

215 Jesus Saves Me.

LOUISE M. ROUSE.   Miss DORA BOOLE.

1. Precious Saviour, thou hast saved me; Thine and only thine I am;
2. Long my yearning heart was trying To en-joy this perfect rest;
3. Trusting, trusting ev'-ry moment; Feeling now the blood applied;
4. Con-se-crat-ed to thy ser-vice, I will live and die to thee:

Oh, the cleansing blood has reached me, Glory, glo - ry to the Lamb!
But I gave all try-ing o - ver: Simply trust-ing, I was blest.
Ly-ing at the cleansing fountain; Dwelling in my Saviour's side.
I will wit-ness to thy glo-ry Of sal-va-tion full and free.

D.S.—Oh, the cleansing blood has reached me, Glory, glo - ry to the Lamb!

REFRAIN.   D.S.

Glo-ry, glo - ry, Je-sus saves me, Glo-ry, glo - ry to the Lamb!

5 Yes, I will stand up for Jesus;
    He has sweetly saved my soul,
    Cleansed me from inbred corruption,
    Sanctified, and made me whole.

6 Glory to the blood that bought me,
    Glory to its cleansing power!
    Glory to the blood that keeps me!
    Glory, glory, evermore!

Trusting Along.

E. E. HEWITT.

JNO. R. SWENEY.

1. Trusting a-long from day to day; Trusting my Saviour all the way;
2. Trusting the guidance of his hand, Yielding my life to his command;
3. Trusting his truth my soul to feed, Trusting for all the good I need;
4. Trusting his own transforming power, Cleansing, renewing, hour by hour,

Fine.

Trusting his love, his grace, his care, Trusting him always, ev'-rywhere.
Taking the joy or work or rest, Taking the pain, as he sees best.
Oft his designs are hid from me, Trusting him when I can-not see.
Car-ry-ing on his work be-gun, Trusting for home when all is done.

D.S.—Trusting each promise that he gives; Trusting for life, for Je-sus lives.

CHORUS.

D.S.

Trusting a-long I praise and pray; Trusting my Saviour day by day;

Copyright, 1890, by Jno R. Sweney.

Scripture Response.

Lento.

Ps. cxix. 11, 12.

E. D. BEALE.

mp

Thy word have I hid in my heart that I might not sin against thee.

Bless-ed art thou, O Lord: teach me thy stat-utes. A-men.

Copyright, 1889, by John J. Hood.

218 **Consecration.**

Mrs. MARY D. JAMES.　　　　Mrs. JOS. F. KNAPP.

1. My bo-dy, soul, and spirit, Jesus, I give to thee, A con-secrat-ed
2. O Jesus, mighty Saviour, I trust in thy great name, I look for thy sal-
3. Oh, let the fire, descending Just now upon my soul, Consume my humble
4. I'm thine, O blessed Jesus, Wash'd by thy precious blood, Now seal me by thy

REFRAIN.

offering, Thine ev-ermore to be.　My all is on the al-tar, I'm
va-tion, Thy promise now I claim.
offering, And cleanse and make me whole.
Spir-it, A sac-rifice to God.

waiting for the fire; Waiting, waiting, waiting, I'm waiting for the fire.

rit.

From "Notes of Joy," by per.

219 **Angels Hovering Round.**

1. There are angels hov'ring round, There are angels hov'ring round, There are
2. They will carry the tid-ings home, They will carry the tidings home, They will

an-gels, an-gels hov'ring round.
car-ry, car-ry the tid-ings home.

3 To the New Jerusalem, etc.

4 Poor sinners are coming home, etc.

5 And Jesus bids them come, etc.

6 There's glory all around, etc.

187

Blow ye the Trumpet.

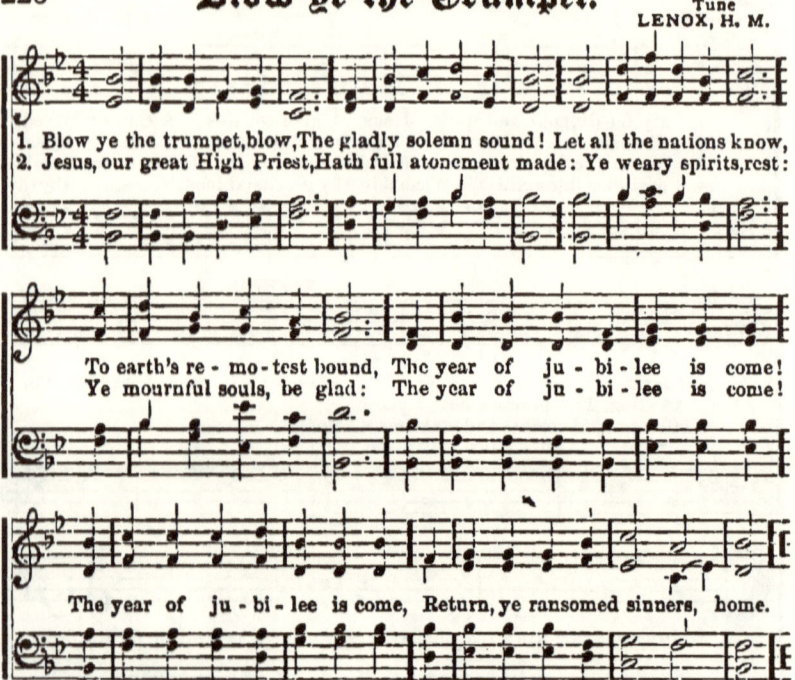

1. Blow ye the trumpet, blow, The gladly solemn sound! Let all the nations know,
2. Jesus, our great High Priest, Hath full atonement made: Ye weary spirits, rest:

To earth's re - mo - test bound, The year of ju - bi - lee is come!
Ye mournful souls, be glad: The year of ju - bi - lee is come!

The year of ju - bi - lee is come, Return, ye ransomed sinners, home.

3 Extol the Lamb of God,
  The all-atoning Lamb;
Redemption in his blood
  Throughout the world proclaim:

4 Ye slaves of sin and hell,
  Your liberty receive,
And safe in Jesus dwell,
  And blest in Jesus live:

5 Ye who have sold for naught
  Your heritage above,
Shall have it back unbought,
  The gift of Jesus' love:

6 The gospel trumpet hear,
  The news of heavenly grace;
And, saved from earth, appear
  Before your Saviour's face:

221   Arise, my soul, arise.

1 Arise, my soul, arise;
  Shake off thy guilty fears;
The bleeding Sacrifice
  In my behalf appears:
Before the throne my Surety stands,
My name is written on his hands.

2 He ever lives above,
  For me to intercede;
His all-redeeming love,
  His precious blood to plead;
His blood atoned for all our race,
And sprinkles now the throne of grace.

3 Five bleeding wounds he bears,
  Received on Calvary;
They pour effectual prayers,
  They strongly plead for me:
"Forgive him, O forgive," they cry,
"Nor let that ransomed sinner die."

4 The Father hears him pray,
  His dear anointed One;
He cannot turn away
  The presence of his Son:
His Spirit answers to the blood,
And tells me I am born of God.

5 My God is reconciled:
  His pardoning voice I hear:
He owns me for his child;
  I can no longer fear:
With confidence I now draw nigh,
And, "Father, Abba, Father," cry.
—CHARLES WESLEY.

"Mizpah."

"Mizpah: . . The Lord watch between me and thee, when we are absent one from another."

E. E. Hewitt.   Gen. xxxi. 49.   Wm. J. Kirkpatrick.

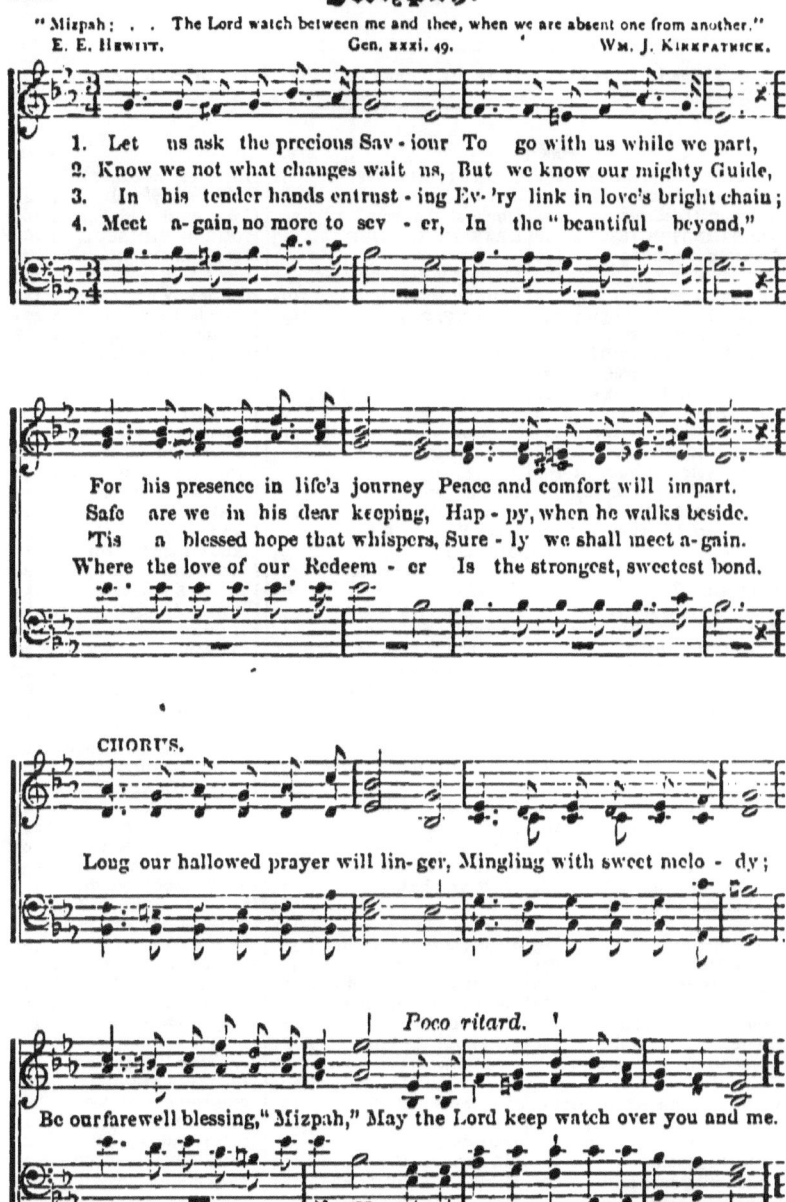

1. Let us ask the precious Sav - iour To go with us while we part,
2. Know we not what changes wait us, But we know our mighty Guide,
3. In his tender hands entrust - ing Ev- 'ry link in love's bright chain;
4. Meet a - gain, no more to sev - er, In the "beautiful beyond,"

For his presence in life's journey Peace and comfort will impart.
Safe are we in his dear keeping, Hap - py, when he walks beside.
'Tis a blessed hope that whispers, Sure - ly we shall meet a - gain.
Where the love of our Redeem - er Is the strongest, sweetest bond.

CHORUS.

Long our hallowed prayer will lin- ger, Mingling with sweet melo - dy;

Poco ritard.

Be our farewell blessing," Mizpah," May the Lord keep watch over you and me.

INDEX.

Titles in CAPITALS; Metrical Tunes in *Italic*; First lines in Roman.